The Nataraja Shiva as cosmic dancer, dancing through
cycles of creation and destruction on the demon of
ignorance in a circle of flame that is samsara.

Cover image Bhavachakra was originally
posted to Flickr by Wonderlane at
https://flickr.com/photos/71401718@N00/5376004435.

Swayambhunath Stupa, Kathmandu, Nepal. The spire represents the thirteen stages to Nirvana, below which are the compassionate all-seeing eyes of the Buddhas, gazing over the world of samsara.

To everyone who has walked this life with me as lights along the path, thank you. And special thanks to my children, Jeremy and Matthew, and to Rob and Marck.

*"As a caterpillar, having come to the end of one blade
of grass, draws itself together and
reaches out for the next, so the Self, having
come to the end of one life and dispelled all ignorance,
gathers in his faculties and reaches
out from the old body to a new."*
Brihadaranyaka Upanishad

*"I maintain that the cosmic religious feeling is the
strongest and noblest motive for scientific research"*
Albert Einstein

SAMSARA – THE WHEEL OF BIRTH, DEATH AND REBIRTH

A journey through spirituality, religion and Asia

"All beings have lived and died and been reborn countless times.
Over and over again they have experienced the indescribable Clear Light.
But because they are obscured by the darkness of ignorance, they
wander endlessly in limitless samsara"
Padmasambhava

REBECCA HARRISON

CONTENTS

"None of us is getting out of here alive…"

CHAPTER ONE

DOWN THE RABBIT HOLE

Loss shoves its way uninvited in to every life sooner or later and was the sharply personal trigger for this book. My partner Rob had just died from hereditary dementia: a traumatic unexpected diagnosis was followed a few years later by a cruel and relentless decline. The illness was cast to him at conception, the enzyme that breaks down toxic proteins missing because of a centuries old genetic error passed into history by an unknown ancestor. Rob himself had no idea he was carrying that genetic time bomb until revealed by a blood test in his late fifties. A happy life in the country surrounded by dogs and horses became brutally unravelled over the next couple of years as the illness robbed him of balance, motor skills and speech, followed by cognitive and personality changes. By the age of sixty-one he was reduced to recognizing no-one in the months preceding his death. His loss knocked me sideways and little guidance was offered by my own Western society increasingly silent as to the meaning of life or death, the latter vaguely unmentionable despite hovering in the wings of every life. I was growing older with no faith to offer solace, like so many millions of others. As Michael Pollan commented in **How to Change Your Mind: The New Science of Psychedelics** "Carl Jung once wrote that it is not the young but people in middle age who need to have an 'experience of the numinous' to help them negotiate the second half of their lives."[1] That insight is valuable but for many at my stage of life from my kind of culture experiences of the numinous are thin on the ground and organized religion offers little or no help.

Life brings unforeseen joys and sorrows to everyone and forces and events beyond our control push their way in be they earthquake, illness, accident or school shooting. Meaning is easy to find in the people we love and what brings us joy in the brief time we inhabit this planet, it's the painful things that are so hard to make sense of. Getting older, as friends began to die and others sicken with terminal illnesses, death and dying were no longer over an invisible horizon but present and insistent. As an agnostic of no particular belief in an increasingly secular materialistic society I had no idea how to deal with the brutal realities of loss and mortality inevitable whatever one's circumstances, beliefs, or lack of them. As eleventh century Tibetan Buddhist poet, teacher and mystic Milarepa bluntly put it: "All worldly pursuits have but one unavoidable and inevitable end, which is sorrow: acquisitions end in dispersion; buildings in destruction; meetings in separation; births in death. Knowing this, one should from the very first renounce acquisition and heaping up ...and set about realizing the Truth ...Life is short, and the time of death is uncertain..."[2] Rob's illness and death forced me to confront the bitter truth of that and the absence of a path to navigate it.

So my journey was born, a search to discover if there were spiritual ideas that could perhaps shed light on not just Rob's illness and death but the suffering and death that comes to everyone. It was simultaneously an internal journey and an exploration of ideas about life, suffering, death and the possibilities of rebirth held by cultures different to my own background as an Australian with English origins. It then became a physical journey through Nepal, Bali, Cambodia and India where those ideas comprise the framework of everyday life. I began my journey perched on the agnostic fence, unable to choose between an empty accidental universe without purpose or meaning on one side, and competing religious explanations all claiming to be right and riddled with cultural baggage on the other. It felt like an impossible choice but one I could no longer wash my hands of. Rob's suffering and death could not be theorized from a distance, they were lived realities and so must understanding of them be. Death and suffering will not go away by ignoring them and come to all regardless of creed, culture and circumstances, our existence on this small fragile planet remaining as mysterious as it has always been. Those are the matters with which spirituality deals so perhaps that could still have meaning in the world of today, even if separating the proverbial sheep of what is worth keeping from the goats of that which is best discarded is a seemingly impossible task.

I found myself drawn to ideas discovered in an earlier part of my life, the spiritual traditions of Hinduism and Buddhism born in India. They became a catalyst to immerse myself in cultures where it is taken for granted that the material world is a stage for our lives in a cycle of repeated lives, deaths and rebirths known as samsara in Sanskrit, the ancient sacred language of India. Could those ideas be of any relevance to someone like me, an agnostic non-believer? Could they offer meaningful understanding of birth, suffering and death to people neither Hindu nor Buddhist? At the very least the ideas of samsara seemed worth investigating. That inevitably led to broader questions. Could spirituality be embraced without taking on religion? Is there any evidence for spiritual dimensions and the continuation of consciousness after death from sources outside religion, such as science, parapsychology, mysticism or psychedelic experiences? What is the nature of consciousness? Does spirituality of any kind have value in a twenty-first century world and what role might it play?

Rob's memorial gathering celebrated the life of a much loved man. He was atheist, or at least strongly agnostic, so it was secular. A kind Christian chaplain co-ordinated the gathering but she didn't say much. Love is the great blessing life offers in the midst of the sorrows of impermanence and death, and the great healer of the awful grief those bring, so we tried to focus on that. Religions frequently describe God as love but it is not easy to reconcile a God of love with the seemingly random suffering life deals out to good people as it did to Rob from an arbitrary throw of the genetic dice, a couple of faulty letters of DNA code dealing him a cruel fate. Buddhism dispenses with God altogether being non-theistic, but death and suffering remain equally puzzling and painful. Without any framework of faith it was hard to know how to farewell him but to make no reference to a spiritual dimension felt something vital was missing, so reading from the **Upanishads**, ancient Hindu texts composed between approximately 800 to 500 BCE, was a response to that. We had shared those together and been greatly moved despite lacking religious belief. They are surprisingly clear of doctrinal or ritual clutter and state that clinging to the outward forms of religion does not provide a solution to being awash on the "sea of samsara." In the words of the **Mundaka Upanishad**:

"… rituals are unsafe rafts for crossing
The sea of samsara of birth and death.
Doomed to shipwreck are those who try to cross
The sea of samsara on these poor rafts."

My grown up children from an earlier marriage looked at me earnestly while I read from the **Shvetashvatara Upanishad**, their love a beacon of comfort for deep grief not just for Rob's passing but for the way death came to him.

"The world is the wheel of God, turning round
And round with all living creatures upon its rim
The world is the river of God
Flowing from him and flowing back to him.
On this ever-revolving wheel of being
The individual self goes round and round
Through life after life, believing itself
To be a separate creature, until
It sees its identity with the Lord of Love.
And attains immortality in the indivisible whole."

Much of the travels that were to come over the following year retraced paths taken at an earlier time with Rob or from a previous part of his life. As his daughter discussed his cremation she quietly asked if some of his ashes could be scattered in Nepal, my first destination. It was a fitting idea. Rob loved the country taking many beautiful photographs there when young, beautiful and free, no shadows of what was to come in a new century in Australia, a long way from his English youth. As Milarepa asks "Strong and healthy, who thinks of sickness until it strikes like lightning? Preoccupied with the world, who thinks of death, until it arrives like thunder?" Those questions certainly applied to me: I had done exactly as Milarepa described and buried my head in the sands of denial and preoccupation.

Facing death and illness are extraordinarily difficult until they actually arrive and then of course there is no escaping them. The office worker at the funeral home passed over all that was left of Rob's physical form, fine grey ash neatly labelled in plastic boxes carefully placed in an attractively decorated paper bag. I mumbled "dust to dust ashes to ashes" while carrying the bag towards the door. She replied 'yes, that's right' and how much it scared her as she followed me through the foyer and out in to the weak late winter sunshine.

We stood next to the building in which the trade of death takes place hidden deep inside, obscured by attractive office spaces and public gathering places designed to make death neat, organized, and as remote and unthreatening as possible. The inside walls were adorned with paintings of idyllic rural scenes and gentle sounds of rainforest birds and tinkling waterfalls looped endlessly from small speakers on the ceiling. Soft lighting, computers humming and artificial flowers created an air of efficient politeness, rendering what happens there strangely surreal. The kind office worker asked why I required a small separate container of ashes. I explained they were going to Nepal so she produced an official letter overcoming prohibitions on carrying human remains, a shocking reminder of the reality that the neat little box and its contents somehow drew a veil over. We talked for a while and she asked if sky burials, where scavenger birds consume the flesh and ground up bones of a corpse, are practiced in Nepal. I confirmed yes, that continues in Himalayan areas bordering Tibet. Despite her job working in a funeral home she was as puzzled by mortality as anyone else.

Modern secular cultures such as Australia have little to say about death which is hidden and sanitized, impermanence and aging denied, the cult of youth, consumption and materialist explanations for the world all reigning supreme. Australia is ordered and prosperous, in many respects 'the lucky country' as sometimes described. Dogs are confined in their back yards away from streets patrolled by council funded officers, no sacred cows wander the streets, almost no garbage is strewn in the gutters, the sight of a begging child, or a mange ridden, starving, street dog covered in weeping sores, unthinkable. Perhaps it is partly the relative order and prosperity of secular Western societies that obscures frames of reference outside of material reality thus rendering those societies increasingly silent in the face of death. European colonialism, with its values of conquest, materialism, private property, competition, individualism and Christianity shattered apart the indigenous cultures it arrived in and gave birth to societies like mine, rich in material blessings but sterile in dimensions of the spirit. Australia rose like a phoenix from the squalor and misery of industrial Britain where those convicted of crimes mostly driven by poverty, or political offenses, were shipped off to an isolated continent "discovered" by Europeans. British colonization was a tale of dispossession and tragedy for Australia's indigenous people who for more than 50,000 years were its sole possessors. Aboriginal spirituality is a profound and ancient tradition premised on non-duality, not separating the natural world from the human world, the sacred from the secular, the body from the spirit, and non-aboriginal Australians such as me have much to learn from it.

My strong desire to be somewhere else following Rob's death was not because somewhere else was better but because it was different. I longed too for a distraction that might offer some escape from the corrosive grief of his loss. And travel is a powerful distraction even if the emotional baggage of our lives comes along for the ride. Rob's illness and dying had been like peering into an abyss of suffering to which my own culture was ill equipped to offer any meaningful response. Asia, with its cocktail of the confronting, inspiring and fascinating along with a rich spirituality, displays the raw truths of life and death, not hidden, not sanitized, not denied as they are where I come from. Perhaps it would be there that the abyss of suffering could find some comprehension. Asia increasingly defies easy conclusions and is changing fast: the subways or huge office towers of Bangkok, the super clean, ordered sterility of Singapore, or high tech communities of Bangalore, are different worlds from the other Asia, and not where I sought to be. Nepal, then Bali, Cambodia and India, each in turn revealed that other Asia where the numinous, suffering and death are present and obvious rather than veiled as they so often are in the comfortable blandness of the modern West. They are all predominantly Hindu or Buddhist, or in the case of Nepal both, so would reveal those spiritual traditions as they are lived and practiced. Perhaps they might offer clues to the questions that many of us in the West have forgotten how to ask. What is this life, and the death that will inevitably follow for all of us, about? Samsara is one response to those questions and is taken for granted by just about everyone in the cultures we visited, offering a startling contrast of perspective to that of my own world.

Travelling alone was a daunting prospect so I was fortunate that a friend Marck was keen to accompany me. He was already in Asia and agreed we would meet in Kathmandu later in the year. Despite the endless variety of cultures and circumstances all people are united in experiencing impermanence, suffering and death. My explorations of samsara, religion and spirituality, and the experiences offered by the rich cultures we visited, became a journey in to a rabbit hole of astounding possibilities bringing many more questions than answers and deepening awareness what incredible mysteries our world, our life, and our consciousness of those, are.

"And only the enlightened can recall their former lives;
for the rest of us, the memories of past existences are
but glints of light, twinges of longing, passing shadows,
disturbingly familiar, that are gone before they can be
grasped, like the passage of that silver bird on Dhaulagiri."
Peter Matthiessen **The Snow Leopard**

CHAPTER TWO

SAMSARA, RELIGION AND SPIRITUALITY

So what precisely does the beautiful Sanskrit word samsara, that occupied so much of my life over the following year, mean? It translates to "wander" or "flow through" describing a cycle of birth, death and rebirth in the world of matter and form. The idea of samsara is central to religions having their source in India, informing the lives of hundreds of millions of Hindus, Buddhists, Jains, and Sikhs. According to those religions samsara is an endless treadmill of births, suffering, aging, deaths and rebirths. We ride different horses in different lives but it's the same painful merry-go-round and the only way to get off is via enlightenment bringing an end to rebirth, only a precious human birth offering the opportunity for escape. The religions born in India understand samsara in differing ways but all perceive it as an unsatisfactory state in which we are trapped unaware of our history as we pass through countless lifetimes across eons of time driven by ignorance and karma. Are we all awash on what the **Mundaka Upanishad** describes as "the sea of samsara of birth and death" being born, dying and reborn, over and over and over again? Could the concept of samsara make any sense of life and death and the cruel suffering that Rob and countless others endure? Could any form of spirituality be meaningful for someone like me: agnostic, sceptical, dissatisfied with both organized religion and lack of a spiritual life, living in a time and a culture that increasingly regards religion as an irrelevance?

My search was to understand what samsara might mean and if spirituality and religion might have relevance in a twenty-first century world. Religion is fascinating but its cultural baggage often is not, so the challenge was to sift insights about spirituality and samsara out from religion to discover what of wider value might lie buried within. The journey required putting aside preconceptions and letting the path go wherever it led, that being occasionally challenging. As an Australian outsider my own background and biases inevitably seeped in: objectivity is not fully possible outside of the laboratory, and even that can be questioned so no claim is made to it. Religion continues to both attract and repel as a cocktail of superstition, cultural tradition, dogmas, beliefs and practices woven through with glimpses of deep truths about the mysteries of the universe and our lives.

Birth and death are universal facts of life but samsara goes far beyond those to include rebirth on the other side of death. That is its challenging aspect, dividing religions from each other and believer from unbeliever. Atheists perceive rebirth as impossible, to agnostics it is unknowable, and to religions that don't accept it it's just plain wrong. A thousand questions and a thousand objections immediately spring to mind in response to the idea that consciousness survives death to be reborn in another physical form. It is in the religions having their source in India that the idea of samsara developed, but other diverse traditions and thinkers such as Pythagoras, Plato, Gnosticism, the American Transcendentalists, Spiritism and Theosophy, also propose ongoing rebirth. Mystical Jewish teachings such as the Kabbalah and Hasidic Judaism, and strands of Sufism refer to it too. In the contemporary West increasing numbers of people accept the possibility and 'past life regressions' are on offer. However the primary focus will be Hinduism and Buddhism and their associated cultures, samsara being central to their understanding of life and death.

So what do Hinduism and Buddhism have to say about samsara? There are deep differences between them but ending rebirth in samsara is the objective of both, and both believe only a human birth makes that liberation possible. For Buddhists, a core teaching is annata or 'no soul,' so rebirth as reincarnation in the Hindu sense does not exist. What is reborn is not a continuous unified self but a bundle of 'karmic resonances' propelled by karma and ignorance into rebirth in one of the 'six realms of samsara'. For Buddhists samsara is a state of inevitable suffering and death so enlightenment or release from samsara in to nirvana, a blissful state beyond death and rebirth, is the aim. Buddhism recognizes no transcendent creator God and no purpose or explanation for samsara, it just is, the Buddha discouraging speculation as to the existence of a creator in his "Fourteen Silences."

For Hindus, the atman, roughly equivalent to the soul, is continually reborn in samsara through evolution in various life forms, including animals, until finally attaining a much desired human birth. Release from samsara follows enlightenment whereby the atman reunites in bliss with its divine source in moksha, no longer being forced back in to rebirth. Hinduism suggests an evolutionary purpose to ongoing rebirths as expressed in the **Shvetashvatara Upanishad**:

"Not a female, male, not neuter is the Self
The Self takes on a body with desires.
Attachments, and delusions, and is
Born again and again in new bodies
To work out the karma of former lives
The embodied self assumes many forms,
Heavy or light, according to its needs
For growth and the deeds of previous lives.
This evolution is divine law."

There are some Hindu thinkers such as Ramana Maharshi, who argue that belief in rebirth results from ignorance as time, matter and samsara are actually without reality and reincarnation presumes they are real. However he does allow for the concept in so far as it makes samsara comprehensible.[3]

Indian spiritual thinker Sri Aurobindo develops his own ideas about samsara and rebirth in his teaching of "evolutionary rebirth" in **Rebirth and Karma**.[4] He describes samsara as providing opportunity for the atman's eventual realization of divinity after it has evolved through ever more complex forms of life giving purpose and meaning to individual human experience. Rather than samsara being a futile cycle of suffering from which escape is the only goal, Sri Aurobindo presents an optimistic and positive view of the purpose of the physical universe, life and rebirth: it is for consciousness to evolve to become ever more self-aware of its oneness with the divine source of the universe. The cycle of samsara is thereby the 'schoolroom of the soul' providing the varying lives and experiences through which the soul learns wisdom, love and compassion until it eventually reunites with what the **Upanishads** describe as the "Lord of Love." Sri Aurobindo's perspective of the evolution of life and consciousness has parallels with ideas put forward by Jesuit priest, palaeontologist and theologian Teilhard de Chardin (1881-1955), that the universe is inevitably evolving towards a point of unification he termed the Omega Point, with divine consciousness or God. According to Teilhard de Chardin human intelligence and consciousness will also evolve inevitably into a transhuman, then finally posthuman future, and that this process will involve a merger of humanity and technology.

Carl Jung, in the prologue to **Memories, Dreams, Reflections**, describes life and death as a process that resembles samsara: "Life has always seemed to me like a plant that lives on its rhizome. Its true life is invisible, hidden in the rhizome. The part that appears above ground lasts only a single summer. Then it withers away - an ephemeral apparition. When we think of the unending growth and decay of life and civilizations, we cannot escape the impression of absolute nullity. Yet I have never lost a sense of something that lives and endures beneath the eternal flux. What we see is blossom, which passes. The rhizome remains."[5] Beneath the transience of an individual life something enduring, the rhizome, persists to blossom again, and again in endless new forms. That echoes the Hindu sacred text the **Bhagavad Gita** that compares each body reborn in samsara to a new suit of clothing for the soul: "Sri Krishna said: As a human being puts on new garments, giving up old ones, the soul similarly accepts new material bodies, giving up the old and useless ones."[6]

Past life, afterlife, or near death experiences suggest tantalizing possibilities that consciousness survives death despite being often dismissed as illusory neurological phenomena or fantasies. Evidence for rebirth has been explored by those such as Ian Stevenson, professor of psychiatry at the University of Virginia. His painstaking research was described in **Twenty Cases Suggestive**

of Reincarnation and was continued by Professor Jim Tucker in **Life Before Life**. Perhaps continuing scientific investigation might eventually demonstrate that consciousness is not annihilated by death and can exist independently of the brain, making rebirth and samsara at least possible and worthy of serious consideration. A concept such as samsara is only meaningful if it is accepted that there exists a spiritual dimension and consciousness survives death. Finding value in the concepts of rebirth and samsara is absolutely not about becoming a Hindu or Buddhist but rather asking could they help illuminate the meaning of life and death? The idea of samsara developed within the framework of the religions that endorse it but is not dependent on those, and if it has value then it does so for everyone whatever religion they follow, or if they have no religion at all as is increasingly the case.

The endless births samsara is believed to propel us all through and the ways those lives are experienced are always shifting according to time and place. Any useful contemporary understanding or evaluation of samsara needs to encompass the massive changes that have occurred in recent centuries. As the pace of change rapidly speeds up the experience of being human is sailing in to uncharted waters leaving spirituality and religious beliefs of all kinds challenged and fractured by historical and cultural forces, globalisation, technology, scientific advancement and materialism. Religion once defined for humans the meaning and purpose of life across time and place but is increasingly becoming an irrelevance, particularly in the modern West. That has left many stranded with no path to make any sense of their life or their death. Around thirty percent of Australians declared in the 2016 census that they have no religious belief (in 1991 it was close to thirteen percent) and probably many 'believers' are actually agnostic. Secularization has left a widespread spiritual vacuum with increasingly thin connections to a sacred dimension. Simultaneously fundamentalism of many varieties offers escape from uncertainty and living and dying without meaning, and some find antidotes in dreams of Caliphates, or Biblical fundamentalism, or adopting Tibetan Buddhism. The present day focus of Western societies on the material, the rational and the secular gives them many fine qualities but doesn't nurture the spirit, reveal any wider meaning to living or dying, or offer a sustaining purpose beyond what humans create for themselves.

Could or should spirituality of any kind, including the concept of samsara, have any place in the contemporary world? As an antidote to the eroding of religious faith some seek spiritual experiences by ingesting consciousness-altering substances, consulting a psychic or astrologer, visiting an ashram or perhaps joining a spiritual community. A thirst for spiritual experiences feeds the growth of spiritual tourism as a new global industry. Gurus in India or Buddhist monasteries in Nepal provide opportunities for foreigners to tread a spiritual path or discover meditation, and healers and shamans are sought as guides to approach the numinous. Some search in indigenous communities of Latin America, Australia, Africa, and Asia where connectedness to nature is a living tradition and transcendent dimensions can be accessed perhaps with the help of a plant substance like ayahuasca, peyote or psilocybin mushrooms. Recently in my home city in Australia a Benedictine monastery arrived with around twenty-four young men devoting themselves to prayer and poverty. They spend long hours in silent contemplation and start their day at four am in their search for a spiritual life. Others have taken a path of retreat from the twenty first century and joined groups who reject modern dress, technology and living to adopt a way of life from hundreds of years ago. It is surprising to discover there are families in Australia in remote communities using horses and carts and adopting the beliefs and lifestyle of the traditional Amish, seeing themselves as refugees from a world that fails to fulfil their needs. How their children will negotiate their lives, the faith of their parents, and withdrawal from wider society, is unknown. These groups may be certain of their beliefs, and their courage to swim against the tide of their culture is remarkable, but that does not in itself make their beliefs true. History is full of people earnestly believing many things that would now mostly be rejected, be those the earth is flat, that women should not have social or political rights, or that God condemns people who are homosexual to an eternity in hell.

According to ancient Indian belief the world is now deeply in the Kali Yuga, an age of spiritual darkness dominated by materialism and loss of belief. Some would argue that is positive and the shackles of ignorance and superstition are finally being broken to build a world based on reason and secular ideals free of the fairy tales told by religion, in which case atheism is a move in the right direction. From that perspective the 'death of God' is a blessing to be celebrated as humans forge a future with reference to nothing but themselves, creating their own meaning, and with the advent of genetic technologies, creating themselves. Interestingly some spiritual leaders agree that atheism is of value: Benedictine monk Bede Griffiths commented "Atheism and agnosticism signify the rejection of certain images and concepts of God or of truth, which are historically conditioned and therefore inadequate. Atheism is a challenge to religion to purify its images and concepts and come nearer to the truth of the divine mystery."[7] Abdu'l-Baha of the Bahai faith states: "If religion becomes the cause of dislike, hatred, and division, it were better to be without it, and to withdraw from such a religion would be a truly religious act... Any religion which is not a cause of love and unity is no religion."[8] Sri Aurobindo observed that "... we shall observe with respect and wonder the work that Atheism has done for the Divine"[9] because it clears away the accretions of dogma and superstition embedded in all religion.

So where does all this leave the concept of samsara, religion and or spirituality? Can they or do they mean anything at all in the world of today? Are there kernels of truth buried deep at in the heart of all religion, spiritual pearls lying at the bottom of a deep, often impenetrable, ocean? Or are all spiritual impulses and religions, including ideas such as samsara and rebirth, just fantasies humans invent rooted in fear and the need to explain or deny death and suffering, a "whistling in the dark of an empty universe, hoping to keep up our spirits"?[10] Would humanity be better off abandoning religion altogether? Religion has done much to bring about its own demise, one of the greatest contributors to atheism being religion itself as it sits on an uneasy border between ideology and transcendent truth, often having slipped into the darkest elements of human nature and history. It is not alone in reflecting the worst of human behaviour but often has done exactly that, fuelling rejection by increasing numbers. Religion has at times terrorized its way through history, beating followers in to obedience with threats of damnation or punishment such as Yahweh of the Old Testament, a self-described jealous God ruling through violence and murder. In Afghanistan, Iran, Malaysia, Maldives,

Mauritania, Nigeria, Pakistan, Qatar, Saudi Arabia, Somalia, Sudan, United Arab Emirates and Yemen the punishment for apostasy of Islam is death.[11] In many of those countries the death penalty is not enforced but is prescribed by Sharia law. Simultaneous with the 'sticks' of rules and condemnation religions have held out the 'carrots' of salvation, moksha, nirvana, heaven or paradise.

Freud described all religion as a collective neurosis and Mao Tse Tung famously remarked to the Dalai Lama "religion is poison": violence, superstition, conflict, hatred, oppression, sexism, homophobia, racism, prejudice, self-righteousness, jihads, caste divisions, burnings at the stake, inquisitions and wars, bear that out. The claims by religions to exclusive truth and the smug belief of some that their particular creed is the only path up the mountain, says much about humanity that is not flattering. If there is a God that God must despair of the strange ways of Homo sapiens sapiens creating so many religions with such contrasting beliefs, believing theirs alone is right and providing exclusive occupancy of a blissful afterlife. Innumerable wars have been fought between and within religions, each religion or sect quoting its own texts to 'prove' its correctness leading to outcomes such as Hindus and Muslims slaughtering each other, the bombing of Jewish synagogues, burning of Christian heretics at the stake, or fighting between Catholics and Protestants in Northern Ireland. With such a dark track record perhaps the world would be a better place without any form of religion and secular ideals would form a surer foundation for human progress? And what of spirituality? Is it possible to hold on to that without the baggage of religion coming along for the ride?

Religions have often failed to create a better kinder world but so too have secular dreams of heaven on earth such as promised by the French Revolution or **The Communist Manifesto.**[12] Utopian communist fantasies of a fair equal world where it would be "From each according to his ability, to each according to his needs"[13] became twisted into brutal repressive regimes in Stalin's USSR, Mao's China, or the Cambodia of Pol Pot. Contemporary capitalism has enshrined materialism, consumption, individualism, profit, competition and greed as core values, making life for many a lonely and alienating challenge. The torturers of the Inquisition, the gulags of the Soviet Union, revolutionary political and social movements, or preachers announcing that if you do not believe in Jesus as saviour then eternal damnation is certain, are all products of the power of organized belief. Humans are great creators of stories and willing to go to any lengths, including war and persecution, to ensure their story is the only one that prevails, religion and social or political ideologies all unfortunately reflecting that.

Outside of traditional societies with strong religious traditions today's world has become a spiritual supermarket where every imaginable form is on offer creating much confusion. If the first choice doesn't work out there are always endless other options. For many people navigating the endless possibilities is so confusing they give up, overwhelmed by the 'tyranny of choice' they resign themselves to no spiritual life at all. The old narratives of religion are no longer convincing for increasing numbers who have no idea what they believe beyond the immediate concerns of their day to day life, loved ones, job, family, pets, sports, hobbies and friends. The vacuum is filled by materialism, consumerism, pornography, technology, alcohol, the tribalism of designer labels, the drowning in digital escapes such as computer games, Facebook, Instagram, Youtube, TV, virtual reality, or surfing the internet. None of those offer refuge from death and suffering or are equipped to provide wider meaning, and their satisfactions are short lived as craving something better or different inevitably arises. In an age where ecstasy comes in tablet form at a ritual of music at dance parties or nightclubs the thirst for transcendence is as strong as it has always been, but the means to satisfy it complex, obscure, difficult, and fraught with contradictions. For many it is not satisfied at all.

In the process of escape from the meshes of superstition and religion how do humans not become stranded on the shore of spiritual emptiness, utterly lost in samsara with no clues to its meaning, not recognizing its existence? Matthew Arnold's poem "Dover Beach" (1867) expresses well the challenges to belief associated with the social and scientific changes of the nineteenth century and the publication of Darwin's **Origin of Species**[14]:

"The Sea of Faith
Was once, too, at the full, and round earth's shore
Lay like the folds of a bright girdle furled.

But now I only hear its melancholy, long, withdrawing roar,
Retreating, to the breath
Of the night-wind, down the vast edges drear
And naked shingles of the world."

That "melancholy, long, withdrawing roar" has loudened as the twentieth and twenty-first centuries have unfolded amputating wider meaning from human experience and leaving little with which to approach death and loss. A gigantic hole has opened in the lives of many in prosperous post-industrial Western societies that consumption and technology cannot fill creating new forms of suffering. As poverty, starvation and disease recede the tides of loneliness, meaninglessness and materialism have swept in. Carl Jung commented in **Memories, Dreams, Reflections** "when I think of my patients, they all seek their own existence and to assure their existence against that complete atomization into nothingness or into meaninglessness. Man cannot stand a meaningless life".

Romantic relationships are seen by many as a solution and become loaded with tremendous weight of expectations for happiness and fulfilment. Online dating services promise a new relationship will bring connection, fill the hole of loneliness and give meaning, but instead they often bring a revolving door of transient and empty encounters generating deeper loneliness. People advertise themselves and are shopped for on websites where there is always a better looking version available with a swipe of the screen left or right. For those seeking no strings or paid for sex, then shopping online offers plenty of that too, with pornography making up a massive volume of internet searches. People being reduced to consumer products to be purchased digs a hole of unhappiness for both the purchaser and the purchased, the latter in many contexts selling themselves because of lack of other choices, gritty realities of economic survival, or compulsion, or having been trafficked in to the sex trade as those from poor countries often are. A flourishing new industry is the provision of advanced AI sex dolls that speak and respond with endearments or compliments. Sex with a robot might bring temporary pleasure but can never bring connection with another person and is likely to erode the possibility of intimate human relationships generating yet more dissatisfaction.

The intense individualism and materialism of post-industrial Western societies has marooned many in a culture of consumption and competition with serious consequences for personal happiness. According to **Time Magazine** in August 2017, thirteen percent of Americans take anti-depressant drugs and that is rising. The commonest cause of death for young men in Australia between seventeen and twenty-four is suicide. The World Health Organization recently published a report predicting that by the year 2030 depression will be responsible for the greatest burden of illness on the planet and suicide the most frequent cause of death. Something is clearly wrong that increasing wealth and technological sophistication are accompanied by increasing misery. Technology has reduced for many millions the pain of medically treatable illness and early death but new forms of suffering such as loneliness, depression and lack of meaning have arisen in cultures dominated by individualism, competition, consumption and materialism. The faces of suffering in samsara are constantly shifting but suffering persists whatever form it takes.

Meaning and purpose are deep human needs and throughout history religions have provided that. They have been a source of the most profound and enriching experiences simultaneous with the bitterest conflicts: generating love, compassion, art, music, architecture, and transcendent experiences, along with war, hatred, prejudice, superstition and oppression. In the process of liberation from religion and its baggage have we perhaps also discarded something valuable? GK Chesterton reputedly commented: "When people stop believing in God, they don't believe in nothing, they believe in everything" so turn to places like magazine horoscopes. Meaning is sought in social movements such as environmentalism, feminism, anti-racism, gay pride, or innumerable social justice organizations, and they have brought positive changes for millions. None of them however are equipped to respond to the reality of death, nurture spiritual needs, or provide a broad vision for what being human means. The perennial questions about living, suffering and dying remain whatever time or place humans live and up until this point in history it has been primarily religion that attempted to respond to those.

Are there any answers to any of this? Is spirituality possible whilst not falling back into the baggage of religion created by culture and history? Do genuine spiritual truths exist that transcend religions? If so they are true because they are the way things really are, but distinguishing what those might be is the tricky contentious part. Does the concept of samsara offer meaningful insights that transcend the religious contexts that accept it as fact? What sources of evidence are there for a spiritual realm beyond the confines of religion and dogmas? Mystical experiences across the religious spectrum, including for people with no beliefs, point to an underlying all encompassing source of truth and love known by direct experience making religious divisions irrelevant. Psychedelic substances also reveal the capacity to unlock altered states of perception explored by self-described psychonauts who take extraordinary occasionally terrifying journeys to the frontiers of the mind where many claim to have discovered spiritual realities that render organized religion an irrelevance. Thinkers such as Aldous Huxley in **The Perennial Philosophy** and **The Doors Of Perception,** Ramakrishna, Vivekananda, Krishnamurti, Paramahansa Yogananda, Sri Aurobindo, and numerous others, have also opened up the possibility of universal truths not attached to specific religions offering a way forward between religion and no spirituality at all. For those like me who have never been blessed with a mystical experience, don't tread the path of the psychonaut and have no framework of spiritual belief, we live without access to spiritual dimensions and have few clues as to what life or death might mean, the loss of Rob starkly exposing that in my own life. As Prem Rawat[15] puts it we have no idea where we have come from, or where we are going when our time is done, describing our brief lives as a "holiday from dirt" in to which we arrive as a collection of atoms born in the dust of stars with those atoms returning to dirt after our death. Our lives really are "dust to dust, ashes to ashes". For many of us the solution is to keep our eyes firmly on the solid realities of every day, its struggles and its gifts, and if we contemplate spirituality we do so hesitantly and privately because it's mostly is in the too hard basket.

Samsara teaches we play out our lives in ever-changing forms through endless time this life being just the tip of the iceberg of what we are. If that is accurate how little we really know about each other and ourselves. Sometimes when catching trains or flights I am struck by the endless to and fro of strangers flowing past each other's gaze, living their lives mostly without awareness that according to samsara they are travelling a cycle of rebirth in countless roles and circumstances through endless time. It is only enlightened beings such as the Buddha who were said to have achieved complete realization of their true nature and awareness of their previous lives, the historical Buddha's past human and animal births being described in the **Jataka Tales** from early Buddhism. The rest of us are unaware of how our own and others' history stretches back through innumerable births. Mahayana Buddhism teaches that because our existence in samsara is without beginning Lam Rim meditations recognizing all sentient beings have been at some time our mother help develop compassion and love for all beings. What we can know about people even in relation to even just one lifetime is extremely limited and often wrong. During years as a teacher of seventeen year olds students often shared surprising stories with remarkable and moving honesty. A beautiful young woman with the world seemingly at her feet, tortured by self-loathing shows me an arm laced with silvery self-harm scars, a young man is consumed by hatred for an abusive father, another sad-faced young woman is caring for an alcoholic poker machine addicted mother and a grandmother with cancer but still trying to complete her schoolwork on time. Every possible variation of circumstance and experience is presented as we travel on the wheel of samsara and its infinite choices and contrasts both light and dark.

According to Hinduism and Buddhism heavy layers of karma accumulated through many lifetimes force us back in to rebirth, but being oblivious to those we are trapped by ignorance on samsara's ever turning wheel until we take the steep path to liberation only possible with a human birth. They teach we travel samsara blind to our true nature, the length of our history and the forces that drive us, the countless lives and roles samsara claims everyone has lived being sealed behind an utterly locked door. We enter this world with memory wiped clean of what precedes birth. Plato refers to drinking of the waters of forgetfulness from the river of Lethe before we return in to a new life in a new body.[16] Because samsara is viewed as inevitably woven through with suffering, impermanence, ignorance and death, it is not in the least surprising that ending rebirth is the aim of both Hinduism and Buddhism. It is in the nature of humans to be plagued with dissatisfaction particularly acute in this age of consumption. Matt Haig comments on this in **Notes On a Nervous Planet** "The whole of consumerism is based on us wanting the *next* thing rather than the *present thing we already have.* This is an almost perfect recipe for unhappiness."[17] Even what gives us happiness is ultimately a source of suffering as it is always impermanent no matter how hard we grasp to hold on to it or seek to find more of it. No one escapes this. Even for those whose lives have been more than usually easy it is not possible for anyone to live a life with no suffering and absolutely no one lives a life not ending in death.

The continuation of existence after death in any form is a startling idea whether that is heaven, hell, or rebirth in samsara. Death as absolute annihilation is equally confronting. Humans are sandwiched between these possibilities and often take refuge from the enormity of that in the minutiae of daily life, a dimly remembered poem describing us as being "...dragged by separate fates, clutching at the straws of livelihood to fend off the infinite." Much of the time that is what we do clinging to spouses, lovers, friends, family, jobs, hobbies, possessions, alcohol, drugs, whatever and whoever distracts us. But no matter what our personal situation may be and how successful or happy our lives impermanence and death are the only absolute certainties. There are periods in many lives when it seems possible to ignore this, shielded by immersion in the business of living, loving, building families, careers, homes, and friendships. Humans sometimes drop anchor in the "sea of samsara" finding temporary haven from its storms and waves of change, but that always passes and according to the concept of samsara there is no choice but to keep travelling lifetime after lifetime.

The human predicament is a poignant one. We find ourselves cast into existence without explanation on to a small blue sphere of rock spinning around a gaseous star giving life, light and warmth, unsure if the earth is the only location for intelligent life in a vast unknown universe. In Carl Sagan's words "The Earth is a very small stage in a vast cosmic arena....a mote of dust suspended in a sunbeam."[18] Are we actors in an incomprehensible cosmic game, unsure why or what we are playing and who designed it for what purpose, planet earth providing the setting for the "sea of samsara" in which we swim, or float, or perhaps struggle and drown, lifetime after lifetime? Is the existence of our universe, and humans as its observers, pregnant with meaning and purpose as religions have always claimed, or is there no meaning or explanation or purpose to any of it? There is no guidebook to enlighten us why we are here and no instruction manual. Are humans just particularly clever animals, a much-improved hominid version of our primate ancestors who accidentally evolved by natural selection from random genetic mutations in a brutal competition of survival of the fittest, with no creator and no purpose apart from that we create for ourselves? Australian comedian and songwriter Tim Minchin sings in "Confessions", "we're just fucking monkeys with shoes." Are we "apes on the way up, or angels on the way down?"[19] Or did Jim Carrey get it right when he described us as atoms playing avatars?

The truth is humans have no certain idea how or why we are here no matter how hard religions try to convince otherwise. According to scientific rationalism there is no 'why' as Homo sapiens sapiens is the random accidental result of blind evolution without inherent meaning or purpose in an utterly indifferent universe that accidentally came in to being, and accidentally gave birth to life, and when we die we will find nothing but annihilation. Ideas such as samsara and rebirth assume something very different: that we are here in samsara living the life we are living because karma drove us here, and rebirth in samsara will continue until such time as karma is purified and enlightenment realized. We have gained a rare and precious human birth after passing through a process of endless births in other life forms. Viewed through the lens of samsara and rebirth our lives, our deaths, and every choice we make, are deeply meaningful and death is not the end.

And where do other animals apart from humans fit in? Are they also traveling around the wheel of samsara? Hinduism perceives the soul, or atman, as reincarnating endlessly in either human or non-human form according to spiritual evolution. Buddhism describes six realms of existence: gods, demi-gods, humans, animals, hungry ghosts and hells. Whatever the place of non-human life in samsara, it is only humans that are conscious of mortality and struggle against the death sentence inevitable from the moment of birth. Homo sapiens sapiens is the only animal capable of self-awareness, self-examination and conscience, building complex cultures and personal bonds and creating art, music, literature and architecture that outlive the individuals that create them, bringing enormous capacity for suffering but also the precious opportunity for liberation from samsara unique to humans.

This life, this reality, and our having awareness of those is astonishing. Everyone and everything from a tree to mosquito is a unique temporary assembling of atoms existing for a brief moment in the vastness of infinite time and space, an extraordinary everyday miracle. As Alan Watts puts it life is: "… a brief light that flashes but once in all the eons of time — a rare, complicated, and all-too-delicate organism on the fringe of biological evolution, where the wave of life bursts into individual, sparkling, and multi-coloured drops that gleam for a moment... only to vanish forever."[20] A person, a butterfly, a flower, a mountain, the venom of a snake or a cancer cell, are all collections of atoms born at the birth of the universe, recycled in myriad ever-changing forms that inevitably pass. When an organism dies its atoms might become part of an ocean, the soil, the air, a plant, or a worm. As Polonius explains in **Hamlet** "A man can fish with the worm that ate a king and then eat the fish that fed of that worm" to which Hamlet responds "Nothing but to show you how a king may go a progress through the guts of a beggar." And this transient collection of atoms that is us possesses that most inexplicable undefinable and mysterious of qualities: consciousness. And every living being is unique despite being almost entirely constructed of the same six elements.

Fear of death drives all religions expressed in yearning for an afterlife where the happiness so difficult to find, and impossible to hold on to in the body, is found after death. It is a strange idea that humans believe they must wait until the death of their living body before eternal bliss can be found, and suffering and death overcome by enlightenment, nirvana, moksha, heaven, paradise, or rejoining spirit ancestors. The fundamental premise of all the world's major religions is that the best life will be after death in whatever afterlife they propose. Hopefully, if we have behaved ourselves and followed the rules of our religion, that will not be a hell. It is extraordinary that a religion such as Christianity once vigorously asserted that the God of 'love' would burn 'his' 'children' in eternal hell for sins and disobediences such as having sex with someone they were not married to, or for Catholics eating meat on Fridays. If human parents behaved like God has so often threatened 'his' human 'children' they would be arrested for child abuse. One positive consequence of the collapse of organized religion is the bizarre twisting of spirituality that turns the creator of the universe in to a petty vindictive tyrant, is seldom heard these days. Priests and ministers thundering from their pulpits about God's 'righteous judgement' and the torments of hell has mostly gone out of fashion, at least from Christianity. Thank God for that.

Other animals undoubtedly also fear death but they do not devote their lives to reflecting on it. In **The Snow Leopard**, Peter Matthiessen describes humans as the "haunted animal that wastes most of a long and ghostly life wandering the future and the past on its hind legs, looking for meanings, only to see in the eyes of others of its kind that it must die." For all of us being born means we die: as Seneca the younger's analogy states the cradle does indeed lie in the grave. Death and what it brings are deeply perplexing, "that undiscovered country from whose bourne no traveller returns."[21] Life is a real-life version of snakes and ladders. Ladders of success, joy, meaning, lift us up, as do snakes of disappointment, failure and loss take us down, but inevitably the big snake of death at the bottom of the board will take everyone out of the game to destination unknown. Much of life in the kind of society I come from is spent in denial and avoidance of that inevitable death, that becoming acutely obvious during the unfolding of Rob's terminal illness. Humans preoccupy themselves with what Ernest Becker describes as "immortality projects"[22] amassing great wealth, composing great music, painting great art, building great buildings or great careers, creating whatever will outlast individuals and defy time and death. Mark Manson points out in **The Subtle Art of Not Giving a Fuck,** refusal to face death and suffering means people are always living in a state of denial and distraction.

Another form of denial, particularly common in the West, is glib 'positive thinking' that evades facing our own suffering or that of others. Industries of life coaches self-help books and gurus of positive thinking are built around helping people wear happy smiles of positivity, that shine from Facebook pages displaying wonderful lives, successful jobs and fabulous holidays. Except much of course is fake, not real life but projections of the happiness we all hope for and believe others to be having. Facebook involves "constantly presenting ourselves, and packaging ourselves, like potatoes pretending to be crisps."[23] Karen Armstrong in **Buddha** points out this "allows us to bury our heads in the sand, deny the ubiquity of pain in ourselves and others and to immure ourselves in a state of deliberate heartlessness to ensure our emotional survival. The Buddha would have had little time for this. In his view the spiritual life cannot begin until people allow themselves to be invaded by the reality of suffering and death, to realize how fully those permeate our whole experience and feel the pain of all other beings, even those whom we do not find congenial."[24]

Because the concept of samsara embraces the reality of suffering and death it might offer ways of understanding that are alternatives to denial or immersion in empty or false distractions. In the religious traditions that hold samsara as central recognizing the inevitability of death is perceived as a step towards enlightenment, both Buddhism and Hinduism embracing spiritual practices that focus on imagining and facing one's own death. Tibetan Buddhism specifically addresses the process of death in the **Bardo Thodol** or **Tibetan Book Of The Dead**. Rob's suffering and death made it impossible to ignore all this, setting me on a path to explore what religions and cultures outside of my own have to say. Could the ideas of samsara and rebirth present possible clues to the riddles of our lives, suffering and death? Before setting off on my travels through Nepal, Bali, Cambodia and India I searched if evidence for spiritual dimensions and samsara might be found outside of religion from the perspectives of science, particularly quantum physics, parapsychology and the experiences offered by psychedelic substances and mysticism. What they revealed does shed light on the possibility of spiritual dimensions beyond material reality, and that consciousness might continue after death, thereby making rebirth in samsara plausible. That evidence is the subject of the following chapter.

"Religion and science are the two wings upon which man's intelligence can soar into the heights, with which the human soul can progress. It is not possible to fly with one wing alone!"
Abu'l- Baha

CHAPTER THREE
SCIENCE, PSYCHEDELICS, MYSTICISM, CONSCIOUSNESS, SPIRITUALITY AND SAMSARA

There is evidence outside of religion that supports the existence of spiritual realms and the possibility that samsara and rebirth might be more than mere religious fictions and have value beyond the cultures they are embedded in. The central question is consciousness: if it dies with the brain then a soul, any kind of afterlife, rebirth and samsara are all impossible. If however consciousness is something else, not dependent on or created by matter, then spiritual possibilities are open. Futurist Ray Kurzweil, an ardent supporter of developing technology based immortality and artificial intelligence acknowledges that the nature of consciousness is the key question, surprisingly stating that the "ultimate spiritual value is consciousness."[25] If the ever-deepening mysteries of consciousness open the doors to spirituality then they also make rebirth and samsara valid possibilities to consider. Research that touches on anything spiritual has often been dismissed as 'pseudoscience' or worse, but if absolutist, either or thinking could be put aside it would permit a spirit of enquiry rather than competition or ridicule. Emerging research in quantum physics and parapsychology, together with accounts from mystics and users of psychedelics, could give clues that compliment each other as to the possibility of spiritual dimensions, revealing from different corners of understanding that the material reality we experience is not at all what it appears.

Mystical experiences provide a rich perspective on consciousness and spirituality. Believers of many kinds, as well as agnostics and atheists, give surprisingly similar descriptions of spiritual ecstasy accompanied by light and a sense of transcendent unity. Psychologist William James gives many examples in his remarkable study **The Varieties of Religious Experience**. They do not involve belief or dogma but are accounts of direct personal numinous experiences separate from religion. The **Mundaka Upanishad** describes the experience of unity with the transcendent reality of Brahman, or the Self, as entirely independent of the intellect:

"Bright but hidden, the Self dwell in the heart.
Everything that moves, breathes, opens, and closes
Lives in the Self. He is the source of love
And may be known through love but not through thought."

In some cases religious beliefs may inform interpretation but the experience itself is one of knowing rather than believing, and religion plays no part in it. Most great spiritual thinkers have had some kind of direct experience of God, or in Buddhist terms the 'clear pure light'. Ironically mystical experiences often become incorporated or developed in to organized religions that then lose touch with the living spiritual experiences that inspired them obscuring them in dogma and ritual. The conversion of Saul to St Paul involving an intense light that blinded him and the voice of Jesus speaking to him as he was on the road to Damascus to persecute Christians, is an example of a personal transcendent experience going on to profoundly shape organised religion.

In the Hindu tradition direct mystical experience is known as samadhi, in Zen Buddhism it is satori: "Satori is a brief flash. Suddenly the light breaks through. For a short timeless time we experience eternity in its unmanifest form. It's comparable to salvikalpa samadhi."[26] A surprising example of samadhi happened to Edgar Mitchell during the Apollo 14 moon landing in 1971. He describes it in an interview: "The descriptions of samadhi, savikalpa samadhi, were exactly what I felt: it is described as seeing things in their separateness, but experiencing them viscerally as a unity, as oneness, accompanied by ecstasy."[27] His time in space completely changed him, and when he returned he founded the

Institute of Noetic Sciences. He explains to Sarah Truman of **Ascent Magazine:** "Science and religion have lived on opposite sides of the street now for hundreds of years. So here we are, in the twenty-first century, trying to put two faces of reality – the existence face and the intelligence or conscious face – into the same understanding. Body and mind, physicality and consciousness belong to the same side of reality – it's a dyad, not a dualism. This is what I've been working toward for the past thirty-five years and why I founded the Noetic Institute. After my experience in space, I believed it was time for us to take a look at spiritual or religious experiences from the point of view of quantum science."[28] Edgar Mitchell is not alone in being opened to spirituality by a transcendental experience of wider truth from travel in space. Astronaut Gene Cernan describes a similar experience: "I felt the world was just... there was too much purpose, too much logic," said. "It was too beautiful to happen by accident. There has to be somebody bigger than you, and bigger than me, and I mean this in a spiritual sense, not a religious sense." Charlie Duke," a lunar module pilot for Apollo 16, became a Christian after seeing earth from space; Jim Irwin of Apollo 15 became a preacher; and Apollo 9 astronaut Russell Schweickart began transcendental meditation and dedicated himself to voluntary work."[29]

Paramahansa Yogananda describes an experience of samadhi in **Autobiography Of A Yogi** conferred by his guru Sri Yukteswar: "He struck me gently on my chest above the heart. My body became immovably rooted; Soul and mind instantly lost their physical bondage and streamed out like a fluid piercing light from my every pore. The flesh was as though dead; yet in my intense awareness I knew that never before had I been more fully alive. My sense of identity was no longer narrowly confined to a body but embraced the circumambient atoms...The roots of plants and trees appeared through a dim transparency of the soil; I discerned the inward flow of their sap.....All objects within my panoramic gaze trembled and vibrated...My body, Master's, the pillared courtyard, the furniture and the floor, the trees and sunshine,...all melted in to a luminous sea; even as sugar crystals, thrown in a glass of water, dissolve...An oceanic joy broke upon calm endless shores of my soul. The Spirit of God, I realized, is exhaustless Bliss; His body is countless tissues of light....The divine dispersion of rays poured from an Eternal Source, blazing into galaxies, transfigured with ineffable auras."[30]

Peter Matthiessen describes in **The Snow Leopard** his own mystical experience after a long Zen Buddhist meditation session: "....on that morning, in the near darkness- the altar candle was the only light in the long room - in the dead hush, like the hush in these snow mountains, the silence swelled with the intake of my breath into a Presence of vast benevolence of which *I was a part*: in my journal for that day, seeking in vain to find words for what had happened, I called it the "Smile". The Smile seemed to grow out of me, filling all space above and behind like a huge shadow of my own Buddha form, which was minuscule now without weight, borne up on the upraised palm of this Buddha-being, this eternal amplification of myself. For it was I who had smiled: the Smile was Me. I did not breathe, I did not need to look; for It was Everywhere.....Wounds, ragged edges, hollow places were all gone, all had been healed; my heart lay at the heart of Creation. Then I let my breath go, and gave myself up to delighted immersion in this Presence, to a peaceful belonging so overwhelming that tears of relief poured from my eyes, so overwhelming that even now, struggling to find a better term than "Smile" or "Presence", the memory affects me as I write." [31]

Mystics, whether they are religious, atheist, or agnostic describe a spiritual reality, beyond name, form, creed or culture. Lao Tzu names this the Tao or "way," the underlying essence of all things, in the **Tao Te Ching**:

"The Tao that can be told is not the eternal Tao;
The name that can be named is not the eternal name.
The nameless is the beginning of heaven and earth.
Ever desireless, one can see the mystery.
Ever desiring, one can see the manifestations.
These two spring from the same source but differ in name;"[32]

For a mystic in deep contemplation, experiencing satchitananda, or truth, bliss, consciousness, alone in their Himalayan cave, wrangling over which religion is true, and who is 'saved' and who is not, are utter irrelevances. Great spiritual saints of India such as Ramakrishna, Krishnamurti, Yogananda, Vivekenanda, Ramana Maharshi, and Sivinananda, all gained their inspiration from profound mystical experiences, Siddhartha Gautama becoming the Buddha, or enlightened one, after intense meditation and spiritual realization under the bodhi tree in Bodgaya, India.

Mainstream Protestant Christian churches are mostly highly suspicious of mystical experiences, describing them in derogatory terms such as as 'mist is schism'. However the Catholic Church has a long and rich history of mystics and saints, as does Sufism in Islam. Saint Teresa of Ávila (1515–1582) a prominent Spanish mystic and Catholic contemplative saint, describes in **The Way of Perfection**, her "Prayer of the Quiet," mystical experience: "The soul rests in peace...all [her] powers are at rest. The soul understands, with an understanding quite different from that given by external senses, that she is now quite close to God and that, if she drew just a little nearer, she would become one thing with him by union. She does not see him with eyes of the body or the soul....The soul understands he is there, though not so clearly. She does not know herself how she understands; she sees only that she is in the Kingdom...."[33]

The sculpture by Bernini in Rome depicting the ecstasy of St Teresa shows her intense longing for oneness with God as a winged youth spears her heart with an arrow. She is stretched out in ecstasy in a way that resembles sexual orgasm, a moment of breaking down the barriers between self and other, or in her case self and God. She describes this mystical union, "It pleased our Lord that I should see the following vision a number of times. I saw an angel near me, on the left side, in bodily form. This I am not wont to see, save very rarely.... In this vision it pleased the Lord that I should see it thus. He was not tall, but short, marvellously beautiful, with a face which shone as though he were one of the highest of the angels, who seem to be all of fire: they must be those whom we call Seraphim.... I saw in his hands a long golden spear, and at the point of the iron there seemed to be a little fire. This I thought that he thrust several times into my heart, and that it penetrated to my entrails. When he drew out the spear he seemed to be drawing them with it, leaving me all on fire with a wondrous love for God. The pain was so great that it caused me to utter several moans; and yet so exceeding sweet is this greatest of pains that it is impossible to desire to be rid of it, or for the soul to be content with less than God." [34]

No doubt the Catholic Church would be appalled at the suggestion but is this so very different from the indescribable bliss and realization said to be experienced in Tantric sexual union, depicted in the Vajrayana Buddhist statues of deities with their consorts in yab yum? The Sufi poet Hafiz writes "I searched for God and found only myself. I searched for myself and found only God". That is not greatly different from the teachings of Advaita Vedanta in Hinduism, that the individual self is identical to the essence of the Self as Brahman, the Lord of Love, or God: Tat Tvam Asi: "thou art that". And neither of them are so utterly different from the Christian Bible that states "The Kingdom of God is within you." At the heart of mystical accounts are direct personal experiences of the same spiritual reality of oneness and love that are utterly independent from religious formulations.

Joseph Campbell drew parallels between the experiences given by substances such as LSD and religious mystical states, concluding that psychedelic drug users drown "in the same pool mystics swim in,"[35] an expanded state of awareness of alternative dimensions. Perhaps what psychedelics do is open the "doors of perception" to experiences similar to mystics as they share elements in common despite their many differences. Researchers are once again, after decades of prohibition, exploring the frontiers of the mind revealed by psychedelics that unlock states of consciousness beyond normal reality. The experiences of psychedelics users suggest, like mysticism, that everyday reality is only one of many dimensions, spiritual forces are real, and consciousness is not dependent on matter. Aldous Huxley accessed transcendent spiritual states through psychedelics such as LSD and mescaline, describing those in **The Doors of Perception.** William Blake wrote in his 1793 poem "The Marriage of Heaven and Hell," "If the doors of perception were cleansed everything would appear to man as it is. Infinite. For man has closed himself up, till he sees all things thro' narrow chinks of his cavern."[36] Perhaps the experiences associated with LSD, psilocybin, mescaline, or DMT give access to spiritual realms hitherto closed or controlled by religion. They also give intriguing clues as to the nature of consciousness and therein lies the key to evaluating the possibility of rebirth and samsara.

Many cultures have used consciousness-altering substances such as soma in ancient India, the oracle at Delphi, kava in the Pacific Islands, the widespread use of opium in the nineteenth century peddled from British colonial India. There is evidence that opium and fermented alcohol have been used for thousands of years in the Middle East. A highly toxic extract from the Iboga plant is used by the people of central Africa to commune with the dead in shamanic rituals that can bring about the death of the participant if the dose is miscalculated. The peyote cactus containing mescaline and psilocybin mushrooms, have both been associated with cultures in Mexico and South America from ancient times. The sadhus of India and Nepal smoke copious quantities of cannabis, or ganja, and hashish to enhance their spiritual quest. The ancient Egyptians utilized extracts from the blue water lily. A pharmaceutically created synthetic drug, LSD, is claimed by some to offer a path to spiritual dimensions as described by Huston Smith in **Cleansing The Doors Of Perception**. Deepak Chopra revealed in an interview that his initiation into spirituality was through a LSD trip at 17, but he stressed mind-altering drugs are not recreational and should only be explored by mature adults with the guidance of an experienced shaman or guide.[37] That is good advice as uninformed, casual experimenting with psychedelics has potential danger, people on LSD trips having jumped off buildings to their deaths believing they can fly.

Some now seek the "sacred medicine" of "mother ayahuasca," a plant brew made by indigenous shamans in Peru and Brazil containing dimethyltryptamine (DMT) as its active ingredient. DMT itself has been the subject of clinical research by those such as Dr Rick Strassman in **DMT: Spirit Molecule**. Ayahuasca does not promote a religion but is claimed to be a spiritual medicine that teaches deep lessons of the soul. William Burroughs and Allen Ginsberg describe in **Yage Letters** their experiences with ayahuasca, or yage, in the 1950's, despite the deep antagonism of American society at that time, and their work contributed to the dawning of the counterculture and the massive changes brought by the 1960's. Many of those who take ayahuasca, or DMT, describe meeting beings that teach or reveal highly significant life changing information in a purposeful meaningful way. The active molecule in ayahuasca is DMT, and the combination of plant extracts contains a monoamine oxidase inhibitor that prevents the DMT from being broken down by the gut so it can be absorbed and thus open the "doors of perception". Timothy Leary, Richard Alpert (later to become Ram Dass) and Ralph Metzner, in their 1964 **The Psychedelic Experience,** explored the capacity of LSD, psilocybin, and mescaline to bring transcendent states of awareness, drawing parallels to **The Tibetan Book Of The Dead**. The opening page of **The Psychedelic Experience** claims "A psychedelic experience is a journey to new realms of consciousness." The writers assert that the phantasms of darkness and light, bliss and terror, revealed by psychedelics, are of the same essence as those experienced in the bardo, the state of consciousness after death. In 1963 Leary was fired from his position lecturing in psychology at Harvard and was imprisoned multiple times being described by President Nixon as "the most dangerous man in America."

The work of brothers Dennis and Terence McKenna also brought mind-altering substances to the attention of a wide audience. Dennis McKenna's **The Brotherhood Of The Screaming Abyss** is a fascinating account of their adventures in the world of psychedelics and the changes in American society from the fifties, through the sixties and seventies and on in to the twenty-first century. It was a genuine thrill when the second hand copy of the book purchased online arrived in the post signed by Dennis McKenna. Some users of DMT and ayahuasca describe meeting with intelligences that disclose knowledge and unity with a transcendent energy that might be called the spirit of nature, a spiritual realm, or God in the language of religion. Dennis McKenna recounts an experience with ayahuasca in Brazil where he becomes one with plants, a little reminiscent of Paramahansa Yogananda's mystical experience where he sees the roots of trees glowing through the soil and the sap of plants rising. During this experience a wise entity communicates to McKenna a message about human destruction of the Amazon, nature and the earth: "You monkeys only think you're running things…you don't think we would really allow this to happen, do you?"[38] It is deeply ironic that non-addictive psychedelic substances that unlock not pleasure but knowledge, are classed as category one banned drugs in the US, whilst seriously addictive destructive drugs like methadone and fentanyl are category two. Destructive drugs like alcohol and tobacco are legally and socially sanctioned. Even more ironic, in the USA the culture of weapons and militarization is revered as patriotic and necessary, whilst the pursuit of self-knowledge associated with psychedelic drugs is feared, condemned, criminalized, and repressed as dangerous. It is easy and legal to own a gun, they can still be purchased at Walmart, but being in possession of a psychedelic drug might well bring arrest and prison.

Opinions as to the nature of the experiences facilitated by psychedelics, are much divided. To a shaman in the Amazon jungle 'plant medicines' are the channel through which spirit and nature entities communicate. Those are regarded as unquestionably real. Many users of DMT and ayahuasca describe meeting with teachers and beings who give them knowledge, awareness and messages from plant and spiritual worlds. Oddly, many people describe the presence of technology in their experiences with psychedelics such as DMT, and spiritual beings trying to impart knowledge that is remarkably consistent. The experiences themselves are felt as deeply meaningful and not random, opening up contact with an alternate reality just as real as that of every day.

Aldous Huxley's view was that the function of the brain is to act as a kind of limiting valve of perception and that psychedelics open that valve to allow awareness of a much wider reality, including dimensions otherwise closed. Spontaneous mystical experiences share common elements with those given by mind-altering substances, a minority of people being able to access those states without psychedelics. Mind-altering substances act to open the doors of perception for the majority who cannot do so without them. Dr Rick Strassman, agrees with Huxley that psychedelics open the limiting valves of perception, the brain being the receiver and mediator of psychedelic experiences but not their source. Strassman argues DMT widens the capacity of the brain to receive access to realms and dimensions of consciousness, otherwise closed, in the manner of adjusting the reception antenna of a TV or radio so as to be able to pick up normally invisible information. "By conceiving of the brain as a receiver of information...one can accommodate the biological model of changing brain function with a chemical. At the same time, it allows for the possibility that what is being received, while not usually perceptible, is consistently and verifiably existent for a large number of individuals. It may, indeed, reflect stable, free-standing, and parallel planes of reality."[39] It has been speculated that psychedelics might enable contact with parallel universes as envisaged by the multiverse theory, or with dimensions usually closed, or even with the invisible dark matter thought to make up the majority of the universe about which almost nothing is known.

A neuroscientist is likely to see psychedelic experiences as nothing more than the result of tickling of particular neuronal pathways and brain chemistry, their usual view being that consciousness is entirely confined to and produced by the biological substrate of the brain. A conventional Christian might regard the visions and beings that appear as demonic evil spirits, whereas to others such as followers of Brazilian religions that utilize ritual use of ayahuasca, they provide channels to God, angels and spiritual entities. In Brazil there are two organizations where ceremonial consuming of ayahuasca is regarded as the medium of communication with the spiritual world: Santo Daime and Beneficent Spiritist Center União do Vegetal or UDV. Ayahuasca is used by the indigenous people of the Amazon under the guidance of an experienced shaman to open contact with spiritual and plant teachers. In a very different context, people in Amsterdam can, and do, head to a psychedelic café to take DMT at lunchtime before returning to work.

A scientific researcher of mescaline, psilocybin, DMT, or ayahuasca, may have little idea what is really going on for the people consuming them, although obviously something significant is going on. How the people and groups using or researching psychedelics view them varies greatly according to their own particular presuppositions and motivations, with no consensus as to what, if anything, the experiences mean even if the experiences themselves show surprising consistencies. Irrespective of how psychedelics are understood they possess the power to profoundly alter, expand and challenge conventional reality and consciousness. They can offer potentially terrifying experiences so it is important only informed adults consume them in a safe environment. In that context they have something significant to reveal as has been understood by ancient and indigenous cultures for thousands of years. It is not only psychedelic substances that have the capacity to induce altered states of consciousness. Music such as drumming, dancing, dehydration and other methods, can and do disrupt the usual mechanisms of the mind thus opening the "doors of perception". Shamans in Africa, whirling Sufi dervishes and Balinese trance dancers are examples where dance and or sound induce an altered state in which their participants believe they enter communion with spiritual forces. Mind-altering substances and practices offer tools with which to explore the riddles of consciousness and in doing so have the potential to shed light on the possibilities of spirituality, rebirth and samsara. It is not a matter of returning to the mindset of an indigenous or ancient culture, but of integrating experiences of altered states of consciousness with scientific investigation and modern knowledge, to bring about a counterbalance to the heavily materialistic, rationalistic, mechanistic, divorced from nature, and closed to inner or spiritual experiences, characteristic of many contemporary societies.

Ironically it is not religion, heavily weighted with dogma and cultural baggage, but science that could show a way forward in territory long claimed as the exclusive preserve of religion. If scientific method could be brought to spiritual matters, as urged by Abdu'l- Baha of the Bahai faith, then truths might be discerned: "…weigh carefully in the balance of reason and science everything that is presented to you as religion. If it passes this test, then accept it, for it is truth! If, however, it does not so conform, then reject it, for it is ignorance!"[40] He continues: "There is no contradiction between true religion and science. When a religion is opposed to science it becomes mere superstition ... The true principles of all religions are in conformity with the teachings of science." According to him spirituality and science are both necessary and complimentary, spirituality providing the 'why' and science the 'how' in relation to life and the universe.

Sri Aurobindo proposes in **The Life Divine** that we live in an exciting phase in history, where science and spirituality might begin to cross the frontiers of knowledge together to explore what lies behind the material universe because the quest for truth will inevitably take humans there: "If modern Materialism were simply and unintelligent acquiescence in the material life, the advance might be indefinitely delayed. But since its very soul is the search for Knowledge, it will be unable to cry a halt; as it reaches the barriers of sense-knowledge and of the reasoning from sense-knowledge, its very rush will carry it beyond and the rapidity and sureness with which it has embraced the visible universe is only an earnest of the energy and success which we may hope see repeated in the conquest of what lies beyond, once the stride is taken that crosses the barrier. We already see that advance in its obscure beginnings."[41] Edward O Wilson argues in **The Meaning of Human Existence** that religion, as a product of culture, should be dispensed with, but exploration of the questions which spirituality addresses is an important task for science to involve itself with.

Science has been deeply reluctant to enter in to spiritual territory, mostly for very good reasons, but not all scientists have refused to do so and some have been sufficiently courageous to tackle questions overlapping with spirituality. Frijof Capra's **The Tao of Physics,** published in 1975, described the strange world of subatomic particles, the relativity of time and space, and what appears dense matter is composed of spinning vortices of empty space and energy, all pointing towards possible openings into spiritual realms. I reread **The Tao of Physics** as Rob was dying. It is an extraordinary fact that our existence is in the vehicle of a perishable flesh and blood body, on a speck of a planet, whirling through an obscure part of the Milky Way galaxy, where everything, including us, is constructed from atoms of stardust. As Carl Sagan observed in **Cosmos** "The nitrogen in our DNA, the calcium in our teeth, the iron in our blood, the carbon in our apple pies were made in the interiors of collapsing stars."[42] It is astounding to contemplate a new born baby arriving in to the world is made from trillions of atoms of mostly six elements created at the birth of the universe believed to have occurred around 13.8 billion years ago. One cannot even begin to imagine where all those atoms of carbon, oxygen, hydrogen, nitrogen, calcium and phosphorus might have travelled on their incredible journey from the first moment of the universe to come together in a moment of time as the miracle of new baby.

Gazing towards the heavens on a dark night everything seems so quiet and still, the stars unmoving fixed points of light in the black empty vastness of space, but that is not so. Everything at both the largest and smallest levels of matter, from galaxies to the tiniest subatomic particles, is moving in mind bendingly fast spirals of energy. The earth rotates on its axis at 1700 miles an hour and revolves around the sun at 66,000 miles an hour. The solar system orbits around the centre of the spiral Milky Way Galaxy at an average velocity of 828,000 km/hr taking about 230 million years to make one complete orbit around our galaxy. The Milky Way galaxy spirals around a huge black hole at its centre and hurtles through deep space at 2.1 million kilometres an hour towards the neighbouring much larger Andromeda galaxy. An infinite variety of forms of matter arise in this whirling dance of energy, and all are impermanent, including, in the context of vast eons of time, planets, stars and galaxies. The Milky Way will in the next four billion years or so collide with Andromeda galaxy to form a giant elliptical galaxy. The view will be spectacular but there will be no one on earth to see it as the gaseous star, our sun, will have burned up making life on earth impossible within the next billion or so years. In around six billion years the sun will have become a white dwarf and collapse in on itself as a black hole taking the solar system into oblivion, an example of impermanence on a cosmic scale.

Around 13.8 billion years ago scientists believe this universe of galaxies burst in the "big bang" from a pea-sized ball, eventually evolving the sentient life on planet earth that observes it such as us. How it is remotely possible for something to spring from nothing, or awareness to emerge from matter, is unknown. The "just right" nature of our universe is perplexing as explored in **The God Theory** by Bernard Haisch: "It is now accepted in astrophysics that several key properties of the Universe and the laws of physics have "just right" values that enable life to arise and evolve. This is essentially undisputed. The explanation for this fine-tuning that appeals to most scientists is that there must be a huge number of other Universes, perhaps even an infinite number, in which the laws of physics are different. Life as we know it could never arise in such universes. Our universe is just one of these, and we find ourselves here because we could not have originated anywhere else."[43] This "just right" universe, our galactic home, is the material reality in to which Indian spiritual traditions claim we are continually reborn in samsara, so where does life fit into its mystery?

Nobel Laureate George Wald comments: "We have good reason to believe that we find ourselves in a Universe permeated with life, in which life arises inevitably—given enough time—wherever the conditions exist that make it possible. Yet were any one of a number of the physical properties of our Universe otherwise—some of them basic, others seeming trivial, almost accidental—that life, which seems now to be so prevalent, would become impossible, here or anywhere. It takes no great imagination to conceive of other possible universes, each stable and workable in itself, yet lifeless. How is it that, with so many other apparent options, we are in a Universe that possesses just that peculiar nexus of properties that breeds life? It has occurred to me lately - I must confess with some shock at first to my scientific sensibilities - that both questions might be brought into some degree of congruence. This is with the assumption that mind, rather than emerging as a late outgrowth in the evolution of life, has existed always, as the matrix, the source and condition of physical reality - that the stuff of which physical reality is composed is mind-stuff. It is mind that has composed a physical Universe that breeds life, and so eventually evolves creatures that know and create: science, art, and technology-making animals. In them the universe begins to know itself." [44] That is a statement with which Sri Aurobindo would have agreed: "Consciousness is the great underlying fact, the universal witness for whom the world is a field, the senses instruments."[45]

All matter, including biological life, is constructed from eighty-five atomic elements, and almost all from six types of atom arranged in myriad combinations, like lego, to form molecules. Living beings are brief coalitions of the "dust and ashes" of atoms born at the start of the universe and return to "dust and ashes" at death. Everything is a temporary coming together of those inconceivably ancient atoms becoming perhaps a blade of grass eaten by a sheep that is roasted on a fire for a meal. Some of its atoms might float as smoke in to the sky to be blown in the wind, some become the bones and muscles of the eater or perhaps pass out of the body to drift through sewers to a river whose waters nourish more blades of grass for another sheep in a never ending shifting of shapes and forms, coming together and dispersing in the eternal cosmic dance of creation and destruction epitomized by the Nataraja Shiva of Hinduism. We breathe in each breath atoms of argon that might have been breathed by Abraham Lincoln or Buddha. How it is possible for life to emerge from collections of atoms, that form compounds, that form molecules, that form cells, that form differing organs of complex biological organisms like ourselves, is an extraordinary mystery, and as the inhabitants of the miracle of a living body we often forget to notice the enormity of that mystery. And how that body comes to exhibit something as inexplicable and incredible as consciousness is the biggest mystery of them all.

The internal world of the atom mirrors the universe: lots of empty space and subatomic particles moving fast, just like the spiralling orbits of stars and galaxies. Calculations show that in an atom of hydrogen, the electron is traveling at about 2,200 kilometres per second. Protons and neutrons whiz around inside the nucleus of an atom at approximately 40,000 miles per second whereas neutrinos, elementary particles with no electric charge, move at approximately the speed of light or 299,338 kilometres a second. Protons and neutrons are composite in nature, bound together by high-velocity forces and at the subatomic level the distinction between particles and forces is blurred. Electrons rapidly orbit around the nucleus of an atom, but it is impossible to know both their speed and location at the same time and they can only be described as probabilities, this being a reflection of the Heisenberg uncertainty principle. This is not due to flaws in the system of measurement but the inherent nature of the subatomic world, where particles are not things, but interconnected patterns revealing a fundamental unity of energy and matter. Most of an atom is empty space, its nucleus equivalent in size to a pea in a football stadium, mirroring the Buddhist understanding that the fundamental nature of existence is emptiness or shunyata, as described by Avalokiteshvara, the Boddhisattva of Compassion, in the **The Heart Sutra**:

"O Sariputra, Form does not differ from Emptiness
And Emptiness does not differ from Form.
Form is Emptiness and Emptiness is Form."

Protons and neutrons inside the atom are made up of even smaller particles, quarks and leptons, which are comprised of a growing list of even smaller particles with such marvellous names as squarks, winos and chameleon, the frontiers of the very smallest particles remaining wild mysterious country. The smashing apart of subatomic particles in particle accelerators such as at CERN, reveals patterns of energy probabilities whirling in and out of forms, the illusion of dense matter being created by the strength of the three forces within the atom: weak force, strong force and electromagnetic force. Peter Matthiessen describes this "… most scientists would agree with the ancient Hindus that nothing exists or is destroyed, things merely change shape or form, that matter is insubstantial in origin, a temporary aggregate of atoms held together by the pervasive energy that animates the electron."[46] Every form of matter that manifests in samsara, be it a person, dog, plant, mosquito, rock or planet, is at the subatomic level a dance of energy and empty space, and the solid, dense material world we believe we inhabit disappears altogether at the quantum level.

Through the course of the 20th century, the view of matter as lifeless particles governed by mechanistic Newtonian laws shifted to understanding that in subatomic particles the boundary between matter and energy collapses. Probing the secrets of subatomic particles has brought recognition that everything, including the human body, is at the tiniest level energy probabilities, be those people or the oxygen they breathe. Swami Vivekananda refers to this in **Raja Yoga**: "By what power is this Akasha[47] (the world of matter) manufactured into this universe? By the power of Prana (energy)."[48] Vivekananda was seeking a scientific basis for Vedanta's understanding that the universe is energy, from which matter emerges. In 1896 he wrote: "All perceptible matter comes from a primary substance, or tenuity beyond conception, filling all space, the akasha or luminiferous ether, which is acted upon by the life giving Prana or creative force, calling into existence, in never-ending cycles all things and phenomena."[49]

Quantum physics is revealing the world to be utterly different from what science, and common sense, once assumed it to be. At the quantum level distinctions between a particle and a wave are meaningless because a photon can be either a wave or a particle as shown by the double slit experiment. If a beam of electrons or photons is passed through an opening they will behave as particles, rather than a wave, only when being observed. "The rules of quantum physics state that an unobserved photon exists in all possible states simultaneously but, when observed or measured, exhibits only one state."[50] The observer effect reveals that consciousness is in some way central to matter because the observation of the observer is what causes subatomic energy probabilities to become fixed in to position as particles that constitute material reality. This has startling implications as to the nature of reality that in no way fits the view that the world is fixed and separate from consciousness irrespective of whether being observed or not.

Many physicists find this intrusion of mind into the world of subatomic particles acutely uncomfortable. It demolishes the old assumption that matter and reality exist entirely independently from perception of them, that the moon is always present exactly as we see it regardless of anyone looking at it, as common sense and science had always taken for granted. The observer effect is a revolutionary discovery as it suggests consciousness produces the material world not the other way around and that we live in a participatory universe. The possibility that consciousness is in some unknown way the source of matter is a startling reversal of the assumption that it is matter, in the form of a brain, that produces consciousness, and it opens massive cans of worms not compatible with earlier scientific assumptions. Many scientists remain extremely reluctant, and others openly hostile, to contemplating that consciousness and matter are entwined in some yet to be understood way. Nonetheless the oddities of the quantum world, and the involvement of mind in those, refuse to disappear. "As the famous Copenhagen interpretation of quantum mechanics argues, we cannot speak about an objective reality other than that which is revealed through measurement and observation."[51]

'Quantum mysticism' as it came to be known is an old debate in quantum physics that began in 1920's Germany with those such as Niels Bohr, Wolfgang Pauli, Werner Heisenberg, and Erwin Schrodinger, all open to the idea that matter and consciousness were connected. Pioneer of quantum physics and Nobel Laureate Wolfgang Pauli, and Carl Jung established a close connection, their letters published as **Atom and Archetype**. Pauli was fascinated by Jung's concept of synchronicity or meaningful co-incidences. Max Planck, founder of quantum theory and winner of the Nobel prize for physics in 1918, adopted the following position in relation to consciousness "...I regard consciousness as fundamental. I regard matter as derivative from consciousness. We cannot get behind consciousness. Everything that we talk about, everything that we regard as existing, postulates consciousness."[52] Einstein was particularly averse to the creeping of what he regarded as mysticism in to physics, accusing Niels Bohr of this in 1927. However Einstein also believed that "the cosmic religious feeling is the strongest and noblest motive for scientific research."[53]The debate continues on in to the present time, many physicists rejecting what they regard as 'woo' interpretations of quantum physics whilst others such as Paul Davies and David Bohm continue to explore the relationship between mind and matter. In **The Mind Of God: The Scientific Basis For A Rational World** Davies concludes the book with the enigmatic statement that the universe is "no minor byproduct of mindless, purposeless forces. We are truly meant to be here."

The discovery of quantum entanglement and non-locality brought further disconcerting dismantling of traditional concepts of matter, time and space. If a photon is split into two entangled photons then those remain entangled so that the state of one instantaneously transfers to the other, even if separated by enormous distances, independent of time and space and in defiance of the usual laws of physics. The implications of this are hotly debated in the physics community who are understandably puzzled and uncomfortable where this is taking a world they once assumed to be solid inert matter that obeyed the laws of physics. The phenomenon of quantum entanglement so annoyed Einstein he termed it "spooky action at a distance". In July 2019, physicists at the University of Glasgow captured for the first time an image of a strong form of quantum entanglement.[54]

Could quantum entanglement offer some explanation for parapsychological phenomena, the morphic fields proposed by Rupert Sheldrake or Robert Lanza's theories in **Biocentrism**? Could this principle of quantum entanglement apply on a cosmic scale, as everything in the universe emerged at the Big Bang from a tiny ball of super condensed energy and matter? Is there some kind of field of energy and consciousness from which all matter and form arises, our individual consciousness being but one expression of that? Is it possible that consciousness is the underlying fabric of reality out of which energy, matter, time, and space are woven? If that were discovered to be the case then concepts such as samsara and rebirth could have legitimate basis irrespective of their religious associations, because consciousness would not be annihilated by death and could feasibly be reborn in a new bodily vehicle. It is a strange irony that simultaneous with the culture of Western societies becoming increasingly materialist and secular, the outer reaches of science are suggesting possibilities with profound spiritual implications that reveal the nature of consciousness, 'reality' and ourselves is not what it is usually assumed to be, making the possibility of ongoing rebirths in samsara worth considering. Many scientists refuse to enter what is condescendingly labelled New Age metaphysics, but the strange truths of the subatomic world are inevitably taking it towards spiritual questions despite understandable resistance.

If the atoms of matter from which brains and neurons are made are mostly empty space and energy, then where in the illusion of matter does consciousness lie? The 1980's version of the **Dictionary of Psychology** describes consciousness as: "A fascinating but elusive phenomenon; it is impossible to specify what it is, what it does, or why it evolved. Nothing worth reading has been written about it."[55] It remains unknown what consciousness is or how it is created: perhaps the brain manifests it rather than creates it? Michael Pollan in **How to Change Your Mind: The New Science of Psychedelics**[56] draws the analogy that locating consciousness entirely in the brain is a bit like searching for a person depicted in a TV program inside the hardware of the television set, rather than recognizing they are a wave transmission manifested by material hardware but not created by it. No one knows how emotions of love, hate, grief, joy and envy emerge from neurons. That is the "hard problem of consciousness",[57] described by David Chalmers: how can a material organ deliver subjective experience and feelings? How does consciousness manifest, as the mysterious 'ghost in the machine' of flesh and blood bodies which are sixty percent water and constructed of atoms that at the subatomic level are patterns of energy probabilities whirling in and out of forms? How does the brain, as a collection of atoms, generate memory, awareness, emotion or a sense of self? As a recent article in **Scientific American** asks: "What is it about the biophysics of a chunk of highly excitable brain matter that turns gray goo into the glorious surround sound and Technicolor that is the fabric of everyday experience?"[58]

Recent theories as to the nature of consciousness explore various intriguing possibilities such as consciousness is a manifestation of the brain's electromagnetic field or related to communication by light. It has been discovered that living beings emit light, or biophotons, and that DNA stores and releases photons. These biophotons are in the ultraviolet and low visible light range but are not visible being equivalent in strength to the light from a candle viewed from a distance of six miles. The role biophotons play is not clearly understood but they show properties of quantum coherence and can communicate with each other, perhaps providing the means of intra and inter cellular communication.[59] Biophotons exist in the brain and neurons and according to Nobel prize nominee for physics, Fritz Albert Popp, biophotons are responsible for awareness and determine the processes of consciousness. The role of biophotons presents fascinating avenues for future research and opens up the possibility that consciousness is in some way a wave function involving light and hence not confined to matter. If this is shown to be the case and consciousness is not dependent on matter that means the continuation of consciousness after the death of the body cannot be ruled out. Rebirth and samsara, as well as phenomena such as telepathy, then become plausible and worthy of investigation. It is interesting that in the language and imagery of religion light is closely associated with spirituality and sacred figures are often depicted with haloes of light around their heads, or glowing like Jesus at the transfiguration described in the **Bible** in Matthew 17: "After six days Jesus took with him Peter, James and John the brother of James, and led them up a high mountain by themselves. There he was transfigured before them. His face shone like the sun, and his clothes became as white as the light." Paramahansa Yogananda's account of the mystical experience conferred by his guru Sri Yukteswar in **Autobiography of a Yogi**, concludes "The Spirit of God, I realized, is exhaustless Bliss; His body is countless tissues of light….The divine dispersion of rays poured from an Eternal Source, blazing into galaxies, transfigured with ineffable auras."[60] The discovery of biophotons in DNA and the brain gives a whole new meaning to the word 'englightenment' to describe the spiritual quest.

There are many theories as to the riddle of consciousness proposed by philosophers, atheists, idealists, dualists, materialists, mystics, agnostics, neuroscientists, psychiatrists, biocentrists, quantum physicists, humanists, theologians, mystics, biophysicists and transhumanists, and they inevitably reach differing conclusions because of differing conceptual presuppositions. Even finding a definition of consciousness acceptable to all has not been achieved. Varying views of what consciousness might be depend on the assumptions of the particular theory used to approach it. A reductionist fundamentalism can appear whereby those who adopt a particular paradigm find it extremely difficult to perceive and interpret anything except through the lens of their particular point of view, and a confirmation bias will set in confirming their own perspective is right. A Hindu sadhu deep in mystical experience of samadhi will inevitably have an utterly different understanding of consciousness from a neuroscientist dissecting a brain, or viewing brain activity with a PET scanner. It is an odd paradox that the tool used to study consciousness is the mind, which is a manifestation of consciousness, it being only with consciousness that consciousness can be explored.

Indian spiritual ideas asserting that the material world has no objective independent existence apart from the consciousness that perceives it, parallel the implications of the observer effect that patterns of wave probabilities only become particles upon observation. Sri Aurobindo expresses this "...the universe exists only or for the consciousness that observes and has not independent reality."[61] Lama Anarika Govinda in **The Way of The White Cloud** explains that the Buddhist "...does not believe in an independent or separately existing external world, into whose dynamic forces he inserts himself. The external world and his inner world are for him only two sides of the same fabric in which the threads of consciousness and of their objects, are woven into an inseparable net of endless, mutually conditioned relations."[62] The Buddhist Indian mystic Ashvaghosha, from around 80AD states " All phenomena in the world are nothing but the illusory manifestation of the mind and have no reality on their own".[63] Tibetan Buddhist Tulku Urgyen Rinpoche explains: "Samsara is mind turned outwardly, lost in its projections; nirvana is mind turned inwardly, recognizing its nature."[64] Physicist John Wheeler shares that understanding that the consciousness of the observer is what creates reality: "We could not even imagine a universe that did not somewhere and for some stretch of time contain observers because the very building materials of the universe are these acts of observer participancy...No elementary phenomenon is a phenomenon until it is an observed (or registered) phenomenon." " [65] His view mirrors the Hindu idea of Brahman, the source of consciousness, the universe and everything we experience in samsara, being one and the same as us the perceivers of that universe. Sri Aurobindo explains: " Matter is a form of veiled Life, Life a form of veiled Consciousness."[66] and "...the universe exists only or for the consciousness that observes and has not independent reality."[67] In the words of the **Shvetashvatara Upanishad**:

"Brahman, attributeless Reality,
Becomes the Lord of Love who casts his net
Of appearance over the cosmos and rules it from
within through his divine power.
He was before creation; he will be
After dissolution. He alone is.....
He projects the cosmos from himself,
he maintains and withdraws it
Back in to himself at the end of time.[68]"

According to Hinduism, the world is lila, the cosmic play of divinity expressed in matter, be it a human, a tree, or a stone. We confuse the play of lila with reality, the map with the territory, and are under the spell of maya or illusion as we continually incarnate into the cycle of samsara compelled by karma. The great insight explored in ancient Vedic literature is that we are all part of and identical with the universal consciousness of Brahman as the Self: Tat Tvam Asi,[69] "thou are that". We too are the Self, the universal consciousness that expresses itself in everything in the universe from a flea to a galaxy. The **Shvetashvatara Upanishad** continues:

"May the Lord of Love who projects himself
Into this universe of myriad forms,
From whom all beings come and to whom all
Return- may he grant us the grace of wisdom.
He is fire and the sun, and the moon
And the stars. He is the air and the sea
And the Creator, Prajapati.
He is the blue bird; he is the green bird
With red eyes; he is the thundercloud,
And he is the seasons and the seas.
He has no beginning; he has no end.
He is the source from whom the worlds evolve.
From his divine power comes forth all this
Magical show of name and form, of you
And me, which casts the spell of pain and pleasure.
Only when we pierce through this magic veil
Do we see the one who appears as many."

The aspiration of a yogi, who seeks satchitananda, (truth, consciousness, bliss) and union with Brahman, is liberation from the illusion that is samsara. In the words of the **Brihadaranyaka Upanishad**:

"We live in accordance with our deep driving desire.
It is this desire at the time of death that determines
what our next life will be. We will come back to earth
to work out the satisfaction of that desire.
But those who are free from desire, ….
They do not die like the others; but realizing
Brahman, they merge in Brahman."

Enlightenment is realized when "the Self, freed from the body, merges in Brahman, infinite light, eternal light"[70] and is able to be "aware of the dream nature of the universe and watch it without being entangled in its complex but ephemeral nature."[71] According to the Hindu perspective Brahman manifests matter in the cosmos through the interplay between consciousness and energy or prana, described in Hindu terms as Shiva and Shakti. Max Planck commented in a speech delivered in 1944 "All matter originates and exists only by virtue of a force….We must assume behind this force the existence of a conscious and intelligent Mind. This Mind is the matrix of all matter." [72] In the language of the **Upanishads** Planck's description of a "conscious and intelligent Mind" as "the matrix of all matter" is one and the same as Brahman, source of the universe and consciousness:

"This universe comes forth from Brahman, exists
in Brahman, and will return to Brahman.
Verily all is Brahman."
The Chandogya Upanishad

The nature of consciousness and its relationship with the brain, are critical for evaluating rebirth and samsara. The vital question is whether consciousness is, or is not, solely a creation of matter and the answer determines the nature of 'reality' and whether ideas such as rebirth and samsara stand or fall. If consciousness is entirely a product of chemical processes and unable to exist apart from matter and the brain, then rebirth and samsara are nonsense. But if it can be shown that consciousness can exist independently from the brain then rebirth, samsara, and Brahman as the Self, offer compelling explanation for spiritual realities and the relationship between consciousness and physical matter. What mystics and yogis have claimed for thousands of years would then be recognized as possible: that we, our consciousness and 'reality,' are far, far more than they appear in materialist explanations. Discovery that matter derives from consciousness, rather than the other way around, would have revolutionary significance and confirm Sri Aurobindo's observation that "… all matter, all "reality", is energy; that all phenomena, including time and space, are merely crystallizations of mind."[73] Consciousness would be the true nature of reality with pure consciousness, Brahman the Self, expressed in infinite forms of which our individual self is one tiny spark. How consciousness relates to the brain, remains a mystery. The religious traditions originating in India have always asserted that the body is a vehicle for consciousness but not its source. Paramahansa Yogananda points to the falsity of identifying of consciousness with the body: "The reflection, the verisimilitude, of life that shines in the fleshly cells from the soul source is the only cause of man's attachment to his body; obviously he would not pay solicitous homage to a clod of clay. A human being falsely identifies himself with his physical form because the life currents from the soul are breath-conveyed into the flesh with such intense power that man mistakes the effect for a cause, and idolatrously imagines the body to have life of its own." [74]

One objection to Hinduism and Buddhism has been their inclusion of animals in their model of rebirth and samsara. Interestingly science now asserts that Homo sapiens sapiens can no longer assume it is the only animal with consciousness. At the University of Cambridge in 2012 leading neurobiologists and cognitive scientists signed the Cambridge Declaration on Consciousness stating "Convergent evidence indicates that non-human animals have the neuroanatomical, neurochemical, and neurophysiological substrates of conscious states….humans are not unique in possessing the neurological substrates that generate consciousness." That would fit with the Hindu idea that the atman evolves as it travels around the wheel of samsara through innumerable life forms, from plants through animals until it manifests in humans who possess uniquely developed consciousness and self-awareness.

Research in parapsychology also offers insight in to the relationship between consciousness and matter with strong implications for spirituality, samsara and rebirth. For example the Global Consciousness project begun in 1998, examines how shifts in consciousness around major world events, or with focussed mass attention, correlate with shifts in the output of random number generators. The results reveal that intense global emotional responses can impact on the material world confirming consciousness and matter are intertwined. The data from computers in over seventy world locations is sent to Princeton University and the results indicate statistically significant results occurring in response to the death of Princess Diana, and the 9/11 terrorists attacks on the World Trade Centre. Controversy surrounds this experiment in psychokinesis as it does parapsychology in general, but sufficient evidence exists to make investigation of phenomena such as PSI, telepathy, precognition, and clairvoyance, intriguing fields of research despite their uneasy fit with traditional science.

As the twenty first century unfolds new and disconcerting theories that relate to consciousness and samsara have been proposed. People taken seriously, from Swedish philosopher Nick Bostrum to Elon Musk, believe that our existence, our world, our every experience, is a simulation somewhat akin to **The Matrix** movie. Dramatic recent advances in the capacity to simulate virtual worlds and people indistinguishable from base reality have led to the inevitable question, are we already there? Is it possible that is what our experiences in samsara are? Our lives as simulation echoes the ancient Hindu idea of lila, the cosmic play of matter, form, and energy, flowing from consciousness and held together by illusion or maya. If our lives in samsara are manifestations of a simulation the questions who or what is simulating us and why, open up yet another set of mysteries. If us and our world are all a simulation, what kind of cosmic sadist would simulate wars, tsunamis, the HIV virus, genocides, the holocaust, and so much suffering? The same question could of course be asked of God. Is it possible that simulation theory reveals the mechanism of samsara, with each rebirth being a new entry into the simulation, shaped by karma from the previous life (or simulation), perhaps offering experiences for the purpose of spiritual evolution such as described by Sri Aurobindo? Simulation theory is highly controversial but it does point to new and intriguing ways of thinking. Others such as Michael Talbot in **The Holographic Universe**[75] view the cosmos, and everything in it including us, as some kind of hologram, again mirroring those ideas. Everything about existence in this universe seems to be getting weirder and weirder the more reality and subatomic particles are probed. As JBS Haldane put it in **Possible Worlds** "The Universe is not only queerer than we suppose, but queerer than we can suppose."[76] Neither the blue pill of easy certainty or waking up from comfortable illusion with the red pill,[77] gives answers to these perplexing possibilities, although at least with the red pill questions get asked.

The conviction that consciousness is utterly extinguished when the brain and body die, has given rise to various materially based attempts to overcome death. Recently in the classroom my students presented persuasive speeches on some issue of interest. One young man spoke of the uploading of a person's mind to a computer avatar to replace the brain, that fragile mortal organ of thought in a perishable body. It was obvious that he had come across transhumanist ideas on the internet which he confirmed. He spoke movingly about the transferring of consciousness to a computer made of plastic, silicone and metal, from the 'computer made of meat' - a transhumanist description of the brain - as a solution to the inevitable death of the brain pursued by futurists such as Ray Kurzweil director of AI for Google. Responses such as this to the impermanence of the body reveal the same refusal to accept death that gives religion so much of its power. Death becomes defeated by technology that anchors humans in a machine version of immortality, rather than heaven, hell or rebirth in samsara as proposed by religions. It presumes consciousness can be transferred to a non-biological computer to produce the result of a human person with memories, feelings, ideas, who can love and hate, and be stirred by an exquisite piece of music, art, or poetry. The Blue Brain Project founded in 2005 by Henry Markram attempts to reverse engineer the brain and recreate it at the cellular level inside a computer simulation. If humans succeed in creating an artificial brain will it have sentience of any kind? Markram admits he has no idea whether a computer version of the brain will possess consciousness. The pursuit of technological immortality continues with the creation of talking heads by Martine Rothblatt's Terasem Movement. Bruce

Duncan, speaking for Terasem, explains they are designed to "test the feasibility of transferring consciousness from a human to a biological or technological body."[78] No matter how lofty the stated aims of the Terasem Movement, a person consisting of nothing but a collection of stored information and responses reproduced in a machine seems a thoroughly depressing way of getting around the inevitability of death, that being ironically the only reality that unites all living beings.

Another twenty-first-century attempt to overcome death of the brain are head transplants. The head and its brain, the sum of all that a living being is thought to be, is transferred to another healthy body with the aim of prolonging life in the transplanted head, perhaps for eternity. What a bizarre immortality that would be! Head transplants of mice have been performed many times in China by Professor Xiaoping Ren. White mice's heads have been grafted on to black mice's bodies and vice versa. A successful transplant of a monkey head was apparently undertaken in China in 2017 and a human head transplant is planned.[79] Another development is the creation of artificial neurons to be implanted in the brain, interact with other neurons and neurotransmitters and be much faster, and more permanent, than biological neurons.[80] So how much of our brains could be wired with artificial neurons and we still be us? All this begs the questions where, if anywhere, would consciousness lie if we became completely artificial neurons? Would biological neurons still be needed to generate consciousness, or is consciousness something which the brain manifests but does not create? If consciousness is merely the product of a collection of neurons that can be replicated artificially, what integrates, experiences and transforms those into a person with self-awareness and feelings?

Yuval Noah Harari, in **Homo Deus: A Brief History Of Tomorrow,** speculates that the next frontier of human striving will be developing technical solutions to death. Our attention will turn from evolving technologies outside of ourselves to upgrading our bodies and brains in the direction of perfection and immortality. He argues we will inevitably recreate ourselves into a post-human future, the quest for bodily immortality having already begun. Google is said to be conducting research and development of the possibilities of artificial intelligence and physical immortality, with Ray Kurzweil, author of **The Singularity is Near**[81] actively involved. The yearning for biological immortality is not new. The ancient

Babylonian **Epic of Gilgamesh** describes the search of King Gilgamesh for a plant that provides the secret to conquering death, his quest taking him through many arduous and dangerous exploits to discover the plant, only to lose it to a wily serpent, the whole undertaking being utterly fruitless. Whether immortality in biological bodies is ever going to be possible, and if so what it will mean for Homo sapiens sapiens, is unknowable.

Are those living now among the last generations who will face inevitable death? What new burdens would this kind of immortality bring? If a person could potentially live forever in their biological body, free of aging and disease, would the terror of losing that due to accident, or war, or natural catastrophe, so haunt them that to climb a mountain, ride a horse, sail wild oceans on a yacht, travel to poor countries, or even cross a road, be considered a risk too far? In which case what sort of eternal life would that be, and would it be worth living as a fearful, colourless, boring, obsessively risk-averse, existence always revolving around such high stakes as preserving an immortal body? Loved ones could also live forever unless accidents or unforeseen events bring about their death, which would make their loss unendurable as it would be the loss of someone who could have lived eternally, rather than a person who is bound to die sooner or later as is the case now. Immortality in the body or in a machine might turn out to be a poisoned chalice that delivers new forms of suffering rather than the hoped for blissful eternity free of aging, disease and death.

Creating immortality by head transplanting, inserting artificial neurons into the brain, transcending the brain of flesh by replicating it in a computer, uploading consciousness to a machine, or achieving biological immortality, are all premised on certainty that consciousness dies with the body and are driven by the same fear of death that drives religions. Achieving immortal physical bodies would neither support nor refute the ideas of samsara and rebirth as no light would be shed on what happens to consciousness if and when death occurs. Humanity has spent it's history fighting wars, building empires, creating cities and sending astronauts to the moon, but the least explored realm is consciousness. It is the great unknown, and the key to the whole puzzle of what we are, what if anything our lives might mean, whether or not spiritual dimensions are real and whether or not samsara and rebirth are possible or impossible. Meditation and mystical experiences, and the explorations unleashed by psychedelic substances, have given insights into consciousness from one side of the conceptual fence. Perhaps science can further the quest to explore the frontiers of consciousness from its side.

The question whether consciousness is or is not a purely material phenomenon, is at the centre of what human life might mean and whether samsara and rebirth have any validity. Are we just clever animals in an accidental universe with no intrinsic higher purpose, who can now engineer increasingly superior versions of ourselves with ever longer life spans and perhaps ultimately immortality? That is an interesting twist on the age-old idea of intelligent design, but a version with only ourselves as the designers and with no meaning to existence other than what we create for ourselves. And what of samsara? Would rebirth and samsara, along with all religion, simply no longer exist, put out of business by the end of biological death? If death is ever overcome by clever technical solutions that will still offer no clue as what consciousness is, what happens to an individual's consciousness if death does happen, and whether consciousness can exist separate from the body. All of this comes back to the same core question, what is the nature of consciousness? If consciousness can be shown to exist apart from the brain then spiritual realities are possible, and samsara and rebirth become plausible.

Evidence for the possibility of rebirth can be found in many fields of study but mere mention of anything pertaining to spirituality, or the involvement of mind in the fabric of material reality, can stir heated debate, even derision. There is deep fear associated with considering ideas that question the dominant paradigm of material realism as providing a total explanation for the world. It would represent a similarly confronting challenge as Benny Shannon discovered in his experimentation with ayahuasca that took him to the boundaries of his scientific rationalist worldview.[82] That represents a very threatening possibility to contemplate as it reopens the door to realms of reality that the scientific revolution hoped to close forever, where spiritual forces, alternative dimensions and perhaps demons, gods and spirits, lurk and penetrate in to human life. Blatant superstition often accompanies acceptance of unseen forces and maintaining boundaries to that is a genuine serious concern. The idea of legitimating a world view that accepts as real unseen supernatural forces is shocking for science which is understandably fiercely resistant to anything that threatens to take it in that direction, be it parapsychology, or accepting that spiritual implications are attached to the observer effect and quantum entanglement in physics, or the possibility that consciousness is not created by matter and might survive death. Religion has also made such a bad name for itself with its absurd, often destructive conflicts, claims, dogmas, superstitions and practices throughout the centuries, bringing the result that anything involving spirituality is vehemently rejected for good reasons. But the need for science to honestly face the implications of some of its own discoveries, even if those lead in the unwanted direction of spiritual questions, will not disappear because science is ultimately about the search for truth. Undoubtedly science does open up possibilities that have spiritual implications. Quantum physics does not 'prove' that material reality is an illusion, or maya in Hindu terms, but strange properties of the quantum world, such as quantum entanglement and the observer effect, make it a reasonable question to ask whether the material world is an illusion created by consciousness, rather than the other way around.

The great theoretical physicist Wofgang Pauli expressed his hope that the time would eventually come when science and spirituality would reconcile in the search for one truth that lies behind them both, but warned that it won't happen easily: "[Regarding] the great unfinished problem of the relationship between science and religion... I will never get tired of emphasizing that this matter is not finished, that a synthesis of science and religion is necessary, that this problem far exceeds the possibilities of a single person, that this question concerns the development of human consciousness in general, that many changes will still be necessary in both sides (science and religion), before a synthesis of the two will be within the realm of possibility."[83] The last word belongs to Abdu'l-Baha: "Religion and science are the two wings upon which man's intelligence can soar into the heights, with which the human soul can progress. It is not possible to fly with one wing alone!"

The next chapter explores the religions that take samsara and rebirth for granted, before my journey to Nepal in chapter four, followed by Bali, Cambodia and India as the subjects of later chapters. Hinduism and Buddhism inform every aspect of all those cultures and so it is to them I will now turn.

"The self is eternal and immutable,
When the body dies, the Self does not die
If the slayer believes he can slay,
Or the slain believes he can be slain,
Neither knows the truth. The eternal Self
Slays not, nor is ever slain."
Katha Upanishad, Yama Lord of Death, to Nachiketa

CHAPTER FOUR
HINDUISM, BUDDHISM, TANTRA, KARMA, SUFFERING AND RELIGION

Religions having their source in India, Hinduism and Buddhism, are the primary religious influences in Nepal, India, Bali and Cambodia that I visited over the course of the year following Rob's death. Both religions hold rebirth and samsara as central, albeit with differences in formulation and emphasis, and it is impossible to explore those cultures without reference to them. They reveal many layers of variety, complexity and subtlety but samsara and rebirth are at their heart. Hinduism is dominant in India, Nepal and Bali. In Nepal it is extremely diverse, encompassing an Indian form along the border with India, whereas in the Kathmandu valley and Himalayas Hinduism is much influenced by Buddhism and animism. The Indonesian island of Bali possesses a unique form of Hinduism found nowhere else and distinct from that of India. Buddhism is also widespread ranging from the Tibetan form of Mahayana Buddhism in the regions of Nepal bordering Tibet, Nepalese syncretic Buddhism that has blended with Hinduism, and a unique form of Buddhism found in the Kathmandu valley. All of them belong to the Vajrayana Mahayana stream of Buddhism and all of them are Tantric in nature. By way of contrast in Cambodia it is Theravadan Buddhism that prevails, although fractured by the years of Khmer Rouge rule. While exploring Hinduism and Buddhism I try to avoid what the Dalai Lama calls the "Shangri La phenomenon":

that spiritual ideas of Eastern origin tend to dazzle and seduce because of their exoticism. Armed with that caution the aim is to observe with an open but critical mind and not avoid questioning because beliefs are from a different culture to my own. Delving deeply in to Buddhism and Hinduism has been an intensely rewarding steep learning curve bringing much inspiration but also questions and reservations.

Given Hinduism was the cradle of the term samsara and the cultural context for the birth of the historical Buddha and Buddhism, it makes a good starting point. The term Hinduism is relatively recent, a creation of British colonialism describing the religion of the people of India, Hindustan as they called it, and is still not used by many who live within its folds. It might be more accurate to describe Hinduism as a way of life, one of its main features being an eclectic diversity of belief, ritual and practice. It has no supreme structure of doctrinal or religious authority, no founding figure like Jesus, or Mohammad, or Buddha, no one sacred text or belief followed by all Hindus, and it encompasses an extraordinary diversity of beliefs, and practices, from strict monotheism to a multiplicity of deities and sacred figures. Hinduism is therefore the most difficult to describe and define of all the world's major religions, expressing high levels of abstract philosophical speculation as to the nature of reality, the cosmos, consciousness and God, at the same time as accommodating millions who follow particular deities of their region, family or caste. Its various philosophical schools express a broad range of ideas while somehow all remaining within the fold of Hinduism. It governs every aspect of a Hindu's life, how they live, how they marry, how they live in a household and family, how they age, and how they die. It encompasses a staggering range of traditions and sects all of which gather under the umbrella of Hinduism. That said it is possible to identify core texts, practices and beliefs that most Hindus would accept in some form or other, rebirth and samsara being central examples.

Hindu belief holds that human life is divided into four stages or ashramas: the first "Brahmacharya" or the student stage, the second "Grihastha" or the householder stage, the third "Vanaprastha" or the hermit stage and the fourth "Sannyasa" or the wandering ascetic stage, there being rites and rituals for all of these from birth till death. The final life stage of sannyasa, or wandering renunciate, is an ancient Indian tradition that contributes to the phenomenon of the sadhu or sadvi, holy man or woman, that are commonly seen in India and Nepal. They may belong to one of many sects but their goal is the same: moksha, or realization of spiritual truth and bliss, enlightenment and release from samsara in to union with the divine source, Brahman. They may be Saivites, followers of Shiva, or Vaishnavites, followers of Vishnu, or belong to a variety of other sects, often being distinguishable from each other by their clothing, or lack of it, hairstyles and markings on their foreheads. Hindus generally accept the literature of the **Vedas** as central to their religion, a vast body of Sanskrit literature having its sources around 800 years BCE. There are four and each has sections on ritual and the Gods with a closing section of philosophical speculation, the **Upanishads**. The **Upanishads** are at the core of that stream of Hinduism known as Vedanta and are central to its philosophical ideas. There are six major strands of Vedanta each with differing emphasis, their own followers and sacred writings. The epic of the **Mahabharata** dated between 400 to 800 BCE, particularly part of its sixth book the **Bhagavad Gita**, is another sacred text central to Hinduism. Apart from those there are a hugely diverse range of other sacred writings and each school of Hinduism will refer to different sources for spiritual inspiration and authority.

Almost all Hindus believe in the existence of the atman, or soul, as the eternal innermost essence of consciousness, the Self. The atman is continually reborn in the cycle of samsara as an actor in lila, the illusory play of the material world spun by the source of consciousness and ultimate reality, Brahman or the Self, which all life and matter are manifestations of. The **Amritabindu Upanishad** expresses this:

"Brahman is indivisible and pure;
Realize Brahman and go beyond all change.
He is immanent and transcendent.
Realizing him, sages attain freedom
And declare there are no separate minds.
.....There is only one Self in all creatures."

Brahman is the ground of all reality, life, energy, time, consciousness and matter, formless, limitless and eternal, the source and sustainer of the universe, sometimes called God by those such as Paramahansa Yogananda. Tantric texts such as the **Mahanirvana Tantra** describe Brahman as "….that which is changeless, existent only, and beyond both mind and speech, which shines as the Truth amidst the illusion of the three worlds.." and contains the following hymn to Brahman, the **Stotra**:

"Om! I bow to Thee, the eternal Refuge of all:
I bow to Thee, the pure Intelligence manifested in the universe.
I bow to Thee Who in His essence in One and Who grants liberation.
I bow to Thee, the great, all-pervading attributeless One…..
The whole universe is the appearance of Thee Who art its Cause.
Thou alone art Creator, Preserver, Destroyer of the world….
O Supreme Lord in Whom all things are, yet Unmanifest in all,
Imperceptible to the senses, yet the very truth.
Incomprehensible, Imperishable All-pervading hidden Essence…
The Self-existent Lord, the Vessel of safety in the ocean of being."[84]

The **Upanishads** define spiritual wisdom as recognition that the Self within every living being, both human and non-human, is the same divine Self that is Brahman. Tat Tvam Asi, "thou art that" is a concept central to the Advaita Vedanta (non dualism) school of Hinduism explored by Aldous Huxley in **The Perennial Philosophy.** Brahman and atman are understood as one and the same, the deathless Self. The aim of Hindus is liberation from rebirth in samsara to merge with Brahman, or ultimate bliss and freedom, beyond birth or death. In the **Katha Upanishad**, Nachiketa, a teenage boy, is told this great secret by Yama Lord of Death:

"The all-knowing Self was never born,
Nor will it die. Beyond cause and effect,
This self is eternal and immutable,
When the body dies, the Self does not die
If the slayer believes he can slay
Or the slain believes he can be slain,
Neither knows the truth. The eternal Self
Slays not, nor is ever slain…..
Hidden in the heart of every creature

Exists the Self, ….
When the wise realize the Self,
Formless in the midst of forms, changeless
In the midst of change, omnipresent
And supreme, they go beyond sorrow…
Wake up! Wake up! Seek the guidance of an
Illuminated teacher and realize the Self."

The **Mundaka Upanishad** expresses the same idea, that the Self within all that lives is identical with the ultimate reality of the universe, Brahman, the Self.

"Bright but hidden, the Self dwells in the heart.
Everything that moves, breathes, opens, and closes
Lives in the Self. He is the source of love
And may be known through love but not through thought.
He is the goal of life. Attain this goal!
The shining Self dwells hidden in the heart.
Everything in the cosmos, great and small,
Lives in the Self. He is the source of life,
Truth beyond the transience of this world.
He is the goal of life. Attain this goal."

According to Hinduism the atman journeys around and around on the wheel of samsara, incarnating in to physical matter, prakriti, in different realms according to karma and the development of consciousness. Atman is manifested in all life but with differing degrees of awareness according to the six kinds of life forms. In plants and aquatics it is dormant and increasingly developed through reptiles and insects, then birds, then animals, and manifested most fully in humans and sacred beings. Interestingly the old dogma that only humans have consciousness has shifted to scientific recognition that consciousness of some kind also exists in animals.[85] Hinduism perceives every being as an expression of atman, that becomes more and more self-aware as consciousness unfolds until it reaches its highest manifestation on earth as human, offering the precious opportunity for liberation from samsara. The Hindu view of the evolution of consciousness through various life forms sits very comfortably with the idea of biological evolution as they mirror each other. The idea that the atman develops increasing levels of consciousness as it passes through progressively sophisticated forms of life, has parallels to Darwinian theory which holds that life evolves in to ever more complex forms from its origins in the sea, through reptiles, birds and insects, to mammals and finally Homo sapiens sapiens.

The Indian belief that animals possess atman, or soul, is totally contrary to deeply laid assumptions that humans are the only creature with consciousness and a spirit. The Christian tradition of the West believes that only humans possess an immortal soul, with an unpassable division between animals and humans, a belief challenged by Darwin's theory of evolution concluding that humans are animals descended from apes. Christianity and the theory of evolution have never sat comfortably together, although some sects of Christianity such as the Catholic Church have made attempts to reconcile them. The work of Jesuit palaeontologist Teilhard de Chardin attempted to bring together Darwinian and spiritual evolution, causing much controversy in the Catholic Church and Chardin was exiled to live in China until his death in 1955. He was forbidden to publish by the Catholic Church during his lifetime but his ideas were published posthumously. In 1962 the Catholic Church imposed a 'Monitum' or warning regarding reading of his work and that remains in place.

Samsara, as an endless cycle of birth, death, and rebirth, is a concept almost all Hindus take for granted as an unsatisfactory state in which the atman is trapped until enlightenment brings liberation from samsara and union with the divine source Brahman, in moksha. The **Katha Upanishad** states:

"Those who lack discrimination, with little control
Over their thoughts and far from pure,
Reach not the pure state of immortality
But wander from death to death; but those
Who have discrimination, with a still mind
And a pure heart, reach journey's end,
Never again to fall into the jaws of death."

The **Katha Upanishad** warns that those who do not achieve enlightenment must keep on returning in to samsara in a new body until such time as they realize union with Brahman.

"If one fails to realize Brahman in this life
Before the physical sheath is shed,

He must again put on a body
In the world of embodied creatures."

The doctrine of rebirth was well developed by the time of the **Upanishads** and the **Bhagavad Gita** and is beautifully described in the **Brihadaranyaka Upanishad**:

"As a caterpillar, having come to the end of
one blade of grass, draws itself together and
reaches out for the next, so the Self, having
come to the end of one life and dispelled all ignorance,
gathers in his faculties and reaches
out from the old body to a new."

Another central idea, closely linked to samsara, is karma, the law of cause and effect created by one's actions. In Hinduism karma means action, not administered by deities but an impartial law that good actions bring good results either in the current life or the next, and bad actions do the opposite. As long as we are subject to maya, or illusion, we are bound by karma to rebirth in samsara, and our karma determines the nature of that rebirth. All actions leave an imprint as the **Brihadaranyaka Upanishad** describes:

"As a person acts, so he becomes in this life. Those
who do good become good; those who do
harm become bad. Good deeds make one
pure; bad deeds make one impure. So we are
said to be what our desire is. As our desire is
so is our will. As our will is, so are our acts,
As we act, so we become.
We live in accordance with our deep, driving
desire. It is this desire at the time of death that
determines what our next life is to be. We will
come back to earth to work out the satisfaction
of that desire."

Hinduism teaches there is no escape from samsara until the bondage of karma is broken and enlightenment realized, setting us free from endless rebirth.

Deeply embedded in Hinduism are the social structures of caste, an extremely ancient system of hereditary social stratification that divides Hindus in to four categories: Brahmins the priestly caste, Kshatriyas the warrior caste, Vaishyas the merchant or farmer caste and Sudras the labouring caste. The four major caste groups each contain numerous sub-groups and categories. Below these four groups are the untouchables, or Dalits, who have no caste status, are given the worst most menial occupations and perceived as ritually impure. Arundhati Roy in her novel **The God of Small Things** describes how people would cross the road to avoid being sullied by the shadow of a passing untouchable. Her character Velutha is beaten to death for violating caste rules by having a sexual relationship with the non-untouchable Ammu. Incidents like this still occasionally occur in India and Nepal where caste rules remain powerful in traditional communities. Villages were traditionally constructed around caste divisions with high caste Brahmins using separate water wells and forbidden to share food or marry someone from a lower caste. This remained unchanged for many centuries, trapping lower caste people in a cycle of poverty, discrimination and social disadvantage. Caste is an important aspect of all varieties of Hinduism in Nepal and Bali, but with different forms and emphasis than in India.

The doctrine that karma determines rebirth is used to justify caste, the highest castes being called 'twice born' and regarded as more spiritually evolved. According to this logic a person's birth in to a particular caste status is the result of good or bad karma from their previous life, and their caste status can be improved in the next life by fulfilling of social and religious duties. The caste system has elaborate religious rationales in texts such as **The Laws of Manu**, but its historical basis lies in the conquest of India by fair skinned Aryan invaders who subjugated the darker skinned preceding inhabitants, and even now high caste people in India have paler skin than those in lower castes. Outsiders such as Europeans were traditionally regarded as without caste status, and therefore ritually impure, which is ironic given their pale skins, material privilege, and position of power as agents of European colonialism. Caste divisions have even crept in to non-Hindu religions such as the Thomasite Christians of Goa and Kerala, and forms of Nepalese Buddhism most influenced by Hinduism. Even the Indian Catholic Church shows the influence of caste as most administrative posts are held by people from a high caste background.

Some Hindus reject caste altogether as contrary to the teachings of their religion. Ghandi named people from the untouchable caste Harijans, or 'children of God', and was murdered by an extremist Hindu as a consequence. Many of India's greatest spiritual thinkers have ignored the social inequality that caste represents, accepted followers and taken their teachings to people from all castes, across all cultures, in all continents, from all religious backgrounds, striving for universal spiritual truths that transcend religious, cultural or social differences. Its good to remember that in the Hindu tradition spirituality can be separated from entanglement with ritual and dogma, and their associated social divisions, the **Mundaka Upanishad** reminding that those are not routes to the highest spiritual truths.

"The rituals and the sacrifices described
In the Vedas deal with lower knowledge.
The sages ignored these rituals
And went in search of higher knowledge...."

Hinduism is diverse, and mostly tolerant and eclectic as to how divinity is conceptualized and worshipped, embracing a range of possibilities from strict monotheism to belief in many Gods. The array of deities in Hinduism are countless and yet are a reflection of the many in one and one in many, all being aspects of Brahman, the attributeless, formless, foundation of all reality. If everything and everyone is a manifestation of Brahman, the source of consciousness, then there is no limit to the forms Brahman may be expressed in and worshipped as. In the words of the **Amritabindu Upanishad**:

"The One appears many, just as the moon
Appears many, reflected in water."

The three main Gods central to Hinduism are known as the Trimurti: Brahma the creator, Vishnu the preserver and Shiva the destroyer so as to allow creation. For monotheistic Hindus these gods and goddesses are all representations of differing aspects of the one cosmic force, Brahman, and have no literal form or existence. For many millions of other Hindus they are perceived as having a literal existence and worshipped as such. The three major deities have many differing manifestations, aspects and forms. For example Vishnu has a huge range of incarnations and the historical founder of Buddhism, Siddhartha Gautama, is sometimes regarded as Vishnu's ninth incarnation. From a Hindu perspective Buddhism then becomes incorporated under the umbrella of Hinduism as just another sect. Krishna is an incarnation of Vishnu and Jesus is also regarded by some as an avatar of Vishnu, or incarnation of Krishna. Shiva might appear as Pashuputi, or Bhairav, or Shankara, having many forms, as does his female consort Parvati, including as Kali the dark Goddess, or Durga the slayer of demons. The offspring of Shiva and Parvati include the elephant headed Ganesha.

An important element of Hinduism, particularly in its Tantric forms, is Shaktism, a recognition and celebration of female energy and power in the form of Goddesses such as Durga and Kali. When travelling in India with Rob it was sometimes difficult to reconcile beautiful texts such as the **Bhagavad Gita** and the **Upanishads** with the endlessly diverse, confusing, and occasionally dark and ugly faces of religion we saw there. The goddess Kali, consort of Shiva, dancing with a string of skulls around her neck, her tongue lolling red out of her mouth wearing a skirt of human arms, her eyes bloodshot in a frenzy of rage, was particularly confronting. Many depictions of her present her as drinking blood from a vessel made of a human skullcap (kapala). Kali and her various manifestations are a particularly strong presence in Nepal. There is much difficult to understand about what Kali represents: to many followers she is Kali-Ma, the divine Mother and a slayer of demons. Ramakrishna, and his disciple Vivikenanda, were devotees of Kali, so I try to not be repulsed by the imagery and animal sacrifices associated with her.

Animal sacrifice has much diminished in Indian Hinduism and many Hindus do not acknowledge or practice it, although it is still occurs in areas of India mostly associated with Shaktism, Tantric or animist rituals, or black magic. It survived in places like Calcutta, home of the Kalighat Temple to Kali until the Indian courts banned it in 2006, in part because it was bad for tourism for visitors to arrive at the temple and be confronted with a bloodbath. The name Calcutta derives from Kali-khat, city of Kali, where human sacrifice, narabali, was reputed to take place prior to and during the time of British rule of India. Animal sacrifice is common in Balinese Hinduism, the word bali being the Sanskrit word for sacrifice. Worship of Shakti deities such as Kali and Durga, is a strong element of Nepalese Hinduism along with animal sacrifices. It is not easy to reconcile Kali and animal sacrifice with a spiritual tradition that gave birth to the **Upanishads**, the **Bhagavad Gita** and the doctrine of ahimsa, or do no harm to any living being.

David Kinsley's book **The Sword And The Flute: Kali and Krsna, Dark Visions of The Terrible And The Sublime in Hindu Mythology**[86] offers insights that are helpful when confronted by Kali images. She is the "wild, black Mother who grants the boon of revealing the world of samsara as it really is: fleeting, painful, and finite. In his transcendent vision the devotee of Kali laughs, sings, and plays, revelling in the Mother's intoxicated creation - affirming his life for what it is, a fleeting episode in Kali's eternal dance of creation and destruction, a sojourn in samsara that may be ultimately redeeming if properly understood."[87] Kali and her consort Shiva, the god of creation and destruction, point towards a reality that religions often struggle to adequately acknowledge or explain: that destruction is manifested in the universe as much as creation and that those opposites are deeply entwined with each other. A fundamental aspect of the universe is devouring: death devours life, humans and other animals devour the flesh of their fellow animals, animals including humans, devour plants, wind and rain devour mountains, winter devours summer, and time devours everything, including eventually the universe itself. Perhaps Hinduism embraces deep truths by encompassing deities such as Kali and Shiva, acknowledging destruction is necessary for creation to emerge and that the universe exists as a dance between opposites.

There is a beautiful statue of Shiva at Elephanta near Mumbai in India that shows Shiva's right face as masculine, his left face as feminine and in the middle depicted as Shiva Mahesvara, the Great Lord of the cosmos. The Ardhanarishvarar form of Shiva combines male and female in one form, the right hand side being male and the left female with a breast, embodying the energies of Shiva and Shakti, male and female, consciousness and energy, the polarities that drive all existence. Shakti deities are strongly associated with Tantra that is a complex dimension of both Hinduism and the Vajrayana Buddhism of Tibet and

Nepal. It is slippery to define, but nonetheless intriguing and practiced widely in India, Nepal, and Bali, so I will take a dive in to its rather murky waters at the end of this chapter.

Symbols central to Hinduism are the lingham, the male organ, which is sculpted in stone and placed at the centre of a stone female organ, the yoni, where together they represent the union of consciousness and energy, Shiva and Shakti, male and female, purusha and prakriti. These Shiva linghams and yonis are to be seen everywhere in Nepal and India, often smeared with red or yellow paste and adorned with flowers or offerings. The worship of Shiva as supreme consciousness, is expressed in veneration of the lingham often involving the pouring of sacred substances such as milk, honey or ghee over the lingham as part of puja rituals. This is to bring consciousness, as masculine purusha, down in to the world of samsara. Tantric temples and sacred buildings dedicated to Shakti deities bring female prakriti, or energy, in to the world and are common in both India and Nepal. Some temples are decorated with incredible erotic carvings and sculptures such as the temple of Khajurajo in India. In Nepal erotic images are particularly common on the roof struts of sacred buildings, depicting scenes of sexual bliss, including a pair of elephants making love, trunks entwined, in the Shiva Parvati temple in Bhaktapur near Kathmandu.

Buddhism is the other major thread of religion in the countries we visited: Mahayana Tantric Vajrayana Buddhism in Nepal, and Theravada Buddhism in Cambodia. Buddhism originated in the world of Indian spirituality so rebirth, samsara and karma are also central ideas, although understood differently from Hinduism. Samsara in Buddhism represents suffering and misery, but no explanation or purpose is given for the universe or for existence as Buddhism does not recognize a creator God, or an ongoing soul or atman. What is endlessly reborn, passing through the six realms of samsara, of gods, demi-gods, humans, animals, hungry ghosts and hells, are bundles of 'karmic resonances' that pass from the old body to the new in the manner of a candle flame passing to a new candle. Anatta, or the doctrine of no soul, and sunyata or emptiness, are at the core of Buddhism, although sunyata is a stronger element in Mahayana than Theravada Buddhism. Duhkha or suffering, and anicca or impermanence, are the primary characteristics of existence in samsara according to Buddhism, and the goal is release from rebirth in to nirvana, a state of bliss, achieved by the realization of enlightenment.

The story of Buddhism begins in Lumbini southern Nepal in the 6th century BC with the birth of Siddhartha Gautama, prince of the Sakya clan who becomes the historical Sakyamuni ("sage of the Sakyas") Buddha ("awakened one"). The facts surrounding the life of the historical Buddha are much debated but the story of his birth and path to enlightenment are recounted in the early Buddhist texts of the Pali Canon, central to earliest forms of Buddhism and Theravadan ("Way of the Elders") Buddhism practiced in Cambodia, Thailand, Laos, Burma, Vietnam and Sri Lanka. His mother Queen Maya dreams that a white elephant with six white tusks enters her side on the night of Siddhartha's conception. The hermit seer Asita prophesies that he will become either a great king, or a great religious leader, to which his father Shuddhodana responds by exerting much effort to shield the young prince from religious teaching and from the truth of suffering.

Siddhartha marries Yasodhara and has a son Rahula, but despite his father's determination to prevent him discovering sickness, aging and suffering, Siddhartha insists he be allowed to leave the confines of the palace. His father has the streets cleared of all the sick, dying and suffering but Siddhartha crosses the path of a sick man. He addresses his charioteer Candaka as follows, described in the **Lalitavistara-Sutra**.

"O charioteer, who is this man, weak and powerless?
His flesh, blood and skin withered, his veins protruding?
With whitened hair, few teeth, his body emaciated,
Walking painfully and leaning on a staff?"
Candaka replies:

"O Prince, this man is oppressed by age
His organs are weak; he is in pain, and his strength and vigor are gone.
Lord this is not unique to his race or his country.
Age exhausts youth and the entire world.
Even you will be separated from the company
Of your mother and father, friends and relatives.
There is no other fate for living beings."

Siddhartha then realizes the folly of his life of pleasure and distractions and sets off on the search for answers to the riddles of suffering, aging, sickness, death, and the imprisonment of all sentient beings in the cycle of samsara. He vows to undertake his quest for spiritual enlightenment until he becomes an "awakened one" or Buddha, (from Bodhi to awaken) released from samsara and its sufferings.

"I desire and wish that,
After attaining the level of awakening
Which is beyond decay and death,
I will save the world.
The time for that has arrived."
Lalitavistara-Sutra

According to the story he studied and practised with groups of extreme ascetics, but eventually becomes dissatisfied with this as a path to enlightenment and adopts the "middle way" between asceticism and worldly indulgence. After being abandoned by his followers for rejecting asceticism, Siddhartha Gautama sits under a Bodhi tree in modern day Bodgaya in India, passing through ever deepening states of meditation. His previous births are revealed to him and he comes to realization of the causes of suffering and the path to end suffering. He is now the "awakened one" or Buddha, freed from rebirth in samsara where all sentient beings are trapped. The central character Siddhartha, in Hermann Hesse's novel **Siddhartha**, is not Gautama Buddha but has strong parallels with him. Hesse's description of Siddhartha through the eyes of his old friend Govinda, is so beautifully expressed that it could be a fitting account of the Buddha and his awakening:

"He no longer saw his friend Siddhartha's face; in its place he saw other faces, many of them a long series, a flowing river of faces, hundreds, thousands, all them arising and dissolving, and yet all seeming to be there at the same time; they all constantly changed and renewed themselves, and yet were all Siddhartha. He saw the face of a fish, a carp, its mouth opened in infinite pain, a dying fish with eyes glazing over- he saw the face of a newborn child, red and full of wrinkles, distorted in weeping - he saw the face of a murderer, saw him plunge a knife into someone's body - in the same second he saw that criminal bound and kneeling and his head being cut off by the executioner...he saw the bodies of men and women naked in the positions and battles of furious love - he saw corpses stretched out, quiet, cold, empty... he saw all these forms and faces interrelating in a thousand ways, each form helping the other, loving it, hating it, annihilating it, giving birth to it again; each one was a death wish, a passionately painful confession of mortality; and yet none of them died, each one was merely transformed, was constantly reborn, constantly received a new face...and all these forms and faces were in repose, flowed, engendered themselves, drifted away and poured into one another; and all of them were constantly covered by something thin, insubstantial, yet existent like a thin layer of glass or ice....and this mask was Siddhartha's smiling face...and Govinda saw that this smile on the mask, this smile of oneness over the flowing shapes, this smile of simultaneity over the thousand births and deaths, this smile of Siddhartha's was exactly the same....quiet, subtle, impenetrable smile of Gotama the Buddha, which he had seen with respect a hundred times. Thus Govinda knew, do the perfect ones smile."[88]

Moved by compassion for all sentient beings trapped in the misery of samsara, the historical Buddha began his life of preaching, delivering his first sermon at the Deer Park of Benares near Varanasi in northern India. There he taught the doctrine of the middle path between ascetic extremism and the world of sensual indulgence. He proclaimed the Four Noble Truths: 1. existence in samsara is characterized by suffering (duhkha), 2. the root of suffering is desire or clinging to maya and the illusions of samsara, which include people, things, ideas or events 3. impermanence is the nature of everything and every being in samsara 4. the means to overcome suffering is to renounce desire and following the Noble Eightfold Path of right views, right intention, right speech, right action, right effort, right mindfulness and right concentration. The Four Noble Truths recognized not just the obvious suffering associated with impermanence, aging, sickness, loss, and death, but that which flows from mental patterns that are never satisfied.

Whatever the mind experiences craving of some kind follows. If it is pain or loss the craving is to escape that. If it is pleasure or happiness the mind grasps to hold on fearing it will pass, as it always eventually does, or longs for the pleasure to intensify with more money, a better car, a better relationship or whatever delivers more pleasure. The mind is always restless and dissatisfied seeking to hold on to happiness, people, or things that are by their very nature transient. Lasting happiness and contentment will thus always evade us until such time, according to Buddhism, the Four Noble Truths are recognized and the Noble Eightfold Path is followed as the path to "waking up". Eliminating craving for pleasure and permanence, as proposed by the Buddhist solution to suffering, is the opposite of modern consumer cultures which seek to immerse us in never ending experiences of pleasure from ever better products, food, technology, sex, or holidays. If that fails we can tackle suffering with pharmaceutical anti-depressant interventions in to the brain, something of a real life version of the drug soma in Huxley's novel **Brave New World**. Buddhism views death as the consequence of birth, so ending rebirth is the aim. In the modern West it is the opposite: death is sought to be overcome or postponed, by medical technologies that fend off aging, such as being developed by Google's company Calico, or the Gilgamesh project. Whether this new vision of an ageless future will make humans any happier is debatable and will probably create as many new forms of suffering in samsara as it solves old ones.

The Buddha continued to preach for around forty five years as he and his followers travelled around India, his teaching based on an understanding of the nature of reality as characterized by Three Marks of Existence: annica (impermanence), duhkha (suffering), and anatta (egolessness). He taught that all phenomena are inherently empty and impermanent: "always changing, always becoming, always dying, and that refusal to recognize these truths leads to suffering." The Three Jewels for a Buddhist are taking refuge in the Buddha, Buddha's teachings or the Dharma, and the Sangha, or community of Buddhist followers. Buddhism teaches that bondage to rebirth, samsara, suffering, and karma, can be overcome. When karma no longer drives rebirth enlightenment is realized as a state of bliss, nirvana, outside of time or individual identity. The Buddha discouraged speculation as to the nature of nirvana: it is to be experienced rather than described, and differing interpretations of nirvana characterize various strands of Buddhism.

After the death of Sakyamuni Buddha his teachings and followers spread throughout India as witnessed by the huge Buddhist complexes at Ajanta and Ellora, the ancient stupa of Sanchi in Bihar, and the Buddhist university of Nalanda in India which operated from 427 until 1129 CE. Buddhism rejected the caste distinctions of Hinduism, and the Buddha accepted low caste Hindus as followers, although caste divisions now feature in some strands of Nepalese Buddhism. Buddhism was adopted by the Mauryan King Ashoka who ruled most of India from 268-232 BCE. He was said to be so moved by the sight of the dead and dying on the battlefield at Kalinga, that he converted to Buddhism and had its central principles inscribed in prominent places across his kingdom, his daughter being the founder of the first Buddhist Sangha in Sri Lanka. Debates between Buddhism and Hinduism are exemplified by the writings of the eighth century Hindu apologist Adi Shankara, who, according to Hindus, effectively neutralized the growth of Buddhism in India after the eighth century. Although Buddhism initially flourished in India it ceased to grow around the eighth century, declined rapidly from the 12th century after Islam arrived, and had all but disappeared from India by the time the Mughuls established their rule in 1526.

Buddhism expanded from India across Asia. The first written Buddhist texts were formulated in Sri Lanka in the language of Pali, the **Tripitaka** or **Pali Canon,** and they contain teachings of Buddhism that remain central to the Theravadan Buddhism of Cambodia, Thailand, Burma, Sri Lanka, the Khmers of Vietnam, and Laos. From around the first century Buddhism spread north in new and diverse directions giving rise various forms of Mahayana Buddhism in Nepal, Sikkim, Bhutan, Tibet, Mongolia, Korea, Vietnam, China, and Japan, where it adapted and incorporated pre-existing beliefs and practices. As Buddhism spread across India and northwards, many texts and teachings such as the Sutras were written in Sanskrit, the sacred language of India, and some of those texts have been preserved only in the Nepalese Buddhism of the Kathmandu valley. It features elements of Indian Buddhism often blended with Hinduism to incorporate a caste system and non-monastic, non-celibate ritual priests. Another form of Mahayana Buddhism, Vajrayana (Thunderbolt Vehicle or Diamond Vehicle) had its origins in India in the fifth century CE and spread to Nepal and Tibet in the six and seventh centuries CE. It is a strongly Tantric and requires initiation by a guru in to teachings that bring power and potential danger, so involves much secrecy and ritual. Mahayana Buddhism is much more overtly religious than Theravada and includes divine beings, multitudes of Buddhas and Bodhisattvas, ceremonies, religious rituals, magical practices, the use of images such as mandalas, and ritual objects such as the Vajra (Tibetan Dorje), Kapala (skullcap vessel), or Damaru (skullcap drum).

In Theravadan Buddhism the aim is for an individual to realize personal enlightenment, to become an arhat and to not return by rebirth in to samsara. This is regarded as only possible for a monk in the body of a man, who has renounced the bonds and pleasures of the world and undertaken a monastic life of strict discipline and self-control. In contrast the Mahayana tradition strongly emphasizes the experiential aspect of realization of Buddhahood, the Buddha nature within every living being recognized through meditation, and the possibility of enlightenment existing for genuine seekers both within and outside of monasteries. The tradition of the Bodhisattva is not part of Theravadan Buddhism but is central to Mahayana traditions, the aim being not personal realization of nirvana but achievement of Buddhahood, or becoming an "awakened one" so as to benefit all sentient beings. A Bodhisattva is one who realizes enlightenment but instead of nirvana, chooses to be reborn over and over again to help all beings find liberation from suffering and samsara. To take the path of the Bodhisattva is to adopt Bodhicitta, an attitude of loving kindness. The Bodhisattva vows are distilled to this resolve: "May I achieve Buddhahood for the benefit of all sentient beings." The eighth century student from the Buddhist University of Nalanda in India, Shantideva, composed the **Guide to the Bodhisattva's Way of Life**. His words are beautiful:

"The Compassionate Heart of the Enlightened Mind
It is the supreme elixir
That overcomes the sovereignty of death.
It is the inexhaustible treasure
That eliminates poverty in the world.
It is the supreme medicine
That quells the world's disease.

It is the tree that shelters all beings
Wandering and tired on the path of conditioned existence.
It is the universal bridge
That leads to freedom from unhappy states of birth.
It is the dawning moon of the mind
That dispels the torment of disturbing conceptions.
It is the great sun that finally removes the misty ignorance of the world."

The following prayer by Shantiveda is a favourite of the current Dalai Lama:

"May all beings everywhere
Plagued by sufferings of body and mind
Obtain an ocean of happiness and joy
By virtue of my merits.
May no living creature suffer,
Commit evil, or ever fall ill.

May no one be afraid or belittled,
With a mind weighed down by depression.
May the blind see forms
And the deaf hear sounds,
May those whose bodies are worn with toil
Be restored on finding repose.

May the naked find clothing,
The hungry find food;
May the thirsty find water
And delicious drinks.
May the poor find wealth,
Those weak with sorrow find joy;
May the forlorn find hope,
Constant happiness, and prosperity.

May there be timely rains
And bountiful harvests;
May all medicines be effective
And wholesome prayers bear fruit.
May all who are sick and ill
Quickly be freed from their ailments.

Whatever diseases there are in the world,
May they never occur again.

May the frightened cease to be afraid
And those bound be freed;
May the powerless find power,
And may people think of benefiting each other.

For as long as space remains,
For as long as sentient beings remain,
Until then may I too remain
To dispel the miseries of the world."

Training in Bodhicitta involves cultivating the four immeasurables:

1.Love, which is the wish that all beings who are unhappy find happiness.

2.Compassion, which is the wish that all who are suffering may be freed from suffering.

3.Sympathetic joy, which is the wish that those who are happy and free from suffering may never be separated from their happiness.

4.Equanimity, which is the wish that those who feel attachment and aversion towards anyone, close or distant, may pacify their attachment and aversion.

The six perfections of Bodhicitta described in the **Prajñāpāramitā Sūtras** and the **Lotus Sutra** are:

Dāna pāramitā: generosity, giving of oneself

Śīla pāramitā : virtue, morality, discipline, proper conduct

Kṣānti pāramitā : patience, tolerance, forbearance, acceptance, endurance

Vīrya pāramitā : energy, diligence, vigour, effort

Dhyāna pāramitā : one-pointed concentration, contemplation

Prajñā pāramitā : wisdom, insight

The aspirations associated with the Mahayana Buddhist ideal of the Bodhisattva, are deeply moving whether one is atheist, agnostic or believer, and important in any spirituality that is to be of universal value. They transcend religion, culture, time and place, and are wonderful to discover at the heart of Mahayana Buddhism.

The Dhammapada, the sacred text central to the Tripitaka from the Pali Canon of Theravadan Buddhism, instructs Buddhists to "Overcome anger with love, overcome evil by good. Overcome the miser by giving, overcome the liar by truth" The Dhammapada also points out "The fault of others is easily perceived, but that of oneself is difficult to perceive; a man winnows his neighbours faults like chaff, but his own fault he hides" which strongly echoes Jesus words from The Bible, Matthew 7:1-5 "Judge not, that you be judged...And why do you look at the speck in your brother's eye, but do not consider the plank in your own eye?" The striking parallels between Buddhist teachings and the message of Jesus, particularly the Sermon on The Mount, has led to speculation of contact between Buddhist ideas from nearly six hundred years before Jesus, and the world in to which he was born. Trade routes between the East and the Middle East had long been in existence, and the New Testament attests to the presence of the three wise men from the East at the birth of Jesus. Buddhist ideas penetrated deep in to modern Afghanistan and Pakistan early in its history, and it is likely they spread in the direction of the Middle East. Buddhist monks were said to be living and teaching in Alexandria, Egypt at the time of the early church father Origen, so perhaps early Christianity was influenced by Eastern spiritual ideas more than is recognized.

Plato described rebirth in the last chapter of **The Republic** and his ideas were also strongly influential in Alexandria and in the earliest Christian church. Although the Roman Catholic church strenuously denies this, there is evidence that those such Origen, and the early Christian Gnostics, accepted rebirth as a process through which the eternal soul travels to purify itself, an understanding that shares much in common with samsara. Teachings as to ongoing rebirth of the soul were said to be reserved for initiates and those considered advanced enough to receive them as secret knowledge. Belief in rebirth was widespread in the earliest centuries of the Christian church, but after bitter doctrinal disputes it was declared heresy at the Second Council Of Constantinople in 553AD, the first anathema declaring: "If anyone asserts the fabulous pre-existence of souls, and shall assert the monstrous restoration which follows from it: let him be anathema." Mention of rebirth was carefully edited from Christian sacred texts at that time, and it has been regarded with hostility and suspicion ever since. The Christian Church continued to persecute those such as Giordano Bruno, Dominican Friar, philosopher and mathematician who was burnt at the stake as heretic in Rome in 1600 AD for denying eternal damnation and transubstantiation, his belief in reincarnation and that the universe is infinite without one centre and with many solar systems. Hence the idea of rebirth, central to the concept of samsara, did not develop in mainstream Christian traditions of the West and any reference to it was effectively silenced from the earliest Christian era onwards. How different history might have been if rebirth had been accepted by Christianity and ideas similar to samsara had been a strong tradition in the West as well as the religions of India.

Central to all schools of Buddhism is recognition that samsara brings inevitable suffering, and the provision of a remedy for that, so perhaps it will offer some insight in to what Rob endured. According to Buddhism the inescapable fact of suffering is caused by desire and craving for permanence in a world of impermanence. There is no joy, or possession, or person, or relationship, or achievement, or experience, or body, absolutely nothing at all, which will not decay and perish. The deep truth of this becomes more obvious as loved ones die and with growing older. The **Hua-yan Sutra** from Chinese Mahayana Buddhism of the Tang Dynasty, describes our lives thus: "Sentient beings bob and sink in the ocean of existence. Their troubles are boundless; they have no place to rest". Buddhism expresses much imagery of samsara as an ocean or sea on which we are tossed as each wave of change washes through our lives, every wave inherently impermanent in our endless wandering through life after life, death after death. Je Tsongkhapa (1357-1419), founder of the Gelugpa sect of Tibetan Buddhism, describes the predicament of all beings in samsara:

"Swept along by the currents of the four powerful rivers,
Tightly bound by the chains of karma, so hard to release,
Ensnared within the iron net of self-grasping,
Completely enveloped by the pitch-black darkness of ignorance,
Taking rebirth after rebirth in boundless samsara,
And unceasingly tormented by the three sufferings —
Generate a supreme mind of Bodhichitta."

The Three Principal Aspects of the Path

Because Buddhism is not concerned with the existence of a divine creator, reconciling suffering with an omniscient, omnipotent, creator God, such as that of Christianity or Judaism, is not an issue. The Buddha offered what he believed was needed: a solution to suffering by realizing the Four Noble Truths and following the Noble Eightfold Path. The Buddha illustrated this with the parable of the poison arrow, it being a waste of time worrying where it came from and who sent it when the primary concern is to remove the arrow and its pain. "It's just as if a man were wounded with an arrow thickly smeared with poison. His friends and companions, kinsmen & relatives would provide him with a surgeon, and the man would say, 'I won't have this arrow removed until I know whether the man who wounded me was a noble warrior, a priest, a merchant, or a worker.' He would say, 'I won't have this arrow removed until I know the given name and clan name of the man who wounded me... until I know whether he was tall, medium, or short... until I know whether he was dark, ruddy-brown, or golden-coloured... until I know his home village, town, or city... until I know whether the bow with which I was wounded was a long bow or a crossbow...' The man would die and those things would still remain unknown to him."[89] The Buddha focussed on what are at the top of the pile of human concerns: suffering, impermanence and death, explicitly discouraging speculation as to the existence of a creator. Central to all Buddhist teaching is ending suffering by the removal of the three poisons of attachment, aversion and ignorance, providing means of escape from samsara by the following of the Noble Eight Fold Path and realization of enlightenment. The details of that vary greatly across the range of Buddhist schools, but all have their roots in the teachings of Gautama Buddha.

Mahayana Buddhism in its Vajrayana form practiced in Nepal and Tibet is a highly esoteric Tantric path with a range of Bodhisattvas, wrathful and non-wrathful deities. It stresses the experiential aspects of religion and utilizes practices such as yidam whereby the practitioner identifies with a particular deity, mantras (esoteric verbal formulas), mandalas (diagrams used in various practices sometimes made of coloured sand), and many other symbols and ritual items. The role of the guru, translated as 'lama' in Tibetan, is central in this tradition. A guru is a teacher who has mastered the philosophical and ritual tradition and passes that knowledge on directly to students, often with Tantric initiation and empowerment rituals. The focus is on a wide range of deities and Buddhas, not only the historical Sakyamuni Buddha. According to Mahayana Buddhism the latter was an emanation of the eternal Buddha Amitabha who will also return as the Buddha to come, Maitreya. Tibetan Varjrayana Buddhism is represented by long lineages of teachers and lamas who are often political as well as religious leaders. These Tibetan Buddhist lineages are all represented and have monasteries and followings in Nepal. The Dalai Lama, spiritual head of the most recent school the Gelugpas, is the most well known of these and regarded as the 14th incarnation of Avaloketishvara (Chenrezig in Tibetan) the Boddhisattva of compassion. Tibetan Buddhism has three other main schools tracing to different lineages of teaching, with differing rules and practice, but they all have the same goal of enlightenment. The Nyingmas (the old school) traces its teachings to Padmasambhava the Indian scholar saint who returned Tibet to Buddhism in the eighth century. The Sakyas were founded in the 11th century and the Kagyus draw on the teachings of and lineage of the twelfth century mystic poet Milarepa and his teacher Marpa.

The pre-Buddhist religion of Tibet, Bon, now closely resembles Buddhism in both its teachings and its practices and has influenced Vajrayana Buddhism, particularly its wrathful deities. The institution of Oracles probably has its sources in Bon and these survive in to the present time with an example being the State Oracle of Nechung. The Dalai Lama consults him for prophecy and advice delivered by the Oracle in a state of trance possession. There are Bon priests and religious institutions in remote regions of Nepal such as Dolpo and Mustang, and also the Triten Nobutse monastery near Kathmandhu. Peter Matthiessen took rather a dark view of Bon as a repository of sorcery, magic rituals to propitiate demons and ridden with superstition. The extraordinary French adventurer in Tibet in the early 20th century, Alexandra David-Neel describes encounters with Bon as well as Buddhist magicians and sorcerers, in **Magic and Mystery in Tibet** and **Journey to Lhasa**. Some of their practices are disturbing including reanimation of corpses, Rolang, and rituals known as Chod in cemeteries. Part of the mission of Padmasambhava, the Indian teacher who returned Buddhism to Tibet in the eighth century, was to overcome supernatural forces, demons and sorcerers using powerful Tantric methods. Schisms and conflict between and within the various strands of Tibetan Buddhism is a reality, like it has been in every major religious tradition. Current tensions involving the Dalai Lama and the Dorje Shugden dispute are an example of this. Religions are quick to label their own beliefs as right and therefore everyone else's as wrong, or of lesser validity, leading to intolerance, rivalry and even violence, and Buddhism has not been immune to this. That tendency contributes to why so many people reject commitment to any form of organized religion and search for a path that does not carry with it religious baggage, or the burden of exclusive ownership of truth.

Mahayana Buddhism in all its forms has much to reveal about samsara, and Bhavachakra images illustrating samsara as the wheel of rebirth are common in temple and religious art in Nepal. Although details vary the core elements of these images are consistent. At the centre of the wheel in the innermost circle are depicted the three poisons of attachment, aversion, and ignorance, represented by a pig as ignorance, a snake as aversion or aggression, and a rooster as attachment, all chasing each other around holding on to each other's tails. The tremendous difficulty I felt letting go of Rob and the life we had together is a clear example of attachment, like the rooster. His loss was a painful experience of the truth of impermanence, as are all the losses everyone will have in their lives in some form or another, and according to Buddhism, it is our clinging to that which is impermanent that is the source of suffering. I think of all the energy and time in my own life expended resisting or feeling angry like the snake, and clinging like the rooster, and how little understanding I have had of those and how to deal with them because of ignorance, just like the Bhavachakra pig. The three poisons chase each other's tails in my life as they do for everyone, creating pain and karma that keep driving us around on the wheel of samsara. Buddhism clearly has a strong message and much to teach about possible ways to manage our life and ourselves skilfully.

The following ring on the Bhavachakra, around the circle of The Three Poisons, is that of karma. On one side people are depicted rising to higher levels and on the other sweeping downwards to lower levels, their place in samsara determined by the karmic law of cause and effect. "We create karma in three different ways, through actions that are positive, negative, or neutral. When we feel kindness and love and with this attitude do good things, which are beneficial to both ourselves and others, this is positive action. When we commit harmful deeds out of equally harmful intentions, this is negative action. Finally, when our motivation is indifferent and our deeds are neither harmful nor beneficial, this is neutral action. The results we experience will accord with the quality of our actions." [90]The next ring on the Bhavachakra diagram depicts the six realms of samsara that beings cycle endlessly through. The three higher realms are those of the Gods or Devas, the angry Gods or Asuras, and human realms, and the three lower realms are the animal, hungry ghost, and hell realms. Birth in these is determined by karma driven by The Three Poisons at the centre of the wheel. David Nichtern, in **Waking From The Daydream,**[91] explores the significance of these six realms to the experience of samsara in modern times, and draws powerful insights as to the patterns and forces that shape our lives from within our own psyche. It is only the human realm that offers the possibility of liberation from samsara but most beings are ignorant of this and miss the opportunity.

The outer rim of the Bhavachakra wheel traditionally shows the "Twelve Links of Dependent Origination" depicting a blind man or woman (representing ignorance); potters (formation); a monkey (consciousness); two men in a boat (mind and body); a house with six windows (the senses); an embracing couple (contact); an eye pierced by an arrow (sensation); a person drinking (thirst); a man gathering fruit (grasping); a couple making love (becoming); a woman giving birth (birth); and a man carrying a corpse (death). Bhavachakra images usually portray the wheel of samsara being held by the demon Mara, who tempted the Buddha to abandon his search for enlightenment, or by Yama, the Lord of Death and hell. Many elements appear in the imagery of Yama, such as a third eye symbolizing understanding of impermanence, and four limbs representing birth, old age, sickness, and death. The image of a moon on the top of the wheel indicates release from rebirth in samsara, often shown with a Buddha pointing to the path of liberation as is the case with the Bhavachakra image on the cover of this book. These graphic Bhavachakra images are to be seen everywhere, constantly reminding that all beings are in samsara, caught in its ever turning cycle and that sooner or later, if we are lucky enough to have a precious human birth, we must take the steep trail to wake up. That is extremely easy to never think about, or forget or ignore in the culture I come from, but is impossible in places such as Nepal, Bali or India that never let one forget for a moment a frame of reference all but invisible in modern, rationalist, materialist cultures like my own.

Buddhism is a wise, rich spiritual tradition, and the Mahayana teaching of Bodhicitta, with its emphasis on boundless compassion for all sentient beings, is profound and moving. Its recognition of the truth and inevitability of suffering have helped a little to accept what happened to Rob, and the Noble Eight Fold Path offers wonderful values to live by. The Mahayana Buddhist doctrine of the Bodhisattva, who chooses to return to samsara to show the way and ease the suffering of all beings, is a particularly powerful teaching of compassion and love. Interestingly a Bodhisattva has choice in relation to samsara and rebirth, not possessed by other beings. The Dalai Lama explains: "there are two ways in which someone can take rebirth after death: rebirth under the sway of karma and destructive emotions and rebirth through the power of compassion and prayer. Regarding the first, due to ignorance negative and positive karma are created and their imprints remain on the consciousness. These are reactivated through craving and grasping, propelling us into the next life. We then take rebirth involuntarily in higher or lower realms. This is the way ordinary beings circle incessantly through existence like the turning of a wheel. On the other hand, superior Bodhisattvas, who have attained the path of seeing, are not reborn through the force of their karma and destructive emotions, but due to the power of their compassion for sentient beings and based on their prayers to benefit others. They are able to choose their place and time of birth as well as their future parents."

Followers of Theravada and Mahayana Buddhism have grown rapidly across the world, and meditation techniques derived from Buddhism have made their way in to modern life with the Buddhist practice of mindfulness making a vital contribution to modern psychotherapy. Buddhism gives deep understanding of the forces of the mind that pull us hither and thither in distraction, craving and dissatisfaction, and how to overcome those forces by immersion in the present moment free of attachment. It teaches skilful management of the mind and a path to realizing our true nature. It also generates deep recognition of impermanence and death in contrast to the denial of death particularly strong in the contemporary West. Buddhism offers much of great value but ultimately its view of the world is pessimistic, it's motivating goal being escape from samsara and rebirth bringing about the end of life and death. It reveals no wider meaning or purpose to living, rebirth or samsara, those being inherently suffering, no evolution of consciousness towards union with its divine source, no ongoing permanent self or soul that learns and grows, and no divine creator. Its stress is rather on emptiness, particularly in the Mahayana tradition. The tendency to become ritualized and formulaic is common to all religious traditions and Buddhism is no exception. For example Vajrayana Buddhism utilizes many Tantric rituals, images and ritual instruments such as vrajas, kapalas, bells, mandalas, specifications of which mantras to repeat how many times, and how many prostrations are required to achieve 'merit'. Some Tantric aspects of Vrajayana Buddhism encompass disturbing rituals and practices. A vast range of Buddhas along with multitudes of protector and wrathful deities abound in Mayahana Buddhism, often becoming objects of worship that obscure as much as enhance the simple and profound message of Gautama Buddha.

Hinduism is similarly pessimistic in that it perceives the outer material world as one of suffering from which liberation in to moksha, or union with the divine source, is the desired aim, thus ending rebirth in painful samsara. Its focus is on the inner world, not the material world ruled by maya, or illusion, so it tends not to bother with remedying suffering such as poverty that manifests in the physical world. If the world, its sufferings, and our bodily life in it, are all illusions to be escaped, then there is little point expending effort and time on fixing that world. From that point of view it is much better to dedicate one's life to the inner journey towards enlightenment, so as to get off samsara's merry-go round of rebirth altogether. Irrespective of that pessimism Hinduism is an extremely rich religious and philosophical tradition that has investigated and categorized the nature of consciousness and our relationship to Brahman the divine source of all matter, time, space, energy and consciousness. Its spiritual teachings have spread the world over leading towards awakening of a path to realize God. Hinduism has given the world great spiritual teachers such as Sri Aurobindo, Ramakrishna, Krishnamurti, Swami Vivekananda, Ramana Maharshi and Paramahansa Yogananda, and been the source of yoga and meditation practices that are have become a global phenomenon bringing peace and healing to millions. It is wonderful to discover Sri Aurobindo's teachings of Integral Yoga and evolutionary rebirth. Although rooted in Hinduism they move beyond it, bringing purpose and meaning to living, karma, rebirth and samsara, rather than focussing on a path to escaping them. Aurobindo's ideas offer optimism, hope and great wisdom for crossing the "sea of samsara" and later visit the Aurobindo ashram and education centre in Pondicherry, India.

On the negative side the bewildering array of Hindu gods and goddesses can be confusing, even at times repellent, and those sometimes appear to become ends in themselves, a distraction obscuring the face of Brahman, the Self, as much as revealing it. Religious practices such as animal sacrifices and caste divisions also sully the face of Hinduism. It embraces such a diverse collection of practices and beliefs it is very hard to form a meaningful conclusion, so perhaps it is better to focus on the beauty and power of the ideas expressed in the **Upanishads** and **Bhagavad Gita**. Their understanding of Brahman, as absolute consciousness and the source of being, with which we are all one, is profound, and reading the **Upanishads** gives that 'aha' moment of recognition that here are great universal truths meaningful to everyone, beyond the confines of Hinduism or any religion.

Before finishing this chapter it is time to turn, as promised, to Tantra, a tricky subject if ever there was one. It is a powerful force in both Hinduism and Mahayana Buddhism, profoundly shaping the religious traditions of Nepal, Bali and India, and there is no avoiding it. Religion in Nepal, and later Bali and India, is not comprehensible without exploring the meaning of Tantra, it is such a strong thread in all those cultures. As an example of this Isabella Tree points to the widespread, powerful but often hidden practices of Tantra in Nepal in her article "Radical Tantra" in **The Economist**. The article reports conversations with foremost Nepalese Tantra expert, Professor Mukunda Raj Aryal: "Tantra is behind the scenes of every state occasion. Every festival is accompanied by rituals conducted by tantric priests. But normal householders can also be tantric practitioners. Many Newars of the high Buddhist castes undergo initiation, as well as Newars and other Nepalis of high Hindu castes," the professor said as he steered me towards the Basantpur Pagoda, the medieval seven-storey look-out tower at the corner of the old palace. "Tantrikas perform two types of worship: exoteric worship, in the open with everyone else, at festivals or temples – and esoteric worship, which is more powerful. They do this in secret shrines in Buddhist courtyards and Hindu temples, or on the top floor of their houses. Tantra, he explained, is the invisible backbone running through both Hindu and Buddhist belief-systems in the valley, and this inner worship is believed to discharge an undercurrent of creative and protective energy into the world."[92]

So what is Tantra? The deeper one digs the more complex and contradictory it appears. Descriptions and opinions of Tantra are much divided across cultural contexts, and with so many divergent Tantric traditions and practices, a single definition cannot encompass them all. Tantra is central to many but not all sects of Hinduism and Mahayana Vajrayana Buddhism. Some strands of Hinduism and Buddhism reject it altogether. To its practitioners Tantra provides a vehicle to transcend good and evil, male and female, life and death, so as to realize the unity that underlies the illusion of opposites and thus achieve liberation from samsara. Tantra derives from the Sanskrit "tan" to expand and perceives "the threads of all forces and all events, of all forms of consciousness and their objects, are woven into an inseparable net of endless, mutually conditioned relations."[93] To its opponents Tantra is to be strongly avoided as a slippery slope frequently associated with magic, animal sacrifice and dark repulsive practices. For example a ritual of initiation for Tantric Hindu Aghori sadhus is the eating of rotten human flesh, to demonstrate their overcoming of all opposites and fear of death. Their rituals routinely employ human skulls and their preferred home is cremation grounds. In Tantric Vajrayana Buddhism rituals such as Chod are performed in charnel grounds in the presence of corpses. The most secret initiation rites of the Kalachakra Tantra describe transgression of prohibitions on sex and alcohol, and repellent rituals involving taboo substances either in symbolic form or in reality, such as menstrual blood, semen, urine, excreta etc. These practices are shrouded in silence and great secrecy.

Tantric practice and thinking are thought to have emerged in India between the fifth and the ninth centuries, but the term Tantra came in to use at the time of European colonization, to describe esoteric rituals in Hinduism and Buddhism. What it means to those that practice it varies widely, so it needs to be approached with that in mind. Type Tantra in to Google and thousands of websites spring forward, many proposing techniques of sexual bliss or magic practices to deal with any life problem. Some of the websites clearly offer black magic Tantra for highly dubious purposes which followers of 'true' Tantra would describe as corrupt and degenerate. Snippets of Tantric concepts are commonplace in references to chakras or kundalini yoga, first revealed to the West through translations of Sanskrit Tantric texts by Sir John Woodroffe. The Tantras reveal that manipulation of physiological factors through various practices, can affect states of consciousness so as to bring spiritual realization. Yoga has roots in Tantric practices such as meditation, breathing techniques, opening of the chakra energy centres and the awakening of kundalini Shakti energy coiled at the base of the spine. The physical postures of Hatha yoga were initially designed to open the energy (prana) channels and centres (chakras) of the body in preparation for spiritual unfolding, but in Western countries Hatha yoga is often practiced as little more than stretching exercises and stripped of its spiritual aspects. The yogis of India appear to have little in common with those attending the local yoga studio in the suburbs of Western cities, but they can both be traced back to Indian spiritual and Tantric ideas.

Because Tantra encompasses such a diversity of forms it is sometimes categorized in to the left hand path (Sanskrit vamachara) versus the right hand path (dakshinachara), the left hand path in Hinduism being strongly associated with Shiva. Although these distinctions are somewhat artificial, they are a useful way of referring to its polarities. This division echoes that of Western traditions involving the occult and magic. Language bears out this same distinction: in Italian the left is sinistra, and in medieval Europe left handed people were persecuted and buried outside church grounds due to their associations with the devil. Madame Blavatsky, the founder of Theosophical Society, wrote extensively of the followers of the left hand path as black magicians, in contrast to the right hand path of "white" esotericism practiced within social and ethical limits. According to some Tantric traditions, both left hand, and right hand Tantra can be used to find enlightenment, but the left hand vamachara path is seen as quicker. It is this that constitutes the "Short Path" in Vajrayana Buddhism. Tantra is regarded as offering reward and peril in both Hinduism and Buddhism, unleashing powerful forces within and without the psyche, so its more extreme vamachara versions are associated with ritual, initiation, the guidance of a Tantric guru and great secrecy. Social transgressions associated with some forms of left handed Tantra involve practices such as sex in a cremation ground, or the practitioner may makes ritual use of taboo substances such as semen, blood, excrement, vaginal fluids, or corpses, either symbolically or sometimes literally. Professor Mukunda Raj Aryal continues: "The Tantrika needs to practice things that are deliberately polluting in Indian culture, that he or she would normally consider repulsive. If they are vegetarian, they eat meat. They drink alcohol. They eat with their left hand – the hand that is normally reserved for wiping away excrement. In Tantra these are all called "vamachari" – left-handed practices. A tantrika has sex with his wife when she is menstruating, or drinks her menstrual blood, or his own semen. If he is high caste, he has relations with someone of a lower caste, or an untouchable, or even an animal, like a dog."[94] Practices such as these are deeply repellent and contribute to the apprehension many people feel about Tantra.

Tantra can have associations with fearful forces and magic. Tantric Buddhist practitioners utilize ritual vessels such as the trumpet made of a human thigh bone (kangling), the cranium from a human skull (kapala), an apron made of human bones, a mala (prayer beads) made of human bones or a drum (damaru) constructed of two joined skull craniums sometimes stretched with human skin. The Hindu Kapalika ascetics evolved in to an outcaste sect of Shakti (Goddess) worship, and they used the same ritual symbolic accompaniments as Naljorpas or Tantric Buddhist practitioners: the skull cap bowl, the thighbone trumpet, the human bone apron, the Tantric staff with a skull (khatvanga) the flaying knife and the damaru drum. In Hinduism Tantric sects such as the Aghori sadhus practice bizarre rites with human corpses and roam cremation grounds smearing their bodies with human ashes.

Radmila Moacanin in her **The Essence of Psychology and Tibetan Buddhism** reveals parallels between Carl Jung's explorations of archetypes, the unconscious and Tantra. They can be transformative and liberating, providing a path to enlightenment, but also present danger, Jung calling the process of journeying in to the unconscious 'individuation'. Tantra is feared and avoided by some, whereas to others it is a necessary dimension of the path of liberation from samsara. Professor Mukunda Raj Aryal describes this further: "Tantra, we might say, is the 'fast track' to enlightenment. It is a way of achieving nirvana within one's own lifetime, without having to wait for aeons on the wheel of rebirth. But, like any short-cut taken at great speed, the tantric way is risky and dangerous. It is easy to crash, to destroy oneself. The guru must steer his pupil safely through the obstacles."[95] At arobuddhism.org Tantra is described as " the direct line to the summit. Mountaineers on longer paths circle around the peak weighted down with the safety equipment of codified philosophy and ethics. Tantra scales the vertical face without oxygen. The climbers ascend naked. At the peak they find liberation: freedom from domination by conflictive emotions, customary rôles, and constricted expectations. They climb quickly...." Many Hindus and non-Mahayana Buddhists regard Tantra as a corrupt form of religion associated with superstition and magic, but Hinduism and Buddhism in Nepal, and the Hinduism of Bali, are strongly associated with a moderate form of Tantra.

It is the sexual aspect of Tantra that most fascinates Westerners and has led to its association with exotic sex practices. People outside of the Tantric tradition are half right: sex does play a central role, but the nature of that role and how it expresses itself are often misinterpreted. The sexual aspects of Tantra cannot be isolated from its broader meaning and context. In Vrajayana Buddhism ritual Tantric sex is performed as visualization or Jhanamudra, but also in reality as Karmamudra. Buddhist Tantric deities are often depicted in sexual union, yab yum, with their female consort, a representation of the integration and transcendence of opposites to realize divine bliss. The practice of Karmamudra with an actual sex partner is for the specific purpose of breaking through in to a state of realization, dakinis or goddesses being represented by the female sex partner. Karmamudra plays a part in the teachings of all Tibetan Buddhist schools including the Kalachakra Tantra of the Gelugpas, and the non-celibate schools such as the Nyingmas, the Sakyas and the Kagyus. It is puzzling how initiation in to Tantra reverses the prohibitions on sex and the restrictions applicable to an ordinary Buddhist monk.

A high level of initiation into the highest levels of Tantra, Anuttarayoga, is required before sexual practice with Karmamudra is permitted for monks, although non-monastic householders can and do practice Tantric sex. Their have been many cases of abuse in Tibetan Buddhism where women have been subject to pressures to perform the role, in secret, of dakini or sexual consort in Tantric rituals. This all seems a long way from the teachings of Siddhartha Gautama, the historical Sakyamuni Buddha, about celibacy. It is even claimed that the Sakyamuni Buddha realized enlightenment through Tantric sexual practices, something Theravadan Buddhists would utterly reject along with all Tantra. This is an extremely controversial issue for Buddhists. For example in an interview with Dr. Nida Chenagtsang published as "Sexuality in the Tibetan Buddhist Tradition" he states this as follows: "According to many Tantric texts, such as the *Kalachakra Tantra* and the *Guhyasamaja Tantra*, Shakyamuni Buddha was transformed into one of the highest *Anuttarayoga Tantra* deities and then he transmitted the teachings of sexual union. We cannot say for sure whether this was his path to final enlightenment, or whether he recognized that this, too, was a method for achieving spiritual attainment after he attained enlightenment, but he transmitted these teachings for us. I am not so sure about that part, but either way, according to Vajrayana Buddhism, there is no doubt about the fact that Shakyamuni Buddha is somehow connected with these teachings."[96]

In Hinduism some sadhus and Tantric practitioners also practice ritual sex for the purposes of transcending taboos and opposites. Hindu Tantric traditions, particularly for followers of Shiva and Shakti (female power) include Tantric sexual practices that mirror the union of the primal forces of Shiva and Shakti, consciousness and energy, to achieve divine realization. Temples, such as Khajaraho in India, explicitly depict these sexual activities in eye watering variety and detail. In both Tantric Buddhism, and Hinduism, the right hand is associated with the male, and the left with the female, and in Tantric art "The goddess is always placed on the left side of the male deity, where she sits of his left thigh, while her Lord places his left arm over her left shoulder and dallies with her left breast." [97]

Professor Mukunda Raj Aryal explains the relationship between Tantra and sex to Isabella Tree while showing to her the erotic carvings on temple roof struts of temples and buildings in Kathmandu's Durbar Square: "In Tantra it is the desires and sensations of the body which are the key to enlightenment. We don't have to look for nirvana somewhere nebulous, out there in the great beyond." He tapped his chest. "It is right here." He goes on: "Sex is important in Tantra because the sexual urge is the most powerful of the body's impulses. There is nothing stronger than the desire to unite oneself physically with another. It is the overpowering instinct for unity, for the male to return to the female, for the female to unite with the male, to enter a state that is beyond all boundaries. Consider, if you will, the phenomenon of orgasm…For a brief moment, at the point of climax, the mind becomes empty of thoughts. It is like a moment of meditation. The ego is extinguished by an experience of supreme bliss. And yet all too soon that moment has vanished – we are left feeling disappointed, dissatisfied, wanting more. Am I right?" I nodded uncomfortably, reluctantly admitting myself into the bedroom of his first person plural. "This is the moment the practice of Tantra aims to expand. The tantrika regains this moment through sexual activity but gradually he – or she – must learn, through meditation and control of their desire, to reach that same experience without releasing energy or becoming the slave of lust…." He goes on: "Mastering the art of orgasm without ejaculation is an act of self-discipline involving the awakening of the kundalini, the serpent of female energy lying dormant, coiled eight times at the base of the spine, blocking the opening of the genital organ with her mouth. When the kundalini is aroused it can be channelled up the body through the chakras – psychic energy centres ranged between the perineum and the brain – piercing them like a shaft of brilliant light. Experienced tantric masters, the professor explained, can raise their kundalini up through these chakras, experiencing different states of awareness, right up to the highest head chakra. From there, they can channel the female Shakti energy through the top of the skull so it can unite with Shiva, the male aspect of Pure Consciousness pervading the whole universe, thereby opening the 1,000-petalled lotus of the sahasrara chakra and flooding the being with indescribable bliss."[98]

Tantra embraces all aspects of samsara and rejects nothing to bring about realization of the true nature of reality. It encompasses many different possibilities, defying easy conclusions. For its practitioners it takes them beyond the confines of religion and ritual to an experience of spiritual power. It takes extremely divergent forms according to culture, context and the intention of its practitioner and stirs highly polarized responses. To its followers, Hindu and Buddhist, it represents the surest and fastest route to spiritual realization, whereas to its detractors it is little more than magic, with extremely disgusting practices added in.

Rituals involving cremation or charnel grounds feature in Tantric practices in both Hinduism and Buddhism. Pashputinath Temple near Kathmandhu is a Hindu Shiva temple where sometimes Aghori Sadhus are to be found. They are feared by many because of rituals they perform with human corpses, embracing death to bring about spiritual realization. We will look out for them when we visit Pashputinath. The sky burial grounds of Tibet and bordering areas of Nepal provide the location for the Buddhist Tantric practices of Chod involving dead bodies and occult forces, and those continue in Himalayan Nepal. Charnel or cremation grounds are viewed by both Hinduism and Buddhism as offering recognition of mortality and impermanence, a necessary first step on the journey towards liberation from samsara. The **Satipatthana Sutta** of early Buddhism describes "Cemetery Contemplations" which "…have as their objects a corpse one of two or three days old, swollen up, blue black in colour, full of corruption; a corpse eaten by crows etc; a framework of bones; flesh hanging from it" or "without flesh and blood, but still held together by the sinews; bones scattered in all direction' bleached and resembling shells; heaped together after the lapse of years; weathered and crumbled to dust". After the contemplation of corpses comes the instruction to reflect upon the impermanence of our human bodies and lives "This body of mine also has this nature, has this destiny, cannot escape it." Death is an inescapable truth of samsara, and according to both Hindu and Buddhist teaching the recognition of that is the starting point of the path to enlightenment. This is the opposite of the predominant perspective on death held in the West. The English Benedictine monk Bede Griffiths (1906-1993) expresses a similar idea: "…Nobody know when he is going to die. It is no good simply putting it off all the time, as we tend to do. If you face it, you realize you hold your life in your hands, and you're ready to let go at any moment. I think that is real wisdom." [99] He later became known as Swami Dayananda ("bliss of compassion") founding ashrams in South India dedicated to understanding between faiths, particularly Hinduism and Christianity.

Hinduism and Buddhism have much to say about our lives in samsara, those being created according to our karma that propels us in to rebirth over and over again. Karma is embedded at their core claiming we are all the authors of our own destiny including the suffering we experience. Karma has difficult aspects to accept: it makes us all responsible for our own circumstances. "Skilful actions that lead to good karmic outcomes are based upon motives of generosity; compassion, kindness and sympathy, and clear mindfulness or wisdom. The opposite motives of greed, aversion (hatred) and delusion, when acted upon, lead to bad karmic results. Karma is not an external force, not a system of punishment or reward dealt out by a god. The concept is more accurately understood as a natural law similar to gravity."[100] That actions have consequences makes sense, but when that is extended towards illness and bad fortune being caused by karma, the implication is people have earned or created those, thus blaming the victim for circumstances often absolutely nothing to do with them or individuals. A good man like Rob being in some way responsible for his own suffering, because of karma, is a deeply shocking idea that I cannot accept.

Karma is a concept open to much abuse. Making people individually responsible for their own suffering is an outrageous idea to apply to a child blown up in a US bombing raid of a Vietnamese village during a war driven by global forces such as the cold war, anti-communism and the end of colonialism, all of which have absolutely nothing to do with the small child or their actions. I recently wandered through the museum in my home city and was struck by a nineteenth century painting of a young Tasmanian aboriginal girl, Mathinna, who suffered terribly from the dispossession of her people and her identity. She was adopted by the wife of the then Governor, Lady Franklin, then abandoned to her fate when they departed Van Diemen's Land. She drowned in a pool of water, drunk, at the age of fifteen, her people, her place, her identity destroyed by colonialism's destruction of the way of life of indigenous people. She is portrayed in nineteenth century European clothing, lost in the world she found herself in with no world of her own to return to. Most of the life experiences of Mathinna were created by British colonialism and the forces of nineteenth century history, so how concepts such as karma could possibly apply to situations such as hers is incomprehensible as it is history, culture, and global social, political and economic forces that mostly drive the circumstances of an individual's life.

Karma is that aspect of samsara I most struggle to make sense of. Self-righteous people sometimes remark that people are suffering in some way because it is 'their karma' and then absolve themselves from doing anything constructive to help, be that alleviate poverty or offer support. Others are extremely smug that they have earned their good fortune because of 'good karma,' inferring that someone experiencing bad fortune deserves it due to 'bad karma' and that the victim is to blame. 'Bad karma' can be used as a weapon of judgement, self-justification, or threat. It is impossible to feel comfortable with easy glib explanations of karma being responsible for cruel and unfair suffering, such as being born blind or afflicted with a hereditary illness such as Rob's. The extreme disparity between the circumstances of people's birth in samsara is often rationalized by reference to karma, and Hinduism uses it to justify the hereditary inequalities and discriminations of the caste system. So to be born at the bottom of the Hindu social pile becomes the karmic fault of the individual. The Bodhisattva ideal of Mahayana Buddhism is positive however. It teaches that although we are responsible for our own karma, we are also responsible for tirelessly working for the release of all beings from samsara, and that eliminating the suffering of others is of far greater importance than eliminating our own.

Suffering remains a confronting mystery of life for which no religion provides a satisfactory explanation. Buddhism is silent as to the existence of God, so at least God is not held responsible. In religions such as Christianity, Judaism or Islam good or bad fortune results from 'God's will' that punishes or rewards, which makes even less sense than karma. Self-congratulation or blame also appears, reflecting human nature rather than 'God's will' or karmic justice. After tragedies or natural disasters people often "thank God" for their survival which begs the question where was God for all the other people who did not survive? Is the implication that because God saved some then God caused others to perish? Did they not survive because that is what God chose or what they deserved? That presents a horrible, cruel, judgemental God, picking and choosing the recipients of 'his' care, not a loving one. It is shocking to discover that various leaders of

Judaism, Hinduism, Islam and Christianity attributed the Boxing Day Asian tsunami of 2004 to God's wrath and vengeance. Gary Stern in **Can God Intervene: How Religion Explains Natural Disasters**, quotes religious leaders claiming that the victims, always from a different group or religion than themselves, were targets of God's vengeance because they had offended God in some way.

In Australia, Phillip Jensen, Dean of the notoriously fundamentalist Australian Sydney Anglican diocese, is quoted by Stern as commenting that the tsunami was a judgement from God: "The Will of God in this world involved his creation of the world, but it also involves his judgment upon the sinfulness of humanity and it also involves his salvation of people through the death and resurrection of his son....And so all the beautiful things we see in this world are an expression of his creative goodness to us and all the disasters of this world are part of his warning the judgment is coming, and both of these things should focus our mind on the death and resurrection of his son and how he saved us." Israeli chief Shephardic rabbi Shlomo Amar said: "This is an expression of God's great ire with the world. The world is being punished for wrongdoing—be it people's needless hatred of each other, lack of charity, moral turpitude."[101] Saudi cleric Muhammad Al-Munajiid describes the tsunami as a punishment from God because "... the Christian holidays [that] are accompanied by forbidden things, by immorality, abomination, adultery, alcohol, drunken dancing and revelry....they spend the entire night defying Allah. ... At the height of immorality, Allah took revenge on these criminals. ... Allah struck them with an earthquake."[102] A Hindu priest from New Delhi claims God caused the tsunami as punishment for "a huge amount of pent-up man-made evil on earth."

These religions all presenting God as vengeful, and responsible for mass murder of thousands of people, effectively turns many towards despair that religion has anything positive to offer. Albert Einstein in a 1915 letter to Swiss physicist Edgar Meyer, put it well: "I see only with deep regret that God punishes so many of His children for their numerous stupidities, for which only He Himself can be held responsible; in my opinion, only His nonexistence could excuse Him.....I cannot imagine a God who rewards and punishes the objects of his creation, whose purposes are modelled after our own — a God, in short, who is but a reflection of human frailty." **God: The Most Unpleasant Person In All Fiction,** is a joint effort between Richard Dawkins and ex-evangelical preacher Dan Barker. It continues the same theme as it explores the murderous, sexist, misogynist, racist, cruel, vindictive ways of the Judeo-Christian male God Yahwey depicted in the Old Testament, and provides powerful evidence that it is long past time for humans to move on from that kind of God in whatever religion 'he' - and it is a self proclaimed he - manifests.

Theologians of the past such as St Augustine, concluded that unbaptized babies, who have committed no personal sin, are condemned to eternal hell because they are contaminated by 'original sin', a monstrous idea in relation to a 'loving' God if there ever was one. Christianity has tangled itself up for millenia over issues such as this, even if it was concluded that hell for unbaptized babies only involved hell's mild outer fringes known as limbo. The comments of the fifth century Pelagian heretic, Julian of Eclanum, cast out of the Catholic Church for his views, says it all: "Tell me then, tell me: who is this person who inflicts punishment on innocent creatures....You answer: God. God you say! God!....He is the persecutor of new-born children; He it is who sends tiny babies to eternal flames...it would be right and proper to treat you as beneath argument...so far from religions feeling, from civilized thinking, so far, indeed form mere common sense, in that you think that your Lord God is capable of committing a crime against justice such as is hardly conceivable even among the barbarians."[103] But it was the views of St Augustine that triumphed in the early Christian Church and the rest, as they say, is history.

Rob was a good man and his suffering was random and cruel, impossible to makes sense of as the result of either the will of God or karma. Christianity has various explanations why God permits evil and suffering, none of them convincing. The three propositions that God is all good, God is all knowing and God is all powerful, are irreconcilable with the existence of evil and suffering that are not the result of free will. The problem of evil in Christianity and Judaism becomes murkier still when Biblical passages are considered such as "I form the light, and create darkness. I make peace, and create evil. I the Lord do all these things." (Isiah

45:7) are considered. It was after all God who sent Satan to tempt Jesus in his forty nights in the wilderness and who sent suffering upon Job in the Bible's Old Testament. Those passages suggest that evil is not an independent force contrary to the will of God, but that God is in some way the source of evil and in control of it, in which case God cannot be all good. Suffering remains deeply perplexing, experienced by some far more than others, in arbitrary, often unfair ways like Rob because he had a genetic glitch in the ITMB2 gene on chromosome thirteen.

Hinduism connects suffering with karma, also having a variety of explanations as to why evil exists and its relationship to Brahman. Gods such as Shiva and Kali explicitly embrace destruction as well as creation as twin aspects of the one reality. Hinduism in Bali explicitly recognizes demonic forces bringing suffering and illness, the aim always being to placate them and keep positive and negative forces in balance. Tantric shakti Mahavidya Hindu deities such as Dhumavati are dark goddesses who bring destruction. Other Hindu goddesses such as Nirriti, goddess of disease, decay, bad luck and misery, and Alakshmi, the goddess of misfortune and poverty are identified by David Kingsley[104] as representing the polarities of good and evil embedded within Brahman who transcends all opposites. Sri Aurobindo offers the following comments: "Brahman is indivisible in all things and whatever is willed in the world has been ultimately willed by Brahman. It is only our relative consciousness, alarmed or baffled by the phenomena of evil, ignorance and pain in the cosmos, that seeks to deliver the Brahman from responsibility for Itself and its workings by erecting some opposite principle, Maya or Mara, conscious Devil or self-existent principle of evil. There is one Lord and Self and the many are only His representations and becomings."[105]

Are suffering and 'evil' required to provide the experiences and challenges through which the soul learns compassion and wisdom as it develops on its journey through repeated births in samsara 'the schoolroom of the soul'? In the **Katha Upanishad** Yama the Lord of Death explains to his questioner, the teenage boy Nachiketa, what happens after death is dependent on the evolutionary progress of the soul at the time of death.

"Now, O Nachiketa, I will tell you
Of this unseen, eternal Brahman, and

What befalls the Self after death. Of those
Unaware of the Self, some are born as
Embodied creatures while others remain
In a lower state of evolution,
As determined by their own need for growth."

If only good existed would it be possible to have the experiences necessary for growth of the soul? Kahlil Gibran in **The Prophet** expresses suffering as somehow redemptive: "Your pain is the breaking of the shell that encloses your understanding." I cannot find anything even faintly redemptive in Rob's suffering that spread ripples of pain across all those that loved him. No answer or response from any religion convincingly explains the age-old problems of evil and suffering, so there seems no choice but to leave them in the too hard basket.

Buddhism and Hinduism gave much to think about, and exhibit the opposite of the death sanitizing and avoidance typical of contemporary Western societies. The latter offer scanty ways of contemplating suffering and death, being mostly orientated towards denial, a purely material explanation of the universe, perpetuating youth, sweeping the ugly realities of aging and death far under the carpet and referencing death with veiled euphemisms such as "passed away," or if an animal is euthanized it is "put to sleep". The concept of samsara, and the honest and direct way that death is acknowledged in Hinduism and Buddhism, present a stark contrast to modern Western societies, where many live with absolutely no idea why or how they come to be here, what their lives might mean and where death will take them. As I was preparing for the journey to Nepal the only clear certainties were Rob was dead, as will be everything that lives, and that everyone will experience suffering, as did Rob.

Om Mani Padme Hum
Hail to the jewel in the lotus

CHAPTER FIVE
NEPAL

Now Rob had been farewelled across the closing frontier of samsara the next step is Nepal, a Hindu and Buddhist country permeated by intense spirituality and a rich culture providing a welcome distraction from grief. I hope to discover if samsara and rebirth could help clarify any aspects of living, dying and what happened to Rob, samsara being woven in to every aspect of Nepalese life. Peter Matthiessen's account of his Nepal travels, **The Snow Leopard**, [106] sowed the seeds for this journey taking place so much water under the bridge and three decades later. I reread his book as Rob was dying, and Matthiessen's struggles with the death of his wife D, and with himself, touched deep chords. He took his hard journey in the 1970's mostly on foot, opening up for the reader Dolpo near Tibet, one of the remotest and most beautiful places on earth. His insights in to the spiritual beliefs and practices of the communities he passes through added a powerful extra dimension to his journey. It was no ordinary travelogue, but something rare, profound, precious. Nepal also appeals because Rob loved it as a young man, taking the hippie trail across the world in search of adventure and hashish, at that time both offered freely. Freak St in Kathmandu is a small reminder of those times albeit in a very washed out version, the hashish shops closed, the hippies rounded up and deported to India decades ago, apparently with compulsory haircuts.

Nepal has much to offer. Extraordinary art and architecture from a remarkable history survive in the ancient cities of the Kathmandu valley, particularly in the Durbar Squares of Lalitpur, Bhaktapur, Kantipur and Kirtipur, all becoming engulfed by the sprawl of greater Kathmandu. As well as enormous cultural, historical and spiritual richness it also possesses astounding natural beauty and diversity. Soaring snow clad peaks of the Himalayas, hot plains bordering India, dry moonscapes on the high plateaux bordering Tibet, verdant valleys of rhododendron, juniper, pine, and birch, sliced by wild torrents born from Himalayan snows. Mountains of incredible beauty and grandeur, home to marvellous creatures such as the blue sheep, the lammergieur, the red panda, the fabled snow leopard, and perhaps, just perhaps, the yeti. In addition to massive mountains, stunning scenery and architecture, warm people, rich history and culture, what attracts me is the all pervasive spirituality.

That requires adjustment to the perceptual frameworks of someone from a secular materially developed society where increasing numbers like myself have no religion at all. In those societies science and rationality are not merely regarded as important, but as possessing total power of explanation despite their silence in the face of impermanence, suffering and death. Nepal presents a smorgasbord of belief, ritual and culture, possessing around one hundred and twenty different languages and a huge range of cultural groups. Samsara is depicted everywhere in the Buddhist Bhavachakra images of the wheel of life, and the presence of suffering and death are inescapable. It is a cocktail of the remarkable, the profound, and the shocking, from mass sacrifice of many thousands of buffalo at Gadhimai[107] on the hot dusty plains near the Indian border, to satisfy a bloodthirsty Hindu goddess of power, to the soaring peaks and plateaux of the Himalayas, where Tibetan Buddhist culture and religion survive in places like Dolpo and Mustang. Buddhist monasteries offer meditation and yoga retreat centres for spiritually thirsty tourists, and shamans practice rituals to heal and exorcise, often for curious foreigners. From animal sacrifices to propitiate demons, gods and goddesses, wandering Hindu sadhus roaming through samsara smeared in ashes, to mantras thrown out to the universe by fluttering prayer flags and turns of prayer wheels, Nepal possesses a wild diversity utterly in contrast to my own tame, dull and well-ordered society.

Strands of Hinduism and Buddhism are woven in to a complex multi-layered tapestry. Simple statistics of religious affiliation disguise the reality that those merge and overlap with not only each other, but animist and magical beliefs and rituals. Some eighty percent of Nepalese describe themselves as Hindu and approximately ten percent as Buddhist, but many follow elements of both, particularly in the uniquely Nepalese forms of religion of the Kathmandu valley and Himalayan foothills. It is a challenge teasing out these many threads of religion but they all have roots in ancient India. Because of this syncretism holy places in Nepal are often simultaneously sacred to Hinduism and Buddhism, such as the temples and stupa at Swayambhunath in Kathmandu, where Newar Buddhists, Himalayan Buddhists and Nepalese Hindus all worship. The complex of temples and chaityas includes prayer wheels for Tibetan Buddhists, Hindu Shiva linghams sitting in their stone yonis carved with Buddhist images, and shrines to various Tantric deities. Both Hindus and Buddhists seek the protection of the smallpox Goddess Harati at her shrine. It is difficult to define what is Hindu and what is Buddhist as deities, art, sculpture and religious imagery often reflect elements of both jumbled up together.

The Shantipur temple at Swayambhunath illustrates how Hindu and Buddhist perceptions of the world directly challenge the rationalist materialist viewpoint that dominates in the West. This small insignificant looking building contains a secret locked room below which, according to legend, Tantric master and magician from the 8th century, Shantikar Acharia, still practices meditation and possesses power over the weather of the Kathmandu valley. The King of Nepal would visit this temple and receive a secret mandala to bring rain, this last occurring in 1658. The temple can only entered by Buddhacaya and Thankali religious leaders and is protected by powerful Tantric spells. The Thankali are an ethnic group who originally practiced a mixture of Tibetan Buddhist, Hindu and Bon beliefs but who have increasingly moved towards Hinduism. All these strands of faith and culture entwine in what seemed like an impenetrable tangle, and many, like belief in the eighth century mystic in Shantipur temple, are impossible to reconcile with a Western way of looking at the world.

In Nepal the veil between the prosaic day to day world of matter, and realms of spiritual power, is porous and thin. There is a palpable sense of some other invisible dimension hovering in the background, present in innumerable shrines, temples, prayer flags, statues, linghams, yonis, vajras set in to pavements, and prayer wheels, that is utterly absent in my own culture. Gods, goddesses, Buddhas, magicians, demons, shamans, spirits, monks, mantras and mystics, and a universe alive with unseen forces that must be managed, represent a very different way of understanding the world from Australia. The shadow side of that cannot be ignored: black magic, sorcery, animal and occasional human sacrifices, caste discrimination, as well as rampant superstition. Dark realities of poverty, high infant mortality, sexism, environmental degradation, corruption, and a society still dominated by the distinctions of caste status, coexist with the extraordinary spirituality saturating all aspects of life. Women are subject to domestic violence, alcohol abuse, family pressures, lack of education, lower life expectancy and misogynist social practices such as chaupadi which castes a menstruating woman as "unclean" from her home in to an isolation hut where she endures freezing cold and wild animals. Another dark side of religion in Nepal is that mental health issues are often blamed on demons, or possession by spirits or angry deities, and fear of these and the use of magic to counteract them, are widespread.

The Nepal of **The Snow Leopard** has irreversibly changed, and Peter Matthiessen is now dead, but his journey remains an inspiration. So too do the accounts of those such as Alexandra David-Neel and Lama Anagarika Govinda, who ventured as Buddhist practitioners in to the world of Himalayan Buddhism early in the twentieth century. Born in Belgium in 1868 Alexandra David-Neel described her extraordinary journey, as an ordained Buddhist Lama during the 1920's, in **Magic and Mystery in Tibet** and **Journey to Lhasa**. She revealed a secret world of Naljorpas, male ascetic Tantric practitioners akin to Indian yogis, and Ngaspas or sorcerers, and gives many alarming accounts of their supernatural powers, rituals and practices, including rolang or the revival of a corpse, the overcoming of demons, and gruesome Chod practices in cemeteries amongst occult forces. She meets an astonishing cast of Lamas and holy men, ascetic recluses, magicians and charlatans, and records a way of life long gone, although elements of it are still to be found in remote Himalayan regions of Nepal such as Mustang and Dolpo. She herself spent two years in seclusion under a Gomchen, or hermit magician, who initiated her in to the secret world of Tantric Buddhism. German born Lama Anagarika Govinda recorded in **The Way of the White Clouds** his journeys in the late 1940's with his wife Li Gotami through a Tibet all but closed to foreigners, revealing a remarkable culture now largely destroyed by the Chinese invasion. A world where bad weather is the work of demons, where trumpets are made from a human thigh bone (kangling) in rituals in cremation grounds (Chod) where the skullcap (kapala) filled with blood is a symbol of the impermanence of the brief journey we take in matter and time that is samsara. This is the Tantric Vajrayana form of Buddhism found in Himalayan Nepal.

I am excited to be travelling to this extraordinary country for myself, Rob had told me so many stories of his time there. A small container of his ashes is tucked in my bag along with the letter from the funeral home. We had planned to visit Nepal together, but neither of us ever imagined it would be happening in this form surrounded by such grief. My flight in to Kathmandu with a lucky window seat gives a brief and startling glimpse of the Himalayas suspended like a dream above the cloud cover, a shimmering white vision against the intense blue of the midday sky. It is an astonishing sight, the snow-capped peaks floating above earth and soaring in to space. They are glowing softly, a silent, looming presence alone on a vast plain of billowing grey white clouds as far as the eye can see. No wonder the Himalayas are seen as the abode of the gods, a sacred landscape. Our journey around on the wheel of samsara inevitably brings suffering and death but also such intense beauty as is now revealing itself. I wish Rob was here to share this moment with me.

As the flight descends the recent devastating floods are visible, rendering millions downstream in southern Nepal and Bangladesh homeless, their lives torn apart by ruthless nature, although perhaps they might see it as the work of demons or angry gods. Wild brown rivers tumble through livid green valleys, hillsides collapsing as de-afforestation and erosion take their toll. Kathmandu from above is a jumbled jungle of half-finished buildings spreading across the valley embracing the old cities of the Kathmandu valley in one great sprawl, the hills and rice fields vanishing in a sea of concrete. Beautiful monasteries such as Kopan occupy many of the ridges and hilltops, small green islands of tranquillity in the grey. Arrival at the terminal does not go smoothly. How easy it is to forget that technologies like Wifi can't be assumed to be always everywhere. In the arrivals sections there are no seats, no food or drink, and the only ATM has no money because the banks are closed due to the festival of Dashain, the Nepalese equivalent of Durga Puja. Marck is arriving on a later flight from Thailand and not contactable which is frustrating, but the airport workers are so helpful while working with few resources that puts it all in perspective. The only thing to do is brave the rows of yelling taxi drivers and take the trip to our hotel in the tourist hub of Thamel to wait for him there.

Kathmandu is the expected shock of dust, anarchic traffic dodging each other with extraordinary skill, cows sleeping on the road, plastic bags, and garbage everywhere. The roads are lined with the incongruities of the 21st century, crumbling ancient buildings covered in signs for technology services, half-finished buildings rising like ugly toadstools from patches of rice field not yet swamped in concrete. It is a sea of dust and concrete laced by grey roads, the surfaces of the roads and laneways of Thamel broken, footpaths non-existent, people picking their way through the anarchy of cars, rickshaws, street vendors, and motor bikes. Little planning for people seems to have accompanied the mushrooming of Kathmandu, turning the once three great Kingdoms of the valley, Lalitpur, Bhaktapur and Kantipur, in to one vast engulfing sprawl without green belts or parks. **Lonely Planet** describes one small park aptly named "The Garden of Dreams" not far from the hotel. We visit this and it is exquisite, but the entry cost puts it way past the affordability of most residents who must grapple with their city every day with no escape from the dust, traffic or chaos. Development is random and uncontrolled, the needs of the car and motorbike being the dominant paradigm. Electricity cabling forms extraordinary tangles of wires like weird games of cat's cradle, spooling around leaning poles and strung along buildings resembling coils of snakes in a wild frenzy. The women in gorgeous gracious kurtas or saris are a riot of colour and beauty as they navigate through the traffic, towing small children with incredible calm and grace.

Spending the afternoon wandering around Thamel brings many surprises. So much artisan skill and beautiful design in objects like a beautiful brass dragon door handle in a shop in a small lane with broken drains, piles of garbage, and sad eyed skinny dogs. Shop after shop displaying exquisite fabrics and objects: Tibetan Buddhist Thangka paintings, brass Shiva statues and Buddhas, beautiful pashminas and cashmere scarves, fake antique prayer wheels, rainbow coloured kurtas and fabrics. Every shop is immaculate and every shop owner in sharp competition with all the others selling much the same products. They are still open and working late in the evening with tight-walleted tourists bargaining. How the shopkeepers manage to smile when they live daily poverty and grinding hours of hard work is a mystery. I am torn by guilt at bargaining for an item that drops fifty percent in price while walking out the door, knowing the hard life and struggle lying behind the shop front and yet not wanting to pay more than the fair going rate. Many shopkeepers tell the same sad story, that since the earthquakes tourism numbers are down and business slow, at the mercy of tourists who pursue bargain hunting as a blood sport and who have the economic power in their wallets to dictate terms. Small shrines are everywhere, some with stone linghams smeared in red and yellow, others with elephant headed Ganesha, son of Shiva and Parvarti, and the overcomer of obstacles. And these people have many obstacles to overcome: poverty, floods, earthquakes, mind numbing traffic, political upheaval, a city growing out of control, and rapid social change, being just a few.

Pedestrians totter along the broken road surfaces narrowly missing being mowed down at every moment and yet strangely no one is. The drivers are oddly patient with being stuck in a tiny street whilst Buddha Water Trucks with lotus decorations, block the passage of motor bikes, cars, rickshaws, itinerant musicians, sellers of just about anything thrusting their goods past one's eyes, monks wandering by, and a great rush of people going about their lives. Pure riotous anarchy but it somehow works with remarkable grace in circumstances that would have driven people in Sydney or New York to road rage or murder. And just about everyone in this wild tapestry of diversity humming with life, is taking it for granted that they are in samsara, living the lives they do because of their karma and the spiritual forces that swirl unseen all around them. It is impossible to tell who are Buddhists and who are Hindus, and whether the shrines dotted everywhere are Hindu or Buddhist or perhaps both.

A group of people are gathered at a small roadside temple, flowers in their hands as they line up to view the image of the deity, each one of them bringing their fears, hopes, gratitude, needs, and dreams, to the attention of the divine presence inside the shrine which is open on three sides. Some of the shrines have a large bell hanging to one side, and as an elderly woman begins her worship she rings the bell as a sign of darshan, or presence of the god. The idol is believed to embody the real spiritual power and energy of the deity that the worshipper can meet with and receive blessings from. This is every moment of every day religion with the deity clearly visible to all who pass by, in utter contrast to the solid neat churches mostly locked except for Sunday services as the face of religion where I come from. Churches still in use are becoming ever scarcer as they are sold to be converted in to homes or restaurants, as church attendance continues to dwindle and funds must be raised to pay vast sums of compensation to victims of sexual abuse perpetrated by priests, pastors, and ministers. I cannot imagine what it would be like to have a strong sense of a spiritual dimension hovering behind what many of the people of Kathmandu would perceive as maya, or illusion, creating their reality as they cross the "sea of samsara," living out in this lifetime what karma has delivered them and hoping that perhaps in the next lifetime things might be better.

The paradoxes of this place are obvious from the first moment. Women haul beautiful handmade bricks in baskets suspended from the top of their heads along ancient laneways of old Kantipur, the original name for Kathmandu, while a Tibetan Buddhist monk earnestly examines his cell phone then plugs in his earphones, his foot tapping against the concrete base of an enormous prayer wheel. The ubiquitous cell phones are everywhere in strangely incongruous contexts, dominating so much time and energy, just as they do now in most places on earth. So much of human experience in samsara in the twenty first century is mediated in some way or another by smart phones: holding memories as photographs, booking flights or hotels, doing banking, keeping us in touch by text message or email, apps that deliver meditation practices, tell us which restaurant nearby is open, mapping the celestial bodies in the night sky, or making it possible for people with diabetes to monitor their blood sugar levels. I remember a snake charmer with his cobra in India, plunging a hand in to a red turban to answer his ringing cell phone, twenty first century meeting twelfth century.

Nepal offers the same startling clashes of worlds I remember from earlier trips to India with Rob. Walking through laneways of the old town of Kirtipur, now part of greater Kathmandu, an elderly Newari man in traditional clothing is sitting on the edge of a broken wall next to a temple at which a buffalo has been sacrificed earlier in the day, utterly absorbed in Eine Kleine Nachtmusik playing on his cell phone. A couple of Shaivite sadhus sit cross-legged beside a Kathmandu highway, consulting their cell phones like a precious oracle as they fish them out from their ochre coloured robes. Rickshaw drivers from past centuries navigate medieval laneways with Google maps, the taxi driver makes us his Facebook friend, internet and wifi are advertised as free in the pizza restaurant occupying a collapsing but utterly beautiful building complete with huge stone lions perched proudly at the entrance where they have been for centuries. But they now have plastic buckets or Hare Krishna brand water bottles stacked on top of them... and so on it goes.

Chaos and contradictions are at every turn. Architecture with exquisite attention to detail, perfect in design and creation, maybe has a whole wall crumbling or the entire building leaning precariously, its roof sprouting a thick crop of grass and shrubs and ugly new chrome door furniture screwed over beautiful, intricate, carved doors from a world of five hundred years earlier. In Bhaktapur's Durbar square a particularly lovely ancient building displays a large sign advertising an internet provider across its worn carved windows, its roof crumbling under the growth of weeds and small trees. An advertisement on a broken ancient doorway proclaims "Experience divinity...with the new American Express card", whilst a group of wild street kids about eight years old, carrying huge bags of possibly garbage, dodge and weave past tourists sipping their café lattes on the steps opposite a temple. They are filthy, dressed in rags and yet so full of vibrant energy it is remarkable. Their skin is noticeably darker than most Nepalese and I wonder what ethnic group they belong to. The locals do not seem pleased by their presence, perhaps they are thieves? Two of the girls have beautiful faces and their future is worrying as many Nepali girls end up in the sex trafficking trade. But the absolutely dominating dimension to all this heady cocktail of beauty, ugliness, contrasts, and paradoxes, is that of religion. There is a palpable sense of the presence of forces and dimensions hovering just beyond the veil of maya, the shadow play of the material world where the wheel of samsara turns and we incarnate over and over again into the vehicle of perishable bodies. According to Buddhism and Hinduism, everything and everyone is whirling through time playing out this life in this body behind the veil of maya's illusion, returning over and over again in to samsara until such time we see things as they really are and wake up.

As evening draws in a bicycle rickshaw propels us through the chaos toward Kathmandu's Durbar Square, the product of a sophisticated culture and a place of great beauty that Rob photographed extensively in the 1970's. It is, as expected, both stunningly lovely and tragically sad. Broken buildings ripped apart by earthquake or neglect still surviving in an utterly different century yet remaining completely captivating, a living culture not a Disneyworld theme park, although much of it has a strangely surreal quality. Temples, stupas, Shiva linghams and yonis, strange collections of stone penises and vaginas as sacred objects, utterly incongruous with a modest shy people, are at every turn. The Shiva linghams are anointed with flowers and coloured powders, representative of Shiva and his cosmic dance of destruction and creation. The linghams sit in their stone yonis or vulvas, representing the polarities of male and female, Shiva and Shakti, parusha and prakriti, consciousness and energy. Many of the temples and sacred buildings of Nepal, particularly in the Durbar squares of Kathmandu, Bhaktapur and Patan, are carved with erotic images on the buildings and roof trusses, showing people and animals in an astounding range of sexual activities reflecting Tantric Shakti ideas, practices and energies.

Professor Mukunda Raj Aryal, retired lecturer from the Department of Culture at Tribhuvan University, is a leading authority on Tantra in Nepal points to the erotic roof truss carvings in Kathmandu's Durbar Square: "So there are two ways of looking at tantric images. You can look at them with the 'innocent' eyes of a lay person, or with the inner eyes of the practising tantrika. "We have some good examples here," he said, peering up at the roof-struts. "You see the couple on the right in the sexual act, and beside them, an attendant? She is holding out a bowl to catch their bodily fluids. This is the nectar of life, the most powerful of all earthly substances. It is drunk by participants in the highest tantric rituals." A couple of passing tourists stopped in their tracks. "Here", continued the professor, "we have an interesting arrangement. The man is being lifted horizontally off the floor by two women, one of whom he has penetrated, the other he is stimulating orally." The tourists, jaws dropping, are rooted to the spot."[108] As well they might.

Our rickshaw driver seems tired and worn trying to navigate his way through the clogged broken lanes and deal with the strange ways of foreigners on whom he depends for a precarious livelihood, and who are at least partially responsible for the whirlwind of change tearing traditional Kathmandu in to another, this time chaotic, form. I sit down overwhelmed and dazzled on the base platform of a broken temple. An elderly woman, dignified, serene with the most beautiful smile, gesticulates to move. I do so only to realize I am in the path of yet another motorbike from which she saves me. She is selling small bags made of a beautiful brocade fabric, probably created in some appalling sweatshop where people work long hours to keep their families fed. She has most likely been there all day selling her bags for a tiny cut of the proceeds, and yet still shows great grace in the midst of her own hard life lived out in dirt, noise, pollution, grinding poverty, and endless hours of thankless labour just to survive. If I could possess just one drop of her dignity and acceptance I would have indeed learned much, but what she shows on a daily basis in the midst of her very tough life is utterly beyond me. We returned a number of times to her patch of Durbar Square and she is always there greeting us with joy, and every time we buy yet more of her bags coloured blue, green, violet, gold, coral, turquoise, like brilliant jewels. She does not pressure, but just smiles and radiates kindness towards visitors from an utterly alien world. In a country with no pensions, no state welfare, no aged care homes, family is all, and for those without family their lives are deeply precarious, as we see later in Bhaktapur as ancient thin beggars shuffle through its Durbar Square.

The following morning the festival of Dashain, the Nepali version of Durga Puja, is in full swing. Durga, a female manifestation of Shiva, akin to Kali slayer of demons and drinker of blood, is widely worshipped in Nepal. Animal sacrifices will be happening in temples all over Nepal as part of Dashain rituals. People in their brilliant new clothes are celebrating and worshipping with intense sincerity in roadside shrines at every turn. Many of the Hindu shrines are dedicated to Ganesha, the elephant headed son of Shiva and his wife Pavarti, and the bringer of prosperity in the commercial districts. Women clad in jewel coloured kurtas wait patiently to present their marigold garlands or offerings in the shrine, light a candle and then ring the darshan bell. Perhaps Ganesha will bring good sales to farangs (foreigners), their accents a babel of Dutch, German, French, Spanish and English. The farangs look oddly mesmerized by their arrival in such an utterly different world, Alices disappearing down bottomless rabbit holes, and being one of them, it is easy to understand exactly how they feel. Small Buddhist stupas and Hindu shrines are hidden in surprising unexpected courtyards everywhere in the old parts of the city. Passing through a tiny door is a levitation into another millennium where plastic bottles litter superb worn pink brick paving, a serene Buddha statue smiles his knowing smile of compassion and recognition, or a worn Shiva lingham covered with vermillion powder and flowers honours Shiva, Lord of Yoga and God of destruction and creation.

Sculpted in bronze, or inserted in to the footpaths, are vajras, a Sanskrit word meaning diamond or thunderbolt. The vajra, used in Hinduism by the God Indra, has made its way in to Vajrayana Buddhism becoming an important ritual implement with many complex layers of meaning. In Tantric Buddhism, the vajra is a symbol for the nature of reality, consisting of a spherical central section, with two symmetrical sets of five prongs. The central sphere represents the underlying unity of all things. Emerging from the sphere are two eight petaled lotus flowers representing samsara and nirvana. In Nepal it is not possible to forget a frame of reference all but invisible in Western societies: the dynamic presence of spiritual power pervading every aspect of life, the world and death. Bede Griffiths described the spirituality of India as being unconscious, permeating every aspect of life [109] and Nepal is no different. Carl Jung referred to this as the numinous, a quality mostly absent in my own society and what I came to Nepal to find. The spiritual aridity of my own clean materially driven world becomes strikingly clear. The irony is not lost that whilst I yearn for the numinous world of Nepal many Nepalese long for the material blessings taken for granted by me as a privileged Westerner.

One taxi driver implores us to organize a visa for Australia, dreaming of a new and better life for his wife and family far away in Sydney in what he perceives as a land of hope and plenty. When it is gently suggested he might not be as happy there as at home, that there will be losses as well as gains, he clearly does not believe it. We write the requested letter and help him navigate the visa application website, knowing all the time he has no chance, his English so poor, his poverty so great, his skills so limited, his life ruled by the heavy debts he has undertaken to buy his taxi. He describes how tired he is of struggling to support his family on a tiny precarious income, battling his way through the unspeakable chaos and traffic of Kathmandu every day, hostage to the vagaries of tourism, earthquakes, and changes of government. Paradox on paradox, we are all caught in utterly different manifestations of samsara, struggling with the universal reality of suffering, dukkha as Buddhism calls it, despite its very different appearances in our very differing lives.

Recognition deepens of the advantages given by birth with a white skin that continues to be a mark of desirability and privilege, and fate casting me this lifetime in to a prosperous Western society. Everywhere in Nepal, just as in India, skin whitening creams such as "Fair and Beautiful" are sold with the fantasy of a better more blessed life enabled by what is seen as a precious patina of paleness. Meanwhile white skinned people spend the equivalent of Nepalese family incomes on tanning products and spray tans, or oiling their white skin to brown on tropical beaches. But that brownness is optional, chosen and temporary, not a destiny, requiring no bleaching creams to remedy and the underlying whiteness utterly taken for granted by those who possess it. On occasions in India I was shocked to be asked to pose with total strangers in photographs at scenic attractions for no other reason than possessing white skin and blonde hair. Indian online marriage sites still advertise spouse availability with skin colour as well as caste as important criteria, a "pale wheatish complexion" being an attribute of great desirability and marriageability.

Caste based discrimination may be fading but it is still a dark reality in Nepal and India, flowing from the religion so omnipresent around us. In India caste itself is strongly demarcated around skin colour, the higher dominant caste possessing paler skin as a historical and genetic legacy of the Aryan conquest of India from the north in the fifth millennium BC. The pale skinned Aryans subjugated the darker skinned preceding peoples and cemented that with social and religious structures such as caste. Their dominance is justified by religious texts such as the **Laws of Manu**. Caste is perceived as a manifestation of karma: good karma equalling high caste and bad karma equalling low caste. It is shocking that in the early 21st century something so arbitrary as skin colour still counts, but it would be ingenuous to imagine that it doesn't continue to demarcate lines of inequality and privilege because unfortunately it clearly still does. The weight of history and its racism is not so easily overthrown, no matter how hard one looks the other way and wishes the world to be different from the way that it sadly often is.

Our hotel is small and friendly and the rooms cheap and pleasant with an ok bathroom. Drugged with exhaustion sleep is fitful, and around midnight heavy, awful, dance music begins thumping through the window, and people screaming at each other four floors below. Very puzzling given that the laneway of the hotel contains an Ayurvedic Health Retreat and an upmarket hotel. The commotion carries on until near dawn and then vanishes as suddenly as it arrived. The next day confirms that underneath the daytime Ayurvedic Health Retreat is a seedy looking over eighteens night time dance club full of heavily made up Nepalese girls and young men. We briefly peek inside as the concrete floors are being hosed of drink, vomit and other human detritus the morning after the night before. Drugs are of course everywhere and freely available. Not as in the Freak St hashish shops before the hippy round up of the late seventies, but offered constantly and randomly in the street. I guess that whatever anyone wants is available, dangerously available, as the police and the dealers are said to have a profitable working arrangement. Sell to a farang, (foreigner), then tip off the local police who arrest the farang who offers a desperate bribe that is then split between the dealer and the police. The drugs that are confiscated are returned to whence they came only to be peddled again. We did later, under very different much safer circumstances, have a little hashish, a kind of toast to Rob, but Thamel is not the place.

The next day is clear and warm and we make our way to Boudhinath Stupa on the north-eastern side of Kathmandu. The first stupa at Boudhinath was built in the 7th century CE, but the enormous existing stupa was probably constructed in the 14th century. It has been for many centuries a sacred place of pilgrimage for Tibetan Buddhists, even more so since the Chinese occupation of Tibet in the 1950's. Many monasteries have developed in its surrounds and Tibetan Buddhist monks of all the major sects circumnavigate the stupa in a clockwise direction, spinning the mantra Om Mani Padme Hum on prayer wheels around its base. Om Mani Padme Hum, "Hail to the jewel in the lotus" is the great Tibetan Buddhist mantra of Avaloketishvara, Boddhisattva of compassion. It's meaning is explained by the Dalai Lama: "OM ... symbolizes the practitioner's impure body, speech, and mind; it also symbolizes the pure exalted body, speech, and mind of a Buddha.... The path is indicated by the next four syllables. MANI, meaning jewel, symbolizes the ... altruistic intention to become enlightened, compassionate and loving.... The two syllables, PADME, meaning lotus, symbolize wisdom.... Purity must be achieved by an indivisible unity of method and wisdom, symbolized by the final syllable HUM, which indicates indivisibility.... Thus the six syllables, om mani padme hum, mean that in dependence on the practice of a path which is an indivisible union of method and wisdom, you can transform your impure body, speech, and mind into the pure exalted body, speech, and mind of a Buddha..."[110]Tantric interpretations of the mantra involve sexual opposites with the jewel as masculine and the lotus as feminine symbols.

The use of sacred sound in the form of mantras, is a tradition common to Hinduism and Mahayana Buddhism. Mantras are a set of sounds that are believed to bring about spiritual effects and energise intentions for particular results. Well known examples are Om Mani Padme Hum in Vajrayana Buddhism, or the Gyatri mantra in Hinduism. The sacred language of Sanskrit is claimed to possess vibrational frequencies that assist in realizing whatever outcome the intention of the mantra is directed at. Mantras are an interesting example of how energy, expressed as sound, resonates with matter that at the quantum level is also energy. Sound having an effect on matter, as mantras are believed to do, does not seem impossible given that both sound and matter are energy, and mantras are believed by both Hindus and Buddhists to unlock spiritual power through the energy they express. If Brahman is the field of consciousness from which energy, matter, space and time have their source, as Hinduism claims, then could it be that the sound energy of mantras combined with the intention they express, perhaps in some way impacts on the field of consciousness and shapes reality? Maybe that is what all prayer and petitions to God, or gods, are about? Do mantras and or prayers work? Personally I have no experience that they are effective but untold millions throughout time and across cultures claim and believe they are.

The words of the Gyatri mantra are thousands of years old and a constant presence in India:

"Om bhur bhuvah svaha
Tat savitur varenyam
Bhargo devasya dhimahi
Dhiyo yo nah pracodayat"
"Oh God thou art the giver of life,
Remover of pain and sorrow,
Bestower of happiness,
O Creator of the Universe,
May we receive thy supreme sin-destroying light,
May thou guide our intellect in the right direction."

Recordings of Om Mani Padme Hum, blare from shops that surround the stupa, often wafting through the air. Spirituality has become big business in Nepal and large religious monuments like Boudhinath attract many spiritually thirsty tourists yearning for some inkling of transcendence and the sacred in a materialistic and troubled world.

Wandering through Kathmandu, signs appear advertising "Spiritual Adventures" and "Sacred Tours" for those seeking experiences that might reveal the presence of a spiritual realm. The tours often include visits to shamans to participate in rituals involving unseen dimensions and forces. I hesitate to do such a tour and don't feel ready to deal with something that might greatly shake my view of the world, as Benny Shanon, Professor of cognitive psychology and philosophy at the University of Tel Aviv was shaken by his experiences of ayahuasca with the indigenous shamans of the Amazon. In a radio interview in 2003 he describes how his scientific rationalist views and assumptions about the nature of the world were challenged by his many ayahuasca journeys in to an alternative reality that was meaningful, educative and once he embraced what ayahuasca was showing him, liberating. The interviewer, Natasha Mitchell, read an extract from Shanon's book **Antipodes Of The Mind – Charting The Phenomenology of The Ayahuasca Experience**, where he comments that ayahuasca "bring us to the boundaries not only to science, but also the entire Western world view and its philosophies."[111]

Buddhist stupas are built to contain holy relics and texts and Boudhinath is claimed to contain a fingerbone of Siddhartha Gautama, the historical Buddha. The stupa is constructed in the form of a giant mandala reflecting sacred geometry. This is common in Buddhist holy places, sometimes on a massive scale such as the extraordinary relic of vanished south Asian Buddhism, Borobodur, on the island of Java in Indonesia. At Boudhinath the base plinth represents earth, above is the dome representing water, and on top of its huge round white belly lies a square tower, or harmika, representing fire. On top of this is a thirteen step pyramid spire, symbolizing the journey through samsara to enlightenment that Buddhism asserts we are all travelling, whatever the many detours we might take and innumerable rebirths we will experience. Numerous prayer flags flutter their mantras out to the skies, urging us on the path to recognize our own Buddhahood, and around the base of the stupa are one hundred and eight Buddha Amitabha images and prayer wheels set in to niches. The all seeing all knowing eyes of the Buddha gaze enigmatically from near the top of the stupa, observing with compassion the foibles, follies and dreams of us navigating our lives in samsara so far below. Surrounding Boudhinath Stupa are streets and narrow alleys lined with restaurants, thangka and singing bowl shops, Tibetan Buddhist monasteries, and street vendors. It is a beautiful clear day and the round enormity of the white dome set against the intense blue of the sky is a strange vision of sacred space amidst the busy surrounding streets.

A tent is set up in front of a Buddhist monastery entrance, and some kind of event is happening as women in traditional Tibetan aprons and skirts prepare drinks. Suddenly a man invites us to join them and explains this is part of the funeral rituals for his grandmother. He offers us traditional Tibetan salted butter tea and much to my surprise it is delicious. In the wilds of Tibet where it is made with pungent yak butter perhaps it might taste less pleasing, but what we sample at Boudhinath is salty and refreshing. He is extremely knowledgeable about Buddhism, and had read many books written by Western Buddhists such as Jack Kornfield. He now lives in Washington, DC, travelling to Nepal for family visits and rites of passage such as the funeral, so has an eye both within and outside of his culture.

Next door a gigantic prayer wheel outside the monastery is set in motion by a small child as a Tibetan Buddhist monk sits beside it deeply absorbed in his cell phone, his ears plugged by earphones, oblivious to the gentle chaos around him. More huge prayer wheels are through a narrow door and vibrant paintings adorn every centimetre of wall space, including a massive wheel of life Bhavachakra painting. It features the core Three Poisons, then concentric rings portraying karma and the six realms of samsara. Yama, the Lord of Death, frames the image consuming everything and everyone in his gaping mouth, as the wheel of samsara relentlessly turns from birth, to death, to birth, over and over again until liberation is found. The lurid colours and wild eyes of Yama jump out from the wall despite the deep shadows of the room. I notice an ancient woman sitting quietly in the corner staring at me with mild curiosity, her white hair pulled on to the top of her head and most of her front teeth long gone. We exchange a brief smile, like ships briefly passing each other as we travel our separate ways across the "sea of samsara."

Monks circle the stupa, their lips moving, the mantras spinning from the ancient prayer wheels at its base as they pass. One man is moving along the ground in prostration, rising to his feet then dropping down to lie completely flat on the ground, doing this over and over again with great fervour and sincerity as he makes his agonizingly slow circuit of the base of the stupa. Prostration is seen as a means of gaining merit and working off bad karma. It is part of Tibetan Buddhist practice and followers will undertake extremely arduous pilgrimages to sacred sites involving long distances incorporating prostration. It is interesting to see many young people also doing the rounds of the stupa, their culture and faith having some resilience in the face of overwhelming cultural impact delivered by technology, cell phones, the internet, TV, Western tourism, Christian missionary activity, and so on. That said, how long that resilience will hold, and what new and ever manifesting forms lie ahead in history's endless dance of change, but it will certainly involve destruction as well as possibilities of creation. How to preserve and celebrate the best aspects of religion so as to foster spiritual growth, peace, tolerance and harmony, without darker aspects such as caste divisions, sexism, homophobia, prejudice, blind superstition, repression, and intolerance, coming along for the ride, is the challenge.

We spend hours at Boudhinath, it is a place where the divisions between the holy and the world are porous and thin, proclaiming yes, this is samsara, but there is a remedy. We can all start the path towards enlightenment no matter how many lifetimes that might take or how much ignorance we will show, or how many mistakes we might make on the way. The all-seeing eyes of the Buddhas, the compassionate ones there to assist us on our journey, are always watching from the top of the stupa. The beautiful dedication and aspiration prayer of Chagdud Tulku Rinpoche (1930-2002), from the Nyingma school of Tibetan Buddhism, comes to mind.

"Throughout my many lives and until this moment
Whatever virtue I have accomplished,
including the merit generated by this
practice and all that I will ever attain,
this I offer for the welfare of sentient beings.

May sickness, war, famine, and suffering
be decreased for every being,
while their wisdom and compassion
increase in this and every future life.

May I clearly perceive all experiences
to be as insubstantial as the dream fabric of the night
and instantly awaken to perceive
the pure wisdom display
in the arising of every phenomenon.

May I quickly attain enlightenment
in order to work ceaselessly
for the liberation of all sentient beings."

My feet are aching badly so we stop for a brief lunch break in a pizza restaurant near the stupa. A group of dogs are fighting, people carefully giving them a wide berth, no-one wanting to get tangled up with fighting dogs in a country where rabies is common. Eventually someone appears with a large bucket of water and hurls it over the snarling animals that, getting the message, slope off towards a laneway between buildings. We eat in silence, watching the passing stream of life, a diverse parade of humanity each person treading their way through samsara with their hopes, fears, sorrows and joys, all facing suffering, aging and death, most of them believing they will return to do it all again, and again, and again. I remember Rob describing this place and now I am here but he is not, time catching us in different moments of present flowing in to past, as this moment too will instantly become irrevocably gone, impermanence being the nature of samsara. It is claimed time is part of maya's illusion as we revolve around on the wheel of samsara endlessly reborn in to a material world that is also an illusion. It feels so odd that it was Rob who described this place to me from his time here forty-five years ago, and now I am in Kathmandu accompanied by his body reduced to fine ashes sitting in the hotel room a few kilometres away. I feel utterly overwhelmed, it is an intensely bittersweet moment. Distractedly I nibble a slice of pizza margherita, unable to stop gazing at the stupa building before us, its enigmatic eyes looking over the scene with an expression I cannot quite read but I hope is compassion.

We reluctantly leave Boudhinath and make our way through the jumble of greater Kathmandu to Kopan Monastery in the hills above. I had heard much of this Gelugpa Tibetan Buddhist monastery, a friend of my son's having spent time here assisting after the earthquake. At a lecture on unconditional love given by Geshe Tenzin Zopa in my home city, I express to him the hope to visit Kopan when in Kathmandu. He kindly gives his brother Nyodrup Tsering as a contact who will show us around. Geshe Tenzin Zopa turns out to be something of a film star, his search for the child reincarnation of his dead spiritual master in a remote Nepalese village on the border of Tibet, being the subject of a fascinating documentary **The**

Unacknowledged. That afternoon at Kopan reveals the depth of learning of the monks and a little of the world of Tibetan Buddhism. The bookshop is extraordinary with a huge range of texts in many languages covering everything from Jungian psychology, to Buddhist writers from many traditions across a wide array of subjects. The library, with its treasure trove of ancient texts in Sanskrit and Tibetan script in loose leaf sheaf form, is an inspiration knowing that here at Kopan this knowledge will be preserved and revered on in to the twenty-first century. We tour the monastery with Nyodrup Tsering who is endlessly patient with our questions and exudes great dignity and serenity. He points out a large throne in the main prayer hall set aside for the Dalai Lama, who cannot visit while Nepal is ruled by a predominantly Maoist government with close ties to China. Quotes from Shantideva are inscribed on the walls, alongside one from the Dalai Lama. "We are visitors on this planet, we are here for ninety or one hundred years at the very most. During that period, we must try to do something good, something useful with our lives. If you contribute to other people's happiness, you will find the true goal, the true meaning of life."

Tibetan Buddhism is complex and easy to respond to with ambivalence. On the one hand something very profound is clearly present, but on the other hand there is a whiff of superstition when reading the instructions with the prayer flags for sale in the monastery shop. They exhort that great care must be taken to select propitious astrological days to hang them, or bad fortune will result. Apparently the monastery gives information on its website as to the right and the wrong days to put up prayer flags. As we tour around Kopan the College of Tantric Studies is on our left, an innocuous looking building to house such deep mysteries as represented by Tantra. There is much difficult to understand about Tibetan Buddhism, which exhibits such a strong sense of the sacred and yet has alarming and threatening dimensions, with wrathful deities, damaru drums made of two joined human skullcaps, human bone ritual implements such as the human thighbone trumpets (kangling), and the use of prophecies delivered by Oracles in trance possession. Tibetan Buddhist communities and teaching centres have sprung up in large numbers throughout Europe, North America and Australia, often with little awareness of its history or shadow aspects. The pre-Chinese invasion history of

Tibetan Buddhism was filled with conflict, even violence, between the various sects and power struggles within Tibet. Tibet's society was feudalistic and backward, dominated by the rule of Lamas, religious power struggles and powerful, wealthy monastic institutions. Belief in spiritual forces and magic dominated every aspect of life giving lamas and religion absolute power. It was truly the "demon haunted world" referred to by Carl Sagan.

The Gelugpa school monks such as at Kopan are committed to celibacy, and yet many Tantric practices revolve around the union of opposites symbolized by deities in postures of sexual union, yab yum, with their consorts. This seems like a slippery slope to sexual exploitation of women by lamas, of which there have been many accusations. The potential for exploitation seems inevitable given that combination of religion, power, ritual and sex in a religion controlled and dominated by men. The sexual abuse scandals engulfing Christian organizations, particularly the Catholic Church, reflect that same combination of sex, religion and male power. Many contributors to a Facebook page dedicated to those escaping Kadampa Buddhism, a breakaway group of the Gelugpa school spreading fast throughout the West, describe their experiences as akin to being in a cult. One commented that Tibetan Buddhism is like the Catholic Church of Christianity, both being holders of deep mysteries but internally racked with power and doctrinal struggles, and wielding vast and sometimes destructive psychological force in the lives of their followers. The image of Buddhism as being always a religion of peace, love, wisdom, and compassion, becomes fractured the more the stranger corners of Tibetan Buddhism are probed, and there are some very strange corners indeed.

Initiations in to the lower levels of the **Kalachakra Tantra** have been given by the Dalai Lama all over the world in large public ceremonies. The highest Kalachakra Tantra initiations are however extremely secret and restricted involving Tantric sexual practices and forbidden substances such as sexual body fluids. Shockingly the **Kalachakra Tantra** text refers to sexual union with young girls as part of its rituals. Warnings have been given to initiates that breaking the rule of absolute secrecy brings death and hell which is in itself shocking that threats of damnation are dealt out by Tibetan Buddhism that describes itself as a religion of compassion. Tantra itself is such a cocktail of the repulsive and the profound, a path to liberation and yet not without danger, employed by some in the service of black magic and yet claimed to provide a way to compassion and enlightenment and overcoming the bonds of samsara by rejecting nothing as a path to liberation. The perception of the Dalai Lama as a jovial and tolerant messenger of world peace and harmony becomes much more complicated when it is realized he is also a powerful Tantric practitioner and master. The most secret Tantric rituals involve practices the opposite of what is permitted to ordinary monks such as sex, and the consumption of alcohol and meat in arcane Tantric rituals. The extent of the Dalai Lama's participation and involvement in the highest most secret Kalachakra initiation rituals is unknown although he underwent his first Kalachakra initiation in 1953 before fleeing Tibet. The text of the **Kalachakra Tantra** contains much that is the opposite of peaceful, with references to war, violence and religious conflict with the Semitic religions, in particular Islam. Tibetan Buddhism clearly has many more layers than the face it presents in the West where it attracts Hollywood stars and large followings.

Tantric rituals involving corpses, taboo substances such as semen, excrement, human blood, vaginal fluids, alcohol, as well as sex, are all components of the Vajrayana Buddhist tradition. It is sometimes claimed, particularly to squeamish Westerners, that this is symbolic but the texts themselves make clear that it involves actual practice. Extreme silence and secrecy coded by secret language references, shrouds the more extreme and controversial Tantric practices that are impossible for an outsider to penetrate. This is the hidden inner world of Tibetan Buddhism that most of its followers in the West, where it has been much sanitized, are utterly oblivious to. Hidden Tantric knowledge is passed to the initiate by their guru only when the student is regarded as ready because powerful forces are unleashed within and without the psyche. Tantric Vajrayana Buddhist practitioners use little cakes made of flour and blood, and refer to human skullcaps full of blood, human body parts, and sexual elements in their rituals.

The Dalai Lama is a voice of reason and inspiration across the planet but still consults the Oracle of Nechung who delivers his messages in a state of trance possession by a spirit. Trance possession raises interesting questions about the nature of consciousness as the possessing spirit occupies the bodily vehicle of the Oracle temporarily displacing them. It assumes that the consciousness of the spirit taking over the Oracle's body is not located in or dependent on physical matter of the brain but rather involves possession of his or her body by a non-physical entity. The Dalai Lama also uses other methods of divination such as Mo, involving the casting of dice to answer questions, the answers being from Manjushri, the Bodhisattva of wisdom. Various divination interpretation manuals based primarily on the **Kalachakra Tantra** are also used. The existence of demons and magic, wrathful deities and superstition, are intrinsic to Tibetan Buddhism, and propitiating demonic forces and exorcising demons remain part of its practice. According to Tibetan legend the great challenge faced by Indian Guru Padmasambhava, when he reclaimed Tibet for Buddhism in the eighth century, was overcoming and controlling the power of demons and forcing them to submit to Buddhism.

The conflict in the Gelugpa school of Tibetan Buddhism, around the status of Dorje Shugden and Kadampa Buddhism, reveals power struggles and competing claims to doctrinal purity that seems to dog all religions in some form or other. Accusations have been made that Kadampa Buddhism and the Dorje Shugden cults are funded by China keen to exploit cracks in the unity of Tibetan Buddhism, and undermine the authority of the Dalai Lama. Investigation of the Dorje Shugden issue reveals much about the shadow side of Tibetan Buddhism, and deep doctrinal and political rifts. Dorje Shugden has been described by the current Dalai Lama as being aligned with dark forces, whereas to others he is a powerful protector deity that to ignore will unleash destructive consequences. Tibetan Buddhism is starting to appear much murkier and more complex than I could have previously imagined and my responses are extremely ambivalent.

The sacred pills, or dutsis, containing substances such as excrement, blood, flesh from corpses and semen, sacred cords blessed by monks, mantras that are believed to transmit protection or spiritual power, resemble the medieval practices of the Christian Church with its relics of saints, talismans, rosary beads, indulgences, and holy water. Much of the ritual practice of Tibetan Buddhism is formulaic of mantras and rituals, claiming they will create merit, guarantee a better rebirth, or avoid a bad future rebirth. I attended a talk at the local Mahayana Buddhist centre in Australia. The speaker was Lama Zopa Rinpoche, a frail elderly man who had survived a stroke. Whilst checking out the website the information given was reminiscent of the superstitious cultish beliefs and practices of the Catholic Church in the Middle Ages, with its emphasis on prayer formulas, mantra recitations and holy talismans. Someone remarked this was spooky Buddhism not California Buddhism, the latter being a highly sanitized, idealized, romanticized version. Like all religions Tibetan Buddhism has its shadow that has been overlooked by many Westerners embracing it as a path of escape from the spiritual emptiness and lack of inner life characteristic of their societies. Stephen Batchelor points out that "In the West we are fond of portraying Buddhism as a tolerant, rational, non-dogmatic and open-minded tradition. But how much is this the result of liberal Western(ized) intellectuals seeking to construct an image of Buddhism that simply confirms their own prejudices and desires?"[112] There is clearly much more to Tibetan Buddhism than is commonly understood and some of it is shocking.

Brendan Neill, in his July 2010 article at **reason.com** "The Truth About Tibetan Buddhism", describes this: "Watching Jennifer Aniston's character Rachel read a collection of the Dalai Lama's teachings in Central Perk on **Friends** a few years ago, you might also think that Tibetan Buddhism is something you can ingest while sipping on a skinny-milk, no-cream, hazelnut latte." He goes on: "Lamaling Temple, like others I visited, is painted in the most obscene colors. No inch of wall or centimetre of roof beam has been left untouched by the possibly colorblind decorators of Tibetan Buddhism's sites of worship. Everywhere you look there's a lashing of red or green or bright blue paint, a weirdly fitting backdrop to the frequently violent imagery of this religion: the statues of sword-wielding demons, the fiery paintings, the images of androgynous Buddhas, some with breasts, others with balls. "Peace" and "calm" are the last words that come to mind when you're inside one of these senses-assaulting places…Yet it is striking how much the backward elements of Tibetan Buddhism are forgiven or glossed over by its hippyish, celebrity, and middle-class followers over here. So if you're a Catholic in Hollywood it is immediately assumed you're a grumpy old git with demented views, but if you're a "Tibetan" Buddhist you are looked upon as a super-cool, enlightened creature of good manners and taste" Westerners are accused of treating "a very old, complex religion as a kind of buffet of ideas that they can pick morsels from, jettisoning the stranger, more demanding stuff—like the dancing demons and the prostration workout—but picking up the shiny things, like the sacred necklaces and bracelets and the BS about reincarnation."[113]

The comment he makes as to the "BS (bullshit?) about reincarnation" is an interesting one. Tibetan Buddhism abounds with claims that people are rebirths of someone else, with great spiritual leaders being reborn as Tulkus. The Dalai Lama is regarded as a rebirth of the Buddha of Compassion, Avalokiteshvara, or Chenrezig in Tibetan. Westerners have also been recognized as Tulkus such as Jalue Dorje, a young boy from Minnesota, was recognized by the Dalai Lama as the eighth incarnation of the Takshem Lama, a Tibetan Buddhist spiritual leader from 16th century Tibet. Osa Hita Torres, born in 1985 in Spain to Spanish parents, was recognized as a rebirth of Thubten Yeshe a teacher of his parents. So where does this leave the idea of rebirth? Is it all bullshit as Brendan O'Neill puts it? The elaborate claims and counterclaims regarding Tulkus are as unconvincing as the Hindu view that people reincarnate in to a high or low position in the hereditary caste system because of karma. There are power and doctrinal struggles hovering in the background of the many disputes over which Tulku is an incarnation of who, and China has meddled in the power politics of recognizing Tulkus which is an odd activity for the Chinese Communist Party. It is puzzling as to how the Tibetan Buddhist belief in Tulkus, who are recognized by tests of their knowledge from their previous life about objects that are familiar to them, can be reconciled with Buddhism's assertion of annatta, or no ongoing identity or soul.

However the idea of rebirth, uncluttered by formulas of religion, is much more convincing than one life followed by everlasting heaven or hell, dispensed by a judgemental God. The idea that one brief life, perhaps ending as a small child, determines an eternity of punishment or reward with no opportunity for ongoing learning or growth, is incomprehensible. Being alive once is astonishing enough so perhaps it is not more astonishing to return many times in to samsara to evolve through a multitude of experiences and incarnations, with that process unfolding over many lifetimes driven by our own actions, our need to grow in compassion and love, and to realize God, Buddhahood, moksha, or nirvana, or whatever the particular religion describes as our spiritual destination. That is an idea that makes some sense, particularly Sri Aurobindo's interpretation he referred to as "evolutionary rebirth". There are many differences between and within religious traditions as to karma and rebirth, but the understanding of rebirth as expressed in Vedanta Hinduism in texts such as the **Bhagavad Gita** and **Upanishads** is personally more convincing than the Buddhist version with its doctrine of anatta. The **Brihadaranyaka Upanishad** describes rebirth of the atman or soul, as follows.

"As a caterpillar, having come to the end of
one blade of grass, draws itself together and
reaches or the next, so the Self, having
come to the end of one life and dispelled all
ignorance, gathers in his faculties and reaches
out from the old body to a new".
4.6 "We live in accordance with our deep, driving
desire. It is this desire at the time of our death that
determines what our next life is to be. We will
come back to earth to work out the satisfaction
of that desire."

A European looking woman of late middle age walks quietly by the Kopan Monastery café. Nyodrup Tsering tells me she arrived from Sweden over twenty years earlier and is still here, her nun's robes and shaved head a testament to her commitment to a spiritual life. I wish I could speak to her but the moment passes and she is gone. Leaving Kopan we visit the large nunnery section of the monastery giving women the chance to practice the Dharma. It is the subject of debate as to whether the historical Buddha regarded it as possible for a woman to achieve liberation from samsara in a female body. There are passages in texts that suggest the possibility "Women, Ananda, having gone forth are able to realize the fruit of stream-attainment or the fruit of once-returning or the fruit of non-returning or arhantship" and others that decree a woman cannot achieve enlightenment. The orders of nuns established in early Buddhism placed many restrictions and rules for women not applicable to monks. Siddhartha Gautama apparently resisted women entering the Sangha but eventually relented, commenting, "in whatever religion women are ordained, that religion will not last long. As families that have more women than men are easily destroyed by robbers, as a plentiful rice-field once infested by rice worms will not long remain, as a sugarcane field invaded by red rust will not long remain, even so the True Dharma will not last long".

Undoubtedly misogyny has been a factor in the history of Buddhism, as has fear and suspicion of sexual passion associated with women who are regarded as the gateway of entry in to samsara and responsible for keeping its wheel turning. Anxiety about women is a common pattern across most religions, including the Semitic religions of Judaism, Christianity and Islam, so it is hardly surprising to find it in Buddhism. Many Buddhist orders and traditions will not ordain women to the same level as men, and regard it as impossible for a woman to realize enlightenment, insisting that to do so she will need to reincarnate as a man first. Prayers undertaken by nuns contain the plea for a better future birth as a man so as to make the achievement of enlightenment possible. However change is happening in part from pressure from Buddhists in Western countries. The Dalai Lama has remarked that he might return in a female body for his next incarnation if that would be useful. Women's role in Buddhist thinking and practice will continue to change, and Buddhism continues to thrive despite the Buddha's warnings that admitting women to the Buddhist community would bring about its early demise. Many accomplished women teachers and practitioners of Buddhism now contribute significantly to Buddhism and so perhaps old gender prejudices may eventually be overcome.

Tibetan Buddhism offers an extremely rich tradition that could absorb many lifetimes and still not be fully comprehended, but also darker much more complex aspects lurk in its shadows. Kopan monastery offers courses and residential programs, perhaps I might return at some point in my life to go deeper in to understanding something profound, but also mysterious and puzzling to those on the outside looking in. We descend from Kopan, high on its hill, back in to the chaotic traffic of Kathmandu. That evening is our first initiation into the wonders of the traditional Nepalese momo, delicious little concoctions somewhat like a

Chinese dumpling filled with chicken, or vegetables, or the ubiquitous buff or buffalo. These are steamed in enormous steel boilers and dumped on a tin plate with a soupy sauce drowning the little momos. Absolutely delicious and hopefully a relatively safe form of streetfood given they are so hot and straight out of the pan. It pays to be careful of perishable foods like meat in Nepal, the regular power outages making refrigeration a very hit and miss affair. The restaurant is filled with local people eating for around sixty rupees a serve of ten momos, and we hope for the best that a dose of Kathmandu belly will not come our way. The choices of food are a cultural hot potch of Irish pub, pizza shop, bakery, Mexican eateries, jumbled up with Tibetan and Nepalese restaurants. Some of them proclaim themselves as serving Nepalese, Tibetan, Chinese, Italian, Pizza, European, icecream and hamburgers, all on the same menu, which is a big ambition for small kitchens. KFC and Pizza Hut have beaten their global path to Kathmandu but thankfully not as yet McDonalds, but no doubt it eventually will and buffalo burgers, rather than the sacred cow, will be on the menu with French fries. We walk the perilous broken road back to the hotel in a contemplative mood, chocolate gelati icecream cones in hand, the polarities of sublime beauty and great ugliness, life and death, samsara and enlightenment, numinous spirituality and deep superstition, giving much to ponder.

The next day we visit Swayambhunath, another sacred stupa complex on another hill just outside Kathmandu. The hill is green and wooded and the site approached by long flights of stone steps from its base, mani stones dotting the way inscribed with the mantra Om Mani Padme Hum. Prayer flags flutter above, and the usual crowds of hawkers sell the same resin Buddhas and fake Tibetan style jewellery that is everywhere around Kathmandu. They are persistent but good humoured. What are their stories that drive them to spend hot thankless days trying to sell items to tourists that mostly don't want them, and who are irritated by the endless pleas to buy? I purchase a few little pendants and am then constantly hounded for the rest of the trip up the hill, some of the sellers possessing an edge of desperation no doubt driven by the relentless all pervading poverty that is the lot of many Nepalese. At the top of the hill a panoramic view over greater Kathmandu is framed by ranges of hills nestling below the Himalayas. What an extraordinary place Swayambhunath is. Sacred to Hindus, Newari Buddhists and Tibetan Buddhists, it is one of the holiest sites in Nepal. It was badly damaged by the 2015 earthquakes but much has been restored and much remains. The white towers around the main stupa that contained secret Tantric texts collapsed in the earthquake, but the main stupa complex is largely intact.

The first building we come to looks so innocuous, so small and insignificant it would be easy to miss. It is Shantipur, where the Tantric Vajrayana priest Shantikar Acharya, a holy man from the eighth century, is believed to reside deep inside this mysterious structure. Although the outer part is relatively modern the temple itself dates back over 1500 years and apparently encompasses three levels down in to the earth. Seven sets of increasingly forbidden and secret locked doors block its innermost mysteries through chambers guarded by secret spells and giant snakes where Shantikar Acharaya is believed to be in deep meditative bliss at its core. Shantikar Acharya is said to have great power and control the weather of Kathmandu over the centuries, and when Kathmandu is crippled by drought he is visited by the King who is presented with a rain bringing mandala. This apparently last occurred in the seventeenth century. The legend has it that the mandala was drawn on the skin of a great and troublesome naga or serpent from the time the Kathmandu valley was a great lake. My Western scepticism rejects all this utterly, but it is an odd slightly forbidding place. Peeking inside the open first door two workers are carrying bricks in baskets suspended on their backs from ropes around their foreheads as they repair an earthquake damaged wall. Apparently the work on the inner areas of the temple involved many Tantric protection spells and invocations to absolute secrecy as to what was seen in there. A set of heavily locked brass doors with the enigmatic eyes painted on them is as far as we can penetrate the mysteries of Shantipur Temple. It is a remarkable example of the completely different way of looking at the world that is typical of Nepal and its spirituality, that perceives the material and the spiritual as two faces of the same coin and the unseen as being as real as the seen.

The young proprietor of the Tibetan singing bowl shop nearby is impressive, with his deep and sincere knowledge of the capacity of singing bowls to use sound to heal and uplift as they effect the vibrational qualities of the body and its energies. Over sixty percent of our physical selves is comprised of water and when the bowls are filled with water and set ringing amazing sounds are produced and patterns of vibration appear on their surface. According to both Hindu and Buddhist tradition, sound vibrational energy possesses power, also expressed through mantras and sounds such as OM, a sacred Sanskrit syllable that is the cosmic primal sound. The singing bowls are considered to create sound waves that heal and raise spiritual energies and different bowls are tuned to the vibrational frequencies of the chakras, or energy centres of the body. He demonstrates the various bowls and their qualities, and they are remarkable. The subject of Shantipur Temple is raised and without the slightest hesitation he confirms the story of Shantikar Acharya he clearly believes to be absolutely true. He tells the tale of the founding of Swayambhunath. According to legend Kathmandu was once a great lake Nagarasa, but Manjusri, a Buddhist Bodhisattva, sliced open with his sword the hill around the lake at Chobar, the water drained and the Kathmandu valley was formed. A beautiful lotus at the centre of the lake transformed in to Swayambhunath, swayambhu meaning self created. The hill has probably been sacred since the first century but the main stupa has been damaged, restored and rebuilt over the centuries, care always being taken to allow passage of air in to the building to allow its spiritual power to flow out to the world around.

It is unknown what exactly is inside the enormous white round dome, as its contents are inaccessible. Some say bones of the Buddha but certainly sacred relics are preserved inside. On top of the dome is the gilded square top, or harmika with a pair of eyes on each of its four cardinal points sides, gazing over the extraordinary scenes of the world of samsara below, with its desires, illusions and suffering. A symbol like a question mark, and the Nepali number one, is between each pair of eyes and represents the unity of all things. A gleaming golden coloured spire with thirteen rings in a spiral representing the thirteen obstacles to enlightenment, rises from the harmika, up to the gilded parasol at the top that represents nirvana and the end of samsara. Pilgrims on their clockwise circuits around the stupa spin the ancient prayer wheels set in to its base. They shine softly in the bright sun as their mantra Om Mani Padme Hum is released to the cosmos and prayer flags flutter against the brilliant blue sky. The inevitable plastic bottles and bags, dogs, hot and tired tourists, laughing children, earnest pilgrims, incense lighting worshippers, souvenir sellers, mischievous monkeys, women in gorgeous coloured kurtas, and jeans clad teenagers, are all embraced by the compassionate eyes of the celestial Buddha painted on the harmika's golden surface. This is a place like no other and we are mesmerized.

The five Dhyani Buddhas shrines at the base of the stupa face the cardinal directions, plus one representing the centre. They are Vairochana, Akshobhya, Ratnasambhava, Amitabha and Amogasiddhi. They are not historical Buddhas like Buddha Sakyamuni, but personify universal divine attributes and aspects of consciousness. Each represents one of the five wisdoms: discriminating wisdom, mirror like wisdom, reality wisdom, wisdom of equanimity, all accomplishing wisdom, and overcoming the five poisons of ignorance and delusion, anger and hatred, desire and pride, malignity, envy and jealousy, that trap us in samsara. The Dhyani Buddhas all have their own colour, symbol and sacred syllable (bija) that can be used as part of a mantra along with the sacred OM syllable. The five Dhyani Buddhas rule the five realms of ether, water, earth, fire and air, and are associated with the five senses of taste, touch, sight, sound and smell. They are often represented in the sacred diagram, the mandala. The **Bardo Thodol**, or **Tibetan Book of The Dead**, makes many references to the presence of the Dhyani Buddhas at the various levels of awareness experienced by the dead person in the Bardo, the period between death and taking rebirth in another round of existence in samsara.

We continue exploration of the maze of buildings, shrines, and monasteries that comprise Swayambhunath, watching women worship at the temple of Hariti the goddess of smallpox who is also protector of children. The goddess Hariti has Hindu origins but has been incorporated in to Buddhism, as is typical of Nepalese syncretism. The story goes Hariti was converted from a child-eating ogress into a goddess by the Lord Buddha, and protects young children and the Swayambhunath site. Now smallpox has been eliminated from Nepal she is invoked to protect against other diseases and attracts a steady stream of supplicants to her beautiful golden temple. The idea that an unseen goddess has the power to prevent infectious disease is at complete odds with Western medicine that regards those as caused by bacteria and viruses not spiritual forces. However parents seeking treatment by Western medicine in modern hospitals also pray for the health and healing of their sick child, so perhaps there is not as much separating those as first appears.

Adjacent to the main stupa is a gigantic gilded vajra or diamond thunderbolt, the ritual implement central to Vajrayana Buddhism and used by both Newari and Tibetan Buddhists. Out of its centre are two sets of five prongs representing at one end the five poisons and samsara, and at the other the five wisdoms and nirvana. We came across these vajra in all sorts of unexpected places such as set in to pavements and in Bhaktapur we unexpectedly discover a huge courtyard with several enormous vajras. We wander around Swayambhunath for hours, a place where divinity and superstition are inextricably and powerfully present. This place presents a way of understanding utterly different from that of my own society. The spirituality of Nepal views the world as an illusion, in to which we are repeatedly cast, lifetime after lifetime in to the cycle of samsara according to our karma. Spiritual forces, holy beings and demonic forces are believed to underlie and govern all aspects of material reality and there is no separation between the sacred and the mundane, the material world being founded on and intricately entangled with invisible supernatural forces. Everything from earthquakes, to the weather, to sickness, or the circumstances of our lives, is seen as the result of the interplay of those spiritual forces with the world and our existence in it

The landscape of Nepal is home to an endless array of gods, demons, spirits and semi-gods, who imbue nature with living spiritual forces that humans are subject to. For example there is a mountain deity for most peaks in Tibet and Nepal, who are invoked as protectors from disease and disasters and who bring rain and good crops. The mountains are also regarded as home to Tsen who are malevolent vampire spirits. In the rivers and lakes lurk the Lu spirits who can, if offended, bring leprosy and disease to humans and animals. The list is endless and these are the forces that Padmasambhava grappled with, but their subjugation to Buddhism was only partial and therefore continuous propitiation and Buddhist ritual practice is regarded as necessary to maintain control over those spirits and demons.

Lama Angarika Govinda wrote extensively about Tibetan Buddhism and was initiated in to several of its sects. He undertook extensive travels across Tibet and the Himalayas described in **The Way of The White Cloud** first published in 1966. He comments about an incident of demonic possession he witnessed during a religious ceremony: "This incident showed us again that invisible forces, whether we call them Gods or spirits, divine or demoniacal powers, that influence the human mind, are not merely abstractions…but realities with which every religion and psychology has to cope. I could very well understand now the type of forces which Padmasambhava had to fight, and that such forces could only be conquered or subdued by calling up counterforces in the human mind, which is exactly the function of ritualistic magic…We are dealing here with spiritual realities, not with theories, with actual forces, and not with religious doctrines."[114]What would it be like to live with the idea that every aspect of reality rests on unseen spiritual dimensions that need to be consulted, propitiated, worshipped, feared, obeyed, controlled or followed, as is also the case in Bali and India? If, as quantum physics suggests, consciousness is the field from which all matter, energy, space and time emerge, then perhaps dismissing all reference to invisible spiritual dimensions as superstitious mumbo jumbo ignores real mysteries and forces? That is a difficult idea for someone like me, sitting on the agnostic fence, to contemplate.

The acceptance of supernatural beings and energies so strongly held in Nepal, is inherent in some form in all religion, be it Jesus casting out demons, Dhyani Buddhas, the Holy Spirit, God, angels, demons, the devil, Shiva, Vishnu, Brahma, Kali, Jinn, saints, or any other deity, spiritual being, or force. Fear of demonic forces haunted earlier periods of Christianity as witnessed by the Inquisition, exorcisms, and witch trials. Astonishingly, belief in demonic possession still persists in twenty-first century Western cultures. The Catholic Church has an official Rite of Exorcism to be performed by specialist trained priests, and various Pentecostal or Evangelical Protestant churches also practice exorcism. The Catholic Church is stepping up training of priests to perform exorcisms as all over the world, demand apparently exceeds supply for those services. It is interesting how an institution such as the Catholic Church, that administers modern hospitals using modern medical treatments and diagnosis premised on a scientific rationalist understanding of illness and the body, continues to sanction the rite of exorcism of demons. It seems a little like having a foot in each camp and how the two fit together is not at all clear.

Perhaps lurking deep below the surface of Western secular rationalist societies is an older deeper strain of belief in supernatural forces, that occasionally bubbles to the surface to make its presence obvious, as reflected in exorcisms and belief in miracles. Fear of demonic powers and the practice of black magic manifests across the world and is widespread in South America, Asia and Africa. In Mexico City the enormous Sonora witches' market does a huge trade in black magic supplies and Brujas, or magic practitioners peddle their trade in back rooms behind the stalls. I remember a friend telling me that satanic worship, rituals and followers are flourishing in my own small Australian city. He had worked for a while with an Evangelical church that provided spiritual cleansing for people seeking exit from Satanism. At the time I was astonished and dismissed his claims as outlandish superstition, but places such as Nepal, India, and Bali suggest that there is much more to the world than previously dreamed of and perhaps it is not possible to be absolutely certain that such realities do not exist.

It is easy to see why religions, whose purpose is in part to grapple with supernatural dimensions, are so vulnerable to superstition. Is all religion deeply irrational, a collective delusion or neurosis as Freud regarded it? Was Karl Marx right that religion is "the opium of the people"[115] and nothing more, or are the many forms of religion all pointing to something that is unseen but as real as the seen? Is this presence of invisible supernatural forces what Carl Jung was alluding to in his descriptions of the unconscious and the archetypes that emerge from the collective unconscious? Is access to these unseen spiritual dimensions what mysticism or psychedelic drugs facilitate, as was claimed by Aldous Huxley in the **The Doors of Perception**?

Ayahuasca, the powerful drink concocted by Amazonian Indians from mixing several plants, has the power to alter perception in a way that those who consume it describe as profoundly meaningful and educative, and it opens its user up to alternative realities and spiritual forces experienced by its users as being as real as everyday reality. To say Benny Shannon found his ayahuasca experiences confronting is a huge understatement. He describes how his left brain, linear thinking, rationalist, materialist world view was challenged as he was forced to confront disconcerting possibilities about the nature of reality, time, and consciousness that profoundly shocked him. Perhaps the spirituality of Nepal presents a somewhat similar challenge in that it is premised on entirely different assumptions about reality, and perceives unseen forces and spirits as having a living presence. I would have previously dismissed this as nonsense but Nepal has the uncanny ability to undermine easy certainties and invite questioning that perhaps there might be a whole lot more going on.

We make our way down the steps at the exit from Swayambhunath navigating through a troupe of squabbling, mischievous monkeys. They have apparently worked out the great attachment humans have to their cell phones and will snatch them to trade for food, so we stuff our phones deep in to pockets and they leave us alone as of no interest. We purchase an ice cream at a pizza joint near the hotel and wander the back streets of Thamel, many shops still open in the forlorn hope a tourist might make a purchase, the street vendors of flutes, bags and bracelets, begging for a sale with a hard edge of desperation in their voices. Street sellers who have given up for the day are stretched out where they will spend the night on the pavement, facing the walls of buildings or tucked in to small spaces like bundles of abandoned rags. Rickshaw drivers are curled in their vehicles where they will sleep before the haggling with customers, the fight to survive, all starts again early the next morning.

We pass many small shrines to elephant headed Ganesha, who is believed to turn around luck and bring financial prosperity. They reflect the belief that economic circumstances are determined by unseen spiritual energies rather than global economic dynamics, or government policies, or lack of tourists, or rice crop failure, or social inequalities, or lack of educational opportunities, or whatever other factors economists and sociologists might attribute them to. The solution to economic problems is therefore sought in the spiritual realm: for example repeating the Vakratunda Ganesha mantra is said to bring riches and good fortune.

"Vakratunda Maha-Kaaya Surya-Kotti Samaprabha
Nirvighnam Kuru Me Deva Sarva-Kaaryeshu Sarvadaa"

"Gracious god with bended trunk, the extensive body whose quality resembles a light of numerous suns, please makes my whole work snag free, until the end of time." That the key to managing all aspects of life, including financial prosperity, lies in spiritual practices, mantras, invisible forces, gods or goddesses, is an utterly foreign concept. We eat momos again for dinner, sitting in an Irish bar with loud Pink Floyd and Steppenwolf music, musing on the challenges places like Swayambhunath make to everything always previously taken for granted. Back at the hotel the male proprietor with a name that sounds oddly like Suzanne, enquires how our day has been. It is difficult to know how to answer that so we smile, nod great, and call it a day.

We have arranged a trip to Nagarkot in the hills outside of Kathmandu, where the views of the Himalayas are supposedly spectacular. This is where Rob's ashes will be scattered in a place of natural beauty. We travel through the ugly urban sprawl of Kathmandu, half-finished buildings like rough concrete skeletons erupting in to what was recently farmland, fragments of old villages and lovely old Newari brick buildings built with great care and a keen aesthetic sense, just visible caked in dust beneath the detritus of advertising, electricity cables, concrete, cars and motorbikes. I wonder what the people of Kathmandu make of what is happening to their city with apparently no planning, no provision for public parks and no regulation to shape the growth of the city in a way that is good for its inhabitants. Money for public works like footpaths is clearly in very short supply, as most of the time there are none, and the roads are broken. Some of this was caused by the 2015 earthquakes, but much of it is the result of poverty, rapid urbanization, a long civil war, corruption, political upheaval, and modernization happening in a random, fragmented, unplanned, way. The route gradually climbs out of the Kathmandu valley and the countryside is beautiful despite the haphazard half-finished buildings all along the road. The hotel is a superb old Newari brick building that was once a fort, carefully and lovingly preserved, with terraced gardens looking straight out to where the Himalayas should be. Except they are completely invisible behind a blanket of clouds, and have apparently been so for months which is disappointing.

The forested hill tumbles down in to a deep valley and the sound of distant horns rings out in the soft late afternoon light. I prepare myself for what now must be done, but have no rituals of faith to ease this final letting go of part of Rob. We find a spot among flower beds that are perched overlooking where the Himalayas lie hidden in cloud, on the edge of a steep drop through the forest to the valley. It is beautiful, the soft green forest blurring in to blue grey misty folds below, a small brook tumbling along somewhere at the bottom, it's waters eventually merging with the Bagmati and finally the holy Ganges. This is where I will scatter Rob's ashes. It is shocking to see a loved person reduced to a fine greyish powder, the reality of mortality is overwhelming and I'm deeply shaken by the experience. Rob's body and bones have been reduced to the same ashes lying beneath the cremation pyres of Bali or India. Different cultures, different people, different kinds of fires, but the same end point of destruction of the fragile perishable body with which we experience our life in samsara, the fine grey powder that was Rob dispersing in to the soil and the air. Our lives really are "dust to dust, ashes to ashes" as the Bible says.

Marck's presence is a great comfort as he reads out a short prayer and I empty the ashes on to the soil and flowers. Strangely once it is done there is a comforting sense that Rob's suffering is finished, and wherever he might be he is now free and at peace. Whether his death brings annihilation for eternity, rebirth or something else, is unknowable, but although his body is gone and he is no longer in this material world I know in some inexplicable way all is well for him. Maybe this is just wishful thinking, or maybe Nepal is beginning to get to me, but the sense of release and peace is real and has lasted. Looking up from a lighted candle placed on the ground it is astonishing to see the dense cloud cover is parting and there is a vision of unearthly beauty. It is a huge Himalayan peak soaring into the late afternoon sky, its whiteness a dazzling contrast to the grey clouds almost as if it is floating ethereal in some other world. I am overwhelmed with gratitude for having known and loved Rob, and for the beauty that has just revealed itself. A strong sense of the continuity of love, and love as the truly important dimension of our time in samsara felt like a gift somehow connected with him.

My mother had a powerful experience the night my father died after being hooked up to a life support machine in a coma for over a month. We were staying near the hospital and early one morning, when asked when we would visit him her reply was astonishing as she was not given to metaphysical experiences. She explained that during the night he had died, and on his way wherever he was going he had come to her as a presence of overwhelming love, peace and joy, so as her whole being was suffused by those as she lay in bed. She glanced at the clock and noted the time as around three am. Sure enough, shortly after recounting this the hospital called to tell her he had passed away during the night. She later enquired as to the time of his death and it matched the time in the night when he had bid her farewell. Her certainty of this was unshakeable conviction which was surprising given neither parent was in any way religious. As a child my father had told me of his near drowning in the Yangtze River in China, long before my birth. This had struck him deeply, not because of almost dying but because of the intense 'life review' experience that accompanied it. His whole life passed by him in an instant, but in such a way that his actions and choices were being shown to him as both an assessment and a lesson. Similar stories of near death experiences have been recounted by innumerable people across all cultures. It has been thought provoking to discover how many personal friends have shared experiences of this kind that plenty of anecdotal evidence suggests are common. What these experiences mean is the subject of much debate. Are they just figments of a brain flooded by chemicals? Or could it be that they point to spiritual dimensions usually invisible in ordinary life but occasionally peeping through when we are close to death or losing a loved one to death?

We walk through the forest, the path and leaves dappled with the fading light and the moon now just visible above the shimmering mountain hovering in the clouds. A small part of Rob will remain here with those incredible mountains watching over him and one day it would be good to return to this extraordinary place. Back at the hotel we are greeted by one of the staff, a small elderly man with the most radiant face and smile who thanks us for coming as our arrival had brought back the mountains. He tells us no one has seen them for months because of heavy cloud. Presumably he is joking, but given that in Nepal everything about the material world, including the weather, is thought of as an illusion produced by unseen spiritual forces, then perhaps he is not entirely joking. It is a bizarre idea that the actions of people can cause cloud cover to part. He tells us that he hopes to see the mountains at dawn the next morning and that the hotel will wake the guests if they appear. Given the mountains have not shown themselves for so long as it has been the rainy season, we are not optimistic, but thank him and go in search of a cup of tea.

Sure enough dawn the next morning brings a chorus of excitement and people everywhere are emerging from their rooms, many in pyjamas, because the mighty Himalayas have appeared in their full and astonishing glory. There across the valley is the most incredible sight. The length of the Himalayan ranges is strung along the horizon glimmering in the pinkish early morning light, their white peaks sharp and clear piercing the sky, a vision of purity and power. We are all overwhelmed. People are running up stairs to get to the roof and we follow them to gaze in awe at what nature has presented. On other buildings we see in the distance the rooftops are filling with people just watching. There is a building site behind our hotel and people are clambering precariously up rickety bamboo scaffolding to get to the top for a better view. Those mountains have brought the world of humans and their busyness to a complete stop, everyone utterly transfixed by the exquisite sight we have been privileged to witness. The Himalayas are a place of holy power to both Hindus and Buddhists, a point where the sacred enters in to samsara and its world of struggle and suffering. We gaze for about an hour and then it is gone, the clouds return and the mountains vanish. Bleary eyed, bare-footed, pyjama clad, guests return in silent contemplation to their rooms as if woken stunned from a dream.

The owner of the hotel is apparently an architect in Kathmandu. We discover on two enormous shelves a remarkable collection of books in English, covering topics from the world of the Himalayas, Jungian psychology, and esoteric spiritual works from many religious traditions. He is clearly an admirer of Krishnamurti and we borrow a couple. Another is **Gita: The Science of Living** by

Jayantilal S Jariwalla exploring the **Bhagavad Gita**. The opening lines of chapter one jump out: here is someone pointing to spirituality as possible without taking on the baggage of religion. "Religion has two aspects: one which is universal in time and space, and the other which is of local and historical value only. In its universal aspect it is the 'Religion of the Spirit' which is neither ancient or modern, but eternal and universal and more or less common to all religions. This is the true Religion which is imprisoned in no forms or rites, and attached to no bodies or institutions. The local aspect consists of the accretions to this pure Religion which give it its local colour or setting, varying from place to place and from time to time.....The pure religion of the Spirit – which is not man-made – is, in the course of interpretation, overlaid with ritual and dogma (with much myth and superstition intermixed) and the overgrowth is often so large as to make it extremely difficult to sift the grain from the chaff. Those who have no patience and understanding to steer clear of this plethora of excrescence lose sight of the Truth and either grow fanatical mistaking these trappings for 'Religion', or go to the other extreme of denouncing all religions as a lie or humbug, and all priests as' quacks or money-mongers..."[116] Bede Griffiths refers to the same idea: "Above all we have to go beyond words and images and concepts. No imaginative vision or conceptual framework is adequate to the great reality."[117] Being sceptical of religion, but not entirely dismissing of the possibility that some universal truth hides deep beneath its cultural accretions, the 'Religion of the Spirit' described by Jariwalla gives hope that spirituality might be separable from dogma and culture.

It is sad to be leaving Nagarkot, it has been inspiring in so many ways. Part of Rob's material form remains here, becoming one with the earth, the plants that grow in it and the surrounding air, the atoms eternal but the forms they manifest in ever changing. The little flowerbed where his ashes are scattered has a spectacular view of the mighty Himalayas, their peaks a symbol of yearning for transcendence, soaring pure, white and holy above the abode of samsara, the earth. Where the consciousness that was Rob has gone is unknown, but in some mysterious and comforting way he is both nowhere, and everywhere, and at peace.

On the way back to Kathmandu the driver drops us at a discreet little viewing point behind a roadside tea-house with a name something like Kantipur

Dreams. Picking the way down a broken path, through lush growth and litter of plastic wrappings, to chairs perched on the edge of a steep hillside, we enjoy a little hashish, 'Nepali chocolate' as it is called. We do not speak, still in the present moment as an island of tranquillity in the constant stream of thought. Rob has gone, his body now fine ash blown to the winds or mingling with the soil, but the Rob that occupied that body, that man I loved so much, where is he? Where are all the infinite others who have occupied fragile mortal bodies of flesh and blood, that appeared and disappeared in the endless flow of time? For a brief moment the beauty and the pain of that slides in, sharp as a knife. A powerful sense of the spinning of samsara's wheel turning around and around, pulling us all in to the material world through birth, life, suffering, and aging, then spinning us out through death, and perhaps, just perhaps, spinning us back in to life again, becomes intensely real in that moment. We sit contemplating the astounding beauty of the Kathmandu valley spreading before us, golden light shimmering over ripening rice fields, the time of harvest having begun.

"Death and Light are everywhere, always, and
they begin end, strive, attend, into and upon
the Dream of the Nameless that is the world,
burning words within Samsara, perhaps
to create a thing of beauty."
Roger Delazny

CHAPTER SIX

MORE NEPAL

Nepal really gets under our skin. People are unfailingly courteous and gracious while carrying so many burdens of poverty, lack of education and services, and difficult lives. The greeting of namaste, "the God in me greets the God in you" is delivered with sincere grace everywhere. But there is so much that foreigners are completely oblivious to, such as caste divisions that strongly impact on every aspect of life but are inaccessible to outsiders. The multitude of ethnic and cultural divisions and their social and economic ramifications are often invisible. The huge gender inequalities that dictate women's lives, their lack of education, their diminished opportunities, their subjection to customs like chaupadi, their lack of economic independence, are all easy to miss in the hustle and bustle of everyday life. The extent of suffering resulting from protracted civil war, rapid social change, terrible earthquakes that destroyed whole communities, grinding poverty, government corruption and inefficiency, lack of infrastructure and poor education, can go unnoticed until someone casually remarks 'in Nepal people choose between lunch and dinner'.

Most Nepalese view their life as one of an endless series of rebirths in samsara dependent on karma, and their understanding of their lives is in those terms. That combined with belief that spiritual forces, gods, goddesses, or demons, shape all aspects of life including illness, weather and natural disasters, puts religion and the management of spiritual forces at the centre of life. It is hard to figure out which is preferable: a world completely barren of any spiritual dimension or a world where everything is controlled by invisible supernatural forces that must be kept under control, propitiated, feared or worshipped.

The strong social, cultural and religious traditions of Nepal give great meaning and purpose but are now also a source of stress and conflict when those traditions clash with twenty first century values, or if challenged by individuals: for example by seeking to marry outside of a caste or religious group. Suicide rates in Nepal have rapidly risen and it now has the seventh highest rate in the world. Extreme poverty, sexism, rapid social change, breakdown of traditional culture, years of political instability and natural disasters such as floods and earthquakes, have also played their part. Human experience in samsara is increasingly uncharted territory as societies the world over undergo rapid transformation. Culture has always determined how life on the wheel of samsara is lived, and cultures are always changing and presenting new challenges wherever people might be, and whatever their religion or beliefs. As most Nepalese view the world through the lenses of karma, rebirth and samsara is it possible for them to reconcile the massive changes going on around them with those traditional beliefs?

A scenic flight has been planned to the Himalayas, the roof of the world and home to the some of the most sacred spaces on earth. It will be like a dream to see those huge mountains close. The Himalayas have been for thousands of years the inspiration of sadhus, rishis, mystics and seers, and the gateway through which ideas and invasions have entered and spread in and out from the Indian subcontinent, be those Buddhism, the arrival into India of the Aryans or Mughuls, or Indian Buddhist holy men such as Padmasambhava. Mt Kailash in western Tibet and sacred to Hindus and Buddhists, lies deep in the Himalayas. Hindus call Kailash Mt Meru, and view it as the abode of Shiva the Lord of Yoga and the divine Tantric master. For a Hindu to journey on pilgrimage to Kailash is to gain release from samsara. It is equally sacred to Tibetan Buddhists who call it Kang Rinpoche and make pilgrimage around its base, often involving long distances of prostration. Holy rivers such as the Ganges, have their sources in the Himalayas and many Hindus believe that they must bathe in mother Ganga's sacred waters at least once in their lives. Bhutanese myth describes Guru Rinpoche riding in from the Himalayas to Bhutan on a flying tiger to overcome the demons and convert Bhutan to Buddhism. Great teachers have trekked across its mountain passes in to Nepal and Tibet carrying with them precious Sanskrit texts and the teachings of Buddhism. The very air is permeated with the sacred and the Himalayas draw holy men and women from across India and Nepal to meditate and contemplate.

It is a clear and perfect morning as we depart Kathmandu at five am and head north with Buddha Air. The mountains soon come in to view and as expected, are jaw dropping in their grandeur and beauty. We soar over various ranges in the direction of Everest, everyone on board awe-struck. We are even allowed in to the Captain's cabin to look from the front of the cockpit, a refreshing experience given the heavy security and restrictions that now surround air travel in this age of terrorism and fear. Tears feel close as those extraordinary peaks come in to view: they are an utter world apart, their intense whiteness and purity rearing towards the sky, symbolizing for millenia the quest to transcend samsara in to the realm of divinity. Finally Everest appears, massive in the milky pink-blue dawn, long shadows over its western sides, its eastern slopes glowing soft and pale, long glittering ridges cutting the sky slicing light from shadow. They stretch along the horizon, range after range of huge peaks cutting the sky shimmering white and dream like in to space, a vision of overwhelming loveliness utterly remote from the gritty world of human existence in samsara. Everest's power to attract climbers numbering in their thousands has spawned a plethora of climbing and trekking businesses, and suppliers of equipment, all of whom now play a big part in the economy of Nepal. Rich country privilege in a poor country manifests in the mountaineering industry as it does in everything else: the Nepalese Sherpas who carry all the equipment up the mountain, get little of the glory, are paid poorly, and sometimes die facilitating the dreams of the many foreigners paying a lot of money to climb. We return from the Himalayas to the dust, noise and chaos of the city as if from a dream to a nightmare, such utterly contrasting worlds playing out in our minds.

The day darkens and thunderclouds threaten ominously as we cross Kathmandu towards the Hindu temple complex of Pashiputinath, dedicated to a form of Shiva, Pashiputi Lord of Animals, and now a World Heritage site. Its origins lie deep in the past perhaps as far back as the fourth century BC, although many of the buildings have been rebuilt and altered with time. An extremely ancient Shiva lingham lies at the centre of its main pagoda style temple building. Animal sacrifices are performed in the Pashuputinath temple complex but we do not observe this, much of the inner temple being closed to non-Hindus. It lies on the banks of the Bagmati, a river sacred to both Hindus and Buddhists, eventually draining in to the Ganges, and Hindus from all over Nepal and India come to worship at Pashiputinath's approximately two hundred and fifty seven shrines and temples. Trash and plastic line the Bagmati's banks, clog its channels, mar its beauty, sully its purity, it has become a river of garbage and refuse. Yet it remains intensely sacred, a metaphor for the filth of the world redeemed by divinity, like the lotus growing in the mud of existence in samsara and blooming with exquisite purity is a central image of Hinduism and Buddhism. Many devout Hindus bathe in the sacred waters of the Bagmati as they do in the Ganges, and I shudder to think of people immersing themselves in water so filthy.

Pashiputinath is huge and we know there are areas forbidden to us as non-Hindus outside of traditional Hindu social structures, without caste and without place. In previous times devout Hindus would not have been willing to pollute themselves by associating with people of no caste, and even now some would not be willing to eat with or accept water from us. Although open discrimination based on caste has been illegal since 1962, caste itself is not prohibited, and caste distinctions and discrimination continue to inform every aspect of life in Nepal. The Dalits, or untouchable caste, still suffer severe disadvantage and discrimination, and caste murders still occur. This is the dark side of spirituality, that it spawns prejudices and divisions in the name of belief. Finding a way between the two unsatisfactory alternatives of spiritual aridity and the dark shadows inherent in every religion, feels as distant as ever. We walk along the banks of the Bagmati, observed by placid cows and yet more mangy, scabbed dogs who are also travelling around the wheel of samsara according to Buddhism and Hinduism. They have not yet received the rare and precious human birth that will make liberation from samsara possible, but with yet more eons of time perhaps they will: certainly Buddhists and Hindus believe so.

Suddenly we find ourselves in the compound of sadhus, or religious ascetics, where hopefully Aghori sadhus, practitioners of rites in cremation grounds who embrace death to discover spiritual light, will be found. Sadhus are an interesting phenomenon of Hindu life in which the final stage of life, sannyasa, is traditionally dedicated to the search for moksha, liberation from samsara and to realize union with Brahman the ultimate reality of the universe. Sadhus often reflect this phase of life, coming from every possible background to turn their back on the material world, devoting themselves to their spiritual search to break free from samsara by leading the life of a wandering ascetic. Most are yogis although not all yogis are sadhus, and women are also represented as sadhvis. In a previous phase of life a sadhu or sadhvi might have been a computer programmer, or a business owner, might speak excellent English and be highly educated. They are mostly regarded with reverence as spiritual seekers and removers of bad karma, although a few are feared as makers of curses. They are estimated to number in their millions in India and Nepal, living by begging and owning nothing except what a sadhu carries. They are mostly celibate, although there are Tantric sadhus who practice sex as a transcendent ritual. Many of them smoke ganga, or hashish, which they use as a spiritual tool and it is not uncommon to see them puffing on an enormous clay chillum pipe. There are numerous sects and types of sadhu wearing different coloured robes, or nothing at all, various hairstyles, or shaved heads, and displaying different markings on their foreheads according to whether they are followers of Shiva, Vishnu or Shakti. The source of their income now includes tourists for whom they are delighted to pose for a few rupees. It is sometimes remarked that they are beggars on to a more lucrative begging method but that is not accurate, as the vast majority of sadhus represent a tradition of spiritual quest almost unknown in the West. For someone to renounce all their material possessions, their work, their family, their usual life, to become a wandering holy man or woman searching for spiritual awakening, and for that to be endorsed as a worthy aim, is utterly foreign to Western culture. Every three years a mass gathering of sadhus from all over India and Nepal takes place at the Kumbh Mela, attracting as many as 30 million pilgrims to that sacred event in a single day. The next Kumbh Mela is in 2021 in Haridwar, India, and I make a mental note to try and visit one Kumbh Mela during my lifetime. Two Shaivite sadhus stand watching us, their yellowish robes remarkably clean given their lifestyle. We approach and they willingly pose for the obligatory photo before wandering off in the direction of the main temple we are not permitted to enter. We look out for the ash smeared Aghori sadhus, the most feared group who practice extreme rituals with corpses and often live in cremation grounds, but see none. Varanasi or the Kumbh Mela in India are the place to be certain of finding them.

The roof struts of the temples at Pashaputinath are carved with erotic images, like the roof trusses of buildings in the Durbar squares of the Kathmandu valley, creating a juxtaposition of sex and death as the opposites that keep the wheel of samsara turning. Sex is at the centre of Tantric ideas and practices, transcending and uniting the opposites of male and female, Shiva and Shakti, and unleashing spiritual power. The rites of death are being performed, large fires burning on the opposite shore of the Bagmati with several cremations in process on circular stone platforms above stone stepped ghats leading down to the river. It looks very much like a smaller version of Varanasi. A priest is reciting mantras and prayers as the dead body is offered to the flames and the soul released to take its next journey in to a new round of rebirth in samsara.

How different this all is to Rob's cremation, hidden away in a sterile modern funeral facility, its crematorium one of high tech efficiency where the body takes its last journey alone, monitored by a computer, the ashes finally finding their way in to neat plastic boxes to be scattered, or stored, or interred in a wall. The same reality of death for the same perishable vehicle of the spirit, but understood so very differently. The same flames burning the corpse to dust, one fuelled by gas, the other by wood, the same smoke carrying the atoms that comprised the person wafting out in to the enormity of space, although the smoke from the modern crematorium is filtered to be almost invisible from the chimney discreetly tucked out of sight at the back of the building. As we gaze the body is identifiable through the dancing tendrils of fire consuming what is left of a life. Rob passed this way, and each and every one of us will sooner or later follow him when we exit samsara.

The corpse clearly emerges in to view as the engulfing fire quietens. A man picks up a long pole and prods the coals, the body collapsing as he does so, the shape of a skull still just identifiable. That burning corpse, disintegrating in to black smoke, charred bones and a pale grey litter of ash, starkly demonstrates the undeniable truth of samsara that once we enter it by birth every one of us will inevitably leave it by death. The soft ashes piling up beneath the smouldering corpse exactly resemble those in the small plastic container of Rob's ashes that came from Australia in my suitcase, and were left to mingle with the soil at Nagarkot. Here however the rendering of the disintegrating body in to ash is starkly visible whereas at home it is hidden deep in a steel furnace, the process obscuring rather than revealing the annihilation of material form.

The gathering clouds become darkly ominous so we hurry along beside the river towards the main temple complexes, keen to avoid a drenching in one of Kathmandu's spectacular thunderstorms. We pass shrine after shrine, compound after compound, some areas littered in plastic bottles yet still deeply sacred. Finally the heavens open in a deluge that turns all the stone paved paths and steps to small rivers, a stream of worshippers, cows, dogs, sadhus shuffling past in the torrential rain and plastic bottles swirling down the stone steps. Fragments of Hindu hymns, Bhajans, muffled by the rain, waft from speakers near the river creating a strange other worldly atmosphere as the storm clouds billow in the gathering dark. A sadhu trailing behind sodden wandering cows looks oddly incongruous with his bright pink plastic umbrella and ancient looking spectacles, throwing us a quick smile as he passes by. I wonder if he has a cell phone tucked under his robes, as some do, and if he did what would a spiritual ascetic and renunciate of the world use it for? Surely not online shopping.

The filthy Bagmati river is rising fast and in its foam plastic bags and bottles are seething under the bridges and through the cremation ghats where the burning flames voraciously consume the dead despite the rain. On the western side of the Bagmati is the main complex of temples most of which we as non-Hindus cannot enter. Between the two sets of cremation ghats is the small 6th century Bachhareshwari Temple containing Tantric and erotic images and said to once be the site of human sacrifice as part of the Maha Shivaratri (Shiva's birthday) festival. The large Guhyeshwari Kali Temple, translating to 'temple of the goddess' vagina' from guhya, vagina and ishwari, goddess, is beside the Bagmati through the wooded area to the East of the main group of temples. It is a Shakti Peeth or Tantric power temple of Shakti or female energy, home of ancient Tantric practices only revealed in secrecy to the initiated and never to the likes of us. The whole complex at Pashuputinath has a most disconcerting sense that something is going on here beyond our understanding and we are not altogether unhappy to leave it and return to the worldly anarchy of Thamel and the safe little haven of the hotel.

Sleep is elusive and it is a vain hope that the nightclub across from the hotel might be having a night off, but once again the thumping and the yelling start in the early hours of the morning dragging thoughts back from the Himalayas and bodies burning to dust and ashes at Pashiputinath, to gritty day to day concerns of tiredness and struggle. The following morning news arrives that a dear friend has just died. She has been ill for a long time but her death comes as a shock. We had arranged to see a movie on my return home and a book of hers sits on the hall table waiting to be returned. The book had outlasted its owner as books so often do, the mystery, fragility and brevity of life underlined by a collection of pages of paper outliving those that write them or read them. As Macbeth says:

"Out out brief candle!
Life's but a walking shadow, a poor player,
That struts and frets his hour upon the stage.
A then is heard no more. It is a tale
Told by an idiot, full of sound and fury,
Signifying nothing".[118]

The first part, that we all die, is undeniable, but whether a life signifies nothing, or something, and what that might be, is uncertain. In Nepal, where death is regarded as endlessly repeated in the cycle of samsara, and karma profoundly important in shaping that unfolding journey, life and death are deeply meaningful. We are urged to 'wake up' while we possess a precious human incarnation and are able to do something towards our own liberation. Buddhism and Hinduism direct us to look inside ourselves to follow, through many lives, the steep journey to enlightenment. What was the story of the person reduced to smouldering ashes in the cremation fire at Pashuputinath? What had been their journey through samsara? Has that journey continued on after the destruction of their body by death and flame, and will they return to the wheel of samsara through eons of time? If karma shapes each rebirth does that mean people return in to samsara with those other beings with whom they have the strongest karmic connections? Practitioners of past life regression sessions consistently claim that is the case, and in Bali it is taken for granted that new born babies are returning family members. Where now are the people I have loved who have also passed through death? Have they returned to the stage of samsara to enact another play in another life? I realize I have been ignoring the questions that really matter for most of my life and Rob's death and Nepal are giving prompts to begin the steep trail to begin what we all are here to do: wake up.

Our remaining time in Kathmandu is filled with yet more temples and visits to ancient towns of the Kathmandu valley, Bhaktapur, Kirtipur, Patan, Khokana, Panauti. The Mallas from India conquered the Kathmandu valley in the twelfth century, ruling for the next six hundred years, and they brought with them a stunning cultural legacy reflected in what were three old Malla kingdoms of Kantipur (the old name for Kathmandu), Bhaktapur and Lalitpur also known as Patan. These in their time were great centres of architectural, cultural and artistic brilliance. The buildings possess exquisite details in door handles, carved window frames, or bronze lions standing proudly at the entrance to small courtyard shrines that might be Buddhist or Hindu or more likely both. Amongst this beauty is glaring twenty first century ugliness of plastic garbage, steel, concrete and glass, glaring advertising signs, broken pavements, tangles of black wiring strung up on sagging house corners and mind numbingly chaotic traffic.

Broken houses in small lanes are ripped by jagged earthquake scars and propped up precariously by massive timber posts, occupied by families who sit in their doorways as we walk by. Who knows what they make of us. Sometimes people smile and sometimes they stare but mostly they completely ignore us. Through tiny doorways daily life unfolds in dark interiors, a family seated on mats eating, a woman cooking, a child's hair being plaited. On one occasion a family is seated around an ipad absorbed in whatever Google delivers up to them. The elderly are in traditional clothes while the young in jeans are clutching their mobile phones and fast disappearing in to an utterly different world from their parents and grandparents. Motorbikes are everywhere stacked against bronze lions, in elaborate carved doorways and across footpaths cluttering any available space. The ancient carved doors on the Newari buildings are bolted shut with hideous gleaming chrome locks roughly attached to their fronts as the magnificent old brass door locks shaped as animals, or as complex wrought designs, no longer serve the purpose.

We pick our way down a narrow street in Bhaktapur admiring the lovely old buildings and small shops filled with huge brass water pots, dodging cars and endless streams of motorbikes, the footpaths either broken or non existent. We are discussing how these beautiful products would be very appealing to Westerners. In India I had longed to fill my suitcase with jewellery, saris, wildly embroidered fabrics, quilted jackets, small delicate traditional Indian style paintings some with Karma Sutra style erotic paintings, but Rob was not enthused by the idea and so it was not to be. I consider starting an online business trying to connect these beautiful products made with such skill and care to people all around the world. Many families and communities depend on the making and sale of these items, but they are haphazardly stacked in shops all competing with each other for the same customers who are small in number since the earthquakes and floods. The traditional skills that create them will wither and be lost unless markets are found to keep those skills alive. In a world flooded with mass produced factory made goods, mostly of no aesthetic value, the ancient knowledge and design traditions of the handmade items seems precious and worth preserving. It is unclear how best to go about this. Exploitation and appalling working conditions in awful sweatshops with people, including children, paid a pittance for their work is a brutal reality. Poverty haunts every aspect of life in Nepal and is a daily survival struggle for all but a few. So the search would be for products that are fair trade and made under decent working conditions paying decent wages and not using child labour. Many good people are involved with handicrafts production such as David from Wales with a big booming voice and big heart. His organization mountainpeople.org has set up schools and craft workshops for the poorest villagers of the Himalayas and recycles the rubbish of Kathmandu in to the most beautiful woven baskets and boxes, and jewellery from discarded tire inner tubes. He began his journey as a mountain climber, then expedition leader, finally leading him to work for the Himalayan communities that service those industries as guides and porters for poor pay in conditions of personal danger and sometimes loss of life. He is a real inspiration and the first of many people who show the best of what people can be.

Our days in Kathmandu are busy visiting more ancient towns manifesting the same contradictions and paradoxes we have seen over and over again. Beautiful children laugh and play around the Bhag Bhairab Hindu temple in Kirtipur where a buffalo has recently been sacrificed, its blood spattered on the walls and buffalo skulls hanging at rakish angles from the roof struts, Bhairab being one of the terrifying manifestations of Shiva. It is a struggle to overcome revulsion and reconcile this with my deep love and respect for Indian spirituality. The momo we will have for lunch will contain buffalo meat, no doubt slaughtered in appalling conditions of cruelty, and I cringe at my hypocrisy that violence and death of an animal in a religious sacrifice is so disturbing but am blind to the same reality that accompanies the eating of meat. Respect for vegans grows as they put in to practice their commitment to not devour the flesh of other sentient beings, nor perpetuate industries such as eggs and dairy where cruelty is endemic. Baby male calves and baby male chicks are brutally disposed of, useless to the mass production of food. Film circulating on the internet of male day old chicks, useless as egg producers, being swept alive into a machine akin to a wood chipper to be processed in to fertilizer and protein meal, certainly brings home the dark practices of the mass egg industry. Racks of hens live out their short miserable lives in small steel cages dropping eggs on to the wire floors to roll on a conveyer belt to end up in pretty cardboard boxes bearing pictures of happy hens to be sold in supermarkets and consumed by the wilfully ignorant like myself.

Close to the Bhag Bhairab temple are small shrines of Shiva linghams standing in their stone yonis, representing the cosmic forces of energy and consciousness, Shiva and Shakti, creation and destruction, male and female, penis and vagina. They are smeared in red kumkum paste, startlingly resembling blood, and in some small shrines it probably is blood as chicken feathers lie in the dirt and the red is wet and fresh looking. Up a small side lane a group of mother chickens is scratching amongst the plastic bags for grains of rice, followed by their baby chicken tribes. They look happy, free, doing what chickens love to do, their babies with them making a contented scene. Then suddenly what is happening becomes apparent and it is shocking. One of the chicks is hobbling weakly and its siblings are brutally pecking it, long strings of what appear to be intestines emerging from its side in to the beaks of the other chicks. Then, horrifyingly, the mother hen joins in and threads of her chick's guts hang from her sharp beak as she gobbles them down. A scene of bucolic bliss in a quiet fifteenth century laneway has become a vision of horror and violence, the merciless face of nature, the cruel face of Kali and the endless dance of Shiva through creation and destruction graphically revealed. **"The Goldfish Pond"** by Douglas Stewart captures that inexplicable twist of darkness and destruction that manifests at the core of creation.

"The devil in the shape of a water-scorpion swam
Across the pool at sunset. Oh, beetle and gnat
And fry of the golden fishes will meet their doom
In those lean jerking arms, that horny throat,
And yet with delight I watched, and with small concern,
The rosy mirror scratched by that secret thorn:
And down where the fantail trailed his flame like a comet
And suns and scaly moons swam round and round
I looked through the eye of God for one clear moment
At naked evil spiking the luminous pond
And thought with satisfaction—or dim remorse?—
That all was well with his strange universe." [119]

An article in **New Scientist** read years before springs to mind in that tiny Kirtipur laneway from another century. It presented evidence that the evolutionary history of Homo sapien reveals cannibalism demonstrated by the presence of protective genes against prions spread by the consumption of human flesh, and by marks on Neolithic skeletons. What strange God could have created nature "red in tooth and claw," and us? William Blake put it well: "tiger tiger burning bright in the forests of the night. What strange hand and eye framed thy immortal symmetry, did the same hand that made the lamb make thee?" Posters displayed outside churches of gorgeous butterflies flitting around statements like "His Creation" and sugary songs such as "All things bright and beautiful the Lord God made them all" are a propaganda whitewash of massive proportions. If the Lord God really made everything then so too the poisonous snake, the cancer cell, the HIV virus, the mate devouring spider and the Bilhazia parasite of Africa bringing death and misery to untold numbers. Its not on to pick and choose only the pretty and the nice so where does this darkness come from in the creation of an all powerful, all knowing and all loving God? Or are we obliged to concede the power of creation to some kind of demonic being who is responsible for the cancer cell and polio virus? That is a possibility too awful to consider but making any sense of suffering, or of Rob's death, feels as far away as ever.

Do Hindu deities such as Shiva and Kali offer insight in to what we just witnessed in their assertion that devouring and destruction are necessary twins of creation, both being embedded and entwined in the dance of life on the wheel of samsara? Every aspect of the world is woven with polarities of good and evil, light and dark, creation and destruction, male and female. That perception is particularly strongly manifested in Balinese Hinduism with its belief in the constant play of antagonistic opposites. Tantra seeks to embrace those polarities and transcend them as a path to enlightenment. Fierce gods such as Shiva and Bhairab, and their female forms Durga or Kali, and the wrathful deities of Mahayana Buddhism, perhaps reveal deep truths. Instead of projecting them on to an evil being such as Satan or the devil they are incorporated as an inherent and necessary dimension of samsara and an aspect of Brahman. Meanwhile the slaying of a baby chick unfolds amongst twenty first century litter engulfing a pretty 15th century lane with a shrine to Shiva tucked against its side-wall.

Perhaps the shrine to Shiva as both destroyer and creator might hold clues? He is pure consciousness, holding us in bondage in time but giving freedom in eternity. He manifests in many forms: as Shiva the Lord of destruction, Shiva the ascetic, Shiva the liberator, Shiva the Lord of Yoga, Shiva the bringer of creation out of destruction and new life from death. It is as Lord of the Dance, the Nataraja Shiva, that all those aspects come together as he dances an ecstatic dance of destruction on the prostrate form of avidya, or ignorance, at the centre of a cosmic ring of fire that symbolizes samsara, the cycle of birth, life and death. In one hand, is a damaru drum on which he beats the passage of time, in another hand a conch shell uttering the sacred syllable of Om, and a third hand holds the flame of vidya, or knowledge. One of Shiva's right hands is held up in Abhaya Mudra, showing fearlessness that comes from realization that although the bodily vehicle will decay and die, the eternal Self, the atman, will continue its endless journey until it reunites in bliss with its source Brahman, the cosmic Self. The mantra to Shiva, Om Namah Shivaya, "I bow to Shiva", beloved by followers of Shiva, passes through my mind.

We continue to walk through Kirtipur past ancient stone walled pools once used for ritual purification, but now pasted with festering green carpets of slime so thick that Coca Cola tins lie scattered on their surface. Stone Cobra heads emerge from the ooze, arching over the bubbling almost fluorescent green water. A small Shiva lingham is at the end of a narrow walkway bridge across the end of one pool. A group of young Nepali boys get off their motorbikes, cigarettes dangling from their lips as they nonchalantly stroll to the stone phallus. The only one wearing a helmet takes it off and thrusts it nonchalantly on to the lingham as he adjusts his Ray Ban lookalike sun-glasses. They laugh and swipe their mobile phones as a tiny old woman dressed in a shabby sarong, her back hunched, hobbles by bearing a heavy load of brightly wrapped boxes. She could be their great grandmother but they inhabit utterly different worlds. As we pass through the cobbled lanes Buddhist and Hindu shrines appear at every turn. Two golden coloured large standing Buddha statues suddenly appear next to a wall, there for no apparent particular reason but not at all surprising in this land where spirituality seeps through every aspect of life.

The next day we visit Dakshinkali Temple up in the hills some distance from Kathmandu, built by a Malla King in the 14th century to appease Kali with sacrifices in the wake of a cholera epidemic. This Kali Temple complex is set in a quiet wooded valley and animal sacrifices of chickens, sheep, goats and occasionally buffalo, are practiced on Tuesdays and Saturdays. We want to visit in the spirit of trying to see the religious life of Nepal as it is, rather than idealized, and to not judge without witnessing it personally, so we decide to go. The taxi driver is not encouraging of our visit but eventually agrees to take us and asks if his wife can come too. She is quiet, young and beautiful, dressed in a gorgeous bright kurta, and we pick her up from their broken down dwelling in a very poor area near the Bagmati River. He later implores me, as did another previous taxi driver, to help him in his quest to move to Australia which I make another feeble attempt to do knowing that he will find that almost impossible to achieve given his poor English, his heavy debt owing for his taxi, and lack of skills.

We journey past lush rice fields and beautiful pine clad hills along broken roads jammed with motorbikes and four wheel drives. There are many glimpses of happy sounding children playing on huge swings constructed of giant bamboo as we pass through village after village. The brightly coloured prayer wheel attached to the dashboard rotates continually as we lurch along pot holed winding roads, its mantras intended to protect from harm. Given the state of the roads the dashboard prayer wheel is not particularly comforting, but nonetheless our journey goes without mishap. The car park is full of worshippers and their families eating in a surrounding circle of restaurants, buying garlands of marigolds and other offerings at small shops. Live animals to offer in sacrifice to Kali as thanks, petition for good fortune, protection, or help to overcome obstacles, are also on sale, the goats bleating piteously, the chickens huddling in their wicker baskets looking miserable, unsurprising given what will shortly happen to them.

Heading down the path to the river the temple complex comes in to view with crowds of people milling around. Sadly masses of plastic bags and bottles litter the banks of the river as in so many other places in Nepal. In a poor country there is little funding for or provision of garbage collection, and plastic litter is a curse of the twentieth and twenty-first centuries. We cross the river and walk behind a large crowd gathered along a brass fence separating the priests and temple workers from the worshippers. Blood is running profusely along channels around and across a stoned paved area, flowing from gutters straight in to the river below to be carried downstream along with chicken feathers. To the rear of the channels running with blood is a statue of Kali covered by an ornately decorated metal canopy. The priest removes coverings from the black statue as drums begin to beat and bells clang and a strange atmosphere of religious fervour builds and continues for around half an hour. It is all most unnerving. Worshippers, their belief in whatever is happening in the temple apparent in their transfixed faces, stand in line to walk through the gate and make offerings to the black Kali idol. The Kali is black stone, her tongue painted red and lolling from her mouth, the garland of skulls painted around her neck, hideous in appearance.

Thankfully we have arrived just after the last animal has had its throat cut and all that is left is blood, but over in another building recently sacrificed animals are being dismembered for their owner to take home to eat. Various legs and body parts of freshly killed goats are piled up on a long table. I try to hold back a sense of horror: this is no more shocking than the reality offered by the butcher's shop in my home suburb, where animal body parts of legs, ribs, shoulders, kidneys, livers, or brains, are artistically presented on neat white plastic trays with decorations of lurid green plastic parsley, ready for us human animals to take home and devour. The familiarity of the local butcher's shop with a cheery butcher handing over parts of dead animals neatly wrapped in white paper to waiting customers, some with small children standing beside them, almost obscures from recognition what is really going on there.

The offerings being taken to the Kali shrine are flower garlands, plates of fruits and coconuts, and the rapt expression on the faces of the worshippers is startling in its intensity. Included amongst the worshippers I am surprised to see our taxi driver and his demure and lovely wife, utterly absorbed by the ceremony in which they are participating. It is odd how ordinary and every day people look in their jeans, tee shirts and gym shoes, whilst their faces are gripped by intense emotion as they take part in what appears to us as a bizarre ritual. Young children are part of the crowd as temple workers start hosing out the blood from the gutters in to channels running down to the river. It is shocking to see the cooing pigeons on the top of the roof of the Kali shrine dropping down on to the blood soaked stone to sip the water stained brilliant red by the fresh blood flowing along the gutters next to the sacrifice area. Empty chip packets appear on the red soaked stone courtyard across which mothers walk carrying their babies. I am utterly outside of my comfort and experience zone and am both revolted and fascinated.

Rituals of animal sacrifice have been part of many religious traditions including Judaism. The language of Christianity with its references to Jesus as the 'lamb of God' who sacrifices himself to save humanity, and the Mass, or Holy Communion, that asks participants to eat the body of Christ and drink his blood in the bread and the wine, also has connotations of blood and sacrifice. The Catholic priest celebrating the Sacrifice of the Mass at a sacrificial altar, repeats the instructions of Jesus at the Last Supper to eat the bread "TAKE THIS, ALL OF YOU, AND EAT OF IT, FOR THIS IS MY BODY, WHICH WILL BE GIVEN UP FOR YOU." and to drink the wine "TAKE THIS, ALL OF YOU, AND DRINK FROM IT, FOR THIS IS THE CHALICE OF MY BLOOD, THE BLOOD OF THE NEW AND ETERNAL COVENANT, WHICH WILL BE POURED OUT FOR YOU AND FOR MANY FOR THE FORGIVENESS OF SINS." What an extremely bizarre concept this would seem to a non-Christian observer, but because of the Christian heritage of the West that is usually not noticed. Apparently the Catholic Church was accused of cannibalism when presenting its teachings on the Eucharist to tribal communities. Ruth Tucker in **Jerusalem to Irian Jaya: A Biographical History of Christian Missions**[120] gives the following example: "To present the gospel to the natives, the Jesuits were willing to compromise in critical areas. For example they did not refer to eating the body or drinking the blood of Christ (an essential aspect of the Mass) because to the Huron it would have been associated with cannibalistic rituals."

As a meat eater I'm willing to eat the body parts of animals as long as there is no requirement to confront the brutal reality of the animal's death, and that death occurs out of sight in a slaughterhouse not in full view in a religious ritual. So why is what happens at Dakshinkali so repellent? The death of the animal is swift as its throat is expertly cut. It is skilfully butchered and used for food just like the meat on little plastic wrapped trays in the supermarket. The animal's death is highly visible and public rather than hidden and sanitized like that of the animal on the supermarket tray, but that does not seem like a fair basis to reject one and accept the other. The animals at the temple must feel terror as they are carried in the queue to be sacrificed, but equally so must the animals herded on to trucks and pushed through the waiting lines to be killed in an abattoir, no matter how well run it is. A friend, who lives in a small Australian town on whose outskirts is a large commercial abattoir, described how the sound of animals screaming are often be heard from a distance. Much shocking film footage of what happens in abattoirs all over the world has been posted online by animal rights activists and it is deeply disconcerting to an ignorant meat eat like myself to become aware of the truth of how what we are eating is created and the suffering involved in the process. At home an elegantly decorated boutique butcher's shop has a large advertising hoarding on the wall outside displaying lamb cutlets. Someone had graffitied "don't believe the human lie, animals don't want to be killed, animals don't want to be eaten." Accusations of animal cruelty at the abattoir used by this elegant shop in part contributed to its eventual closure. I still eat meat, although albeit with increasing qualms, but have great respect for those who take the path of becoming vegetarians. Vegetarians, and even more so vegans, seem to be the people who have the most right to condemn what happens at places like Dakshinkali.

In the winter of 2017 a performance by Belgian artist Hermann Nitsch was staged as part of David Walsh's MONA museum Dark Mofo arts festival in Hobart, Tasmania, amidst a huge outcry. It involved a bull slaughtered humanely in an abattoir and then taken to a performance space where people wallowed in its blood and draped themselves in its entrails as part of the public theatre event. The outrage was intense, much of it by people who were also willing to eat a beef sausage or steak for dinner, probably killed in the same slaughterhouse as the bull in the performance. It struck me what immense hypocrites so many of us are and that perhaps only vegans are sufficiently on the moral high ground as to comment as to the ethics of such an event. Or is it that making death of an animal the centre of a religious or theatrical ritual what makes is so upsetting and shocking? Is it ok to kill animals if that is hidden and veiled, but much too confronting when animal death is revealed in a temple or theatrical ritual? Is that just too honest a revelation of a truth that most meat eaters would prefer not to think about, that they actually consume the flesh of a once living being? Much of my distaste for the shedding of blood at Dakshinkali is no doubt due to the latter factors, and that evening, when eating yet more buffalo momos, my hypocrisy stares at me from the plate. I have no illusions as to where and how the buffalos that ended up in dinner would have been killed. It would have been a cruel death in a horrible and most likely unregulated slaughterhouse.

The creative director for MONA, Leigh Carmichael, acknowledged the work of Nitsch would stir passionate outrage and debate but urged people to "reflect deeply" before responding. "His work seeks to confront the truth of reality. It exposes reality, and it's an intense experience of reality. It deals with the sanitation of war, horror, and slaughter. It is grounded in ancient ritual, religion, and mythology. It is about death and sex." Mr Carmichael said the festival aimed to show the "full spectrum of human emotion" and encourage a deeper understanding of the nature of existence, "an existence that encompasses the terrible abyss, and the glorious splendour ....Ultimately, no one can justify the killing of an animal, not for food or for art....Art sometimes has the power to influence a community, and although it would be an indirect outcome of this performance, we would consider a reduction in the consumption of meat a positive result.....If we cancel this event, not one bull will be saved. There is currently no specific animal earmarked for slaughter for this event....Yes, we could select a random animal to live peacefully in a paddock for the rest of its life. This would amount to no more than a futile attempt to reduce our guilt, and in the process further suppress the truth and reality that we are seeking to understand."[121]

Issues like this stir passionate and contradictory responses. It is in the nature of samsara that violence, bloodshed and brutality are woven through its every aspect. Nature is "red in tooth and claw," and animals killing other animals to eat them is a universal reality that includes us humans, the most intelligent of animals who hunt or farm animals to consume their flesh. The festive Christmas ham or turkey served at gatherings to celebrate the birth of Jesus, the "prince of peace," was a once living sentient being, and in the case of ham a very intelligent living being, a pig, who probably lived a short miserable life on a commercial pig farm before dying in terror in a slaughterhouse to have its legs dismembered to be transformed in to ham. It is easy to forget this is what lies behind the beautifully glazed ham studded with cloves prepared for Christmas lunch.

I love my pet Labrador and am very aware of her intelligence and personality. It is disconcerting to contemplate that the dog food placed in her bowl is manufactured from the body parts of many other animals such as kangaroos, old cows, old worn out laying chickens, and most horribly of all, horses. Up until very recently I kept several horses, and the realization that the meat of old sick or unwanted horses is probably in the dog food is appalling, and another reminder of humans capacity to selectively love, pamper and respect some animals, and yet eat other animals and feed them to our pets with total lack of awareness or concern. Homo sapiens sapiens are deeply hypocritical and inconsistent creatures, able to rationalize just about anything without even noticing it is happening. Facebook is full of posts showing cute pictures of animals and animal rescue videos and people protesting loudly at the cruelty of others to animals, but who share meat recipes and eat pork, lamb or beef for dinner without a second thought. Perhaps the condemnation of others is in part a guilt relieving and deflecting mechanism with denial and projection thrown in. They can set themselves apart from the tendency for humans to be cruel and violent and take a position of moral superiority that makes them feel good. But of course none of us can successfully pretend we are not capable of the darker aspects of human nature, as witnessed by war, violence, genocide, murder and oppression that have been the hallmark of human history. That seems to be written in to our DNA as demonstrated by our extremely close relative the chimpanzee, revealed by David Attenborough to kill and eat their own kind.[122]

Violence and cruelty appear endemic to human behaviour as every century brings yet another round of awful conflicts, genocides and wars, this being entangled at the very heart of human history and experience. What can this tells us about samsara, about ourselves and about any God that might have created us? The Hindu deities of Kali, Durga and Shiva embrace the opposing faces of life and death, creation and destruction, peace and violence, that are entwined in every aspect of samsara and the living beings who journey through it. Thinking about Dakshinkali, the Aghori sadhus and the practitioners of Tantric rituals in cremation grounds in the light of the comments about Nisch's work encompassing the "terrible abyss", forces me to recognize the strength of my fear and avoidance of death. I could not even say farewell to Rob's body after he died. Animal sacrifice in the name of religion remains abhorrent, particularly in places like Ghadimai in southern Nepal where hundreds of thousands of buffalo were brutally slaughtered in a frenzy of bloodletting every four years. In 2009 an estimated 250,000 animals were killed and over five million people attended. That is barbaric and should have no part in any culture anywhere, whatever the religious rationale, and as of 2015 it was thankfully banned. Dakshinkali, and the other examples of animal sacrifice we find in Khokana, Kirtipur and Chaupati, continue to be troubling and provoke serious questioning of meat eating which is exactly what Hermann Nitsch hoped his work would achieve.

Later, chatting with a Nepali friend back home about Dakshinkali as we sit in an Italian café eating olives with prosciutto made from a pig, a highly sentient animal, he explains he has been part of the animal sacrificing rituals at Dakshinkali. It is apparently a very powerful Tantric temple where what he calls paranormal powers manifest and the power of Kali fulfils the wishes of those that worship her. He explains with great sincerity that the animal sacrifices are given in thanks to Kali for her bringing about whatever the person offering the sacrifice has requested. It is believed that the animal sacrificed will be helped because it will achieve a better incarnation, perhaps as a human, in its next rebirth, and that will give it the chance to work towards enlightenment and liberation from samsara. A more kind person would be hard to find and the contradictions and moral murkiness of sacrificing animals is deeply puzzling. We talk about Nepal and the odd sense of the numinous hovering there, in such contrast to the clean, ordered, materially blessed but spiritually arid world of Australia. The animal sacrifice issue will resurface during a later trip to Bali, an island outpost of Hinduism in Indonesia, where unseen spiritual forces also permeate every aspect of life and the natural world. Its many religious practices reflect complex realities similar to Nepal, the name Bali being the Sanskrit word for animal sacrifice, which is commonly performed to placate demons and to keep harmony and balance between forces of good and evil. The Balinese, like the Nepalese, live with intense awareness and also fear of invisible supernatural realities hovering just beyond the veil of everyday life.

On our way to visit Patan and its Durbar square the following day, we detour south to the small Newari town of Khokana with a population of around five thousand. Traditional life continues here as it has for many centuries co-existing with inroads of the modern world, cars, trucks, buses and motorbikes jamming its ancient streets strewn with the usual litter of plastic bags and bottles. Cobs of corn hang in strings and ropes of chillies and garlic are drying in the sun. Toothless ancient women winnow rice on flat trays some using electric fans to blow the husks from the grain. Elderly men, dignified in their traditional Newari clothing of a long shirt or tapalan over tight fitting trousers or suruwa, pass by, the traditional neat Newari cap on their heads. We walk the narrow streets and once again the sense assails us of being in some strange time warp where the twenty first and fifteenth centuries have mixed together creating a hybrid world where a woman spins on a hand held wheel outside the front door of a electronics store where ancient stone lions squat outside on steps surrounded by plastic buckets.

Khokana like the rest of Nepal suffered badly in the earthquakes of 2015 but the soft pink brick Newari buildings are still beautiful and many have survived the earthquake devastation, their balconies, window frames and screens intricately carved. The surrounding fields growing mustard are surrendering to the invasion of Kathmandu's sprawl but it is still an important centre for mustard growing and mustard oil production for Nepal. The usual shrines and temples are at every turn and tucked up small alleys and in secret courtyards. In the centre of the town is the Shekali Mai Mandir or Rudrayani Temple built in the 16th century, dedicated to the goddess Rudrayani a manifestation of the Hindu goddess Durga. Khokana is a town with no chickens. The villagers believe that to raise chickens will anger the goddess. It presents a delightful picture of a quiet and deeply religious community in a Unesco world heritage listed environment. It is shocking to discover that this place is the scene for a brutal annual event, the Deopokhari held in August and dedicated to Rudrayani, religion once again providing the rationale for terrible cruelty. This event involves the throwing of a young female goat in to the ancient Chwe Lachi pond near the Rudrayani Temple, where she is chased, caught and torn and bitten to death by groups of contesting young men thrashing about in the water as they throw, rip and tear at her alive. The young man who delivers the final death blow is considered the winner, hailed as a hero and becomes the leader of the town festival procession.

The contrasting and complex faces of these religious practices are hard as an outsider to fathom. This is Nepalese Hinduism, but still Hinduism, the religion of the **Upanishads**, and the **Bhagavad Gita**, of teachers such as Yogananda, Krishnamurti, and Sri Aurobindo, and of great leaders of peace such as Ghandi and his message of satyagraha "passive resistance," where peaceful protest overcomes oppression. Hinduism holds as central the doctrine of ahimpsa, or no harm to any living being. How can that face of Hinduism coexist with a religious rite involving the agonizing, slow, terrifying death that the goat would suffer in an atmosphere of great noise and commotion as she is tortured in the pond? I find YouTube footage of this event and am aghast. This is much worse than the goat sacrifices at Dakshinkali or the buffalo sacrifice at Kirtipur, both of which would be quick and efficient and not more cruel than a commercial slaughterhouse where meat begins its journey from live animal to dinner. The tearing apart of a live goat as a spectacle watched by townsfolk, including many children, is reminiscent of the Romans watching humans and animals tear each other to pieces as entertainment in the Colosseum, or the bullfighting of Spain, with the added dimension of religious fervour in Khokana. The annual slaughter of thousands of buffalo in appalling circumstances of cruelty at Gadhimai in southern Nepal has been successfully stopped and there is hope that the goat killing at Khokana will be too.

Goddess Rudrayana is a manifestation of Durga who, like Kali, is a female aspect of Shiva. The awful goat killing at Khokana deepens my confusion as to the role of Shakti goddesses such as Durga and Kali, and also Shiva. Kali and Durga are worshipped and propitiated as Tantric Shakti deities possessing real power that manifests in the lives of their followers. Kali embraces a wide range of attributes, possibilities and followers, and her multiple aspects and strong associations with Tantra are clear: "She is a symbol of Mother Nature herself – primordial, creative, nurturing and devouring in turn, but ultimately loving and benevolent. In Tantric meditation, Kali's dual nature leads practitioners to simultaneously face the beauty of life and the reality of death, with the understanding that one cannot exist without the other.....Today, her image reflects her duality. Kali is depicted in the act of killing but smiles engagingly. Her protruding red tongue signals both modesty (a Bengali tradition) and her thirst for blood. Her dishevelled hair hints at unrestrained blood lust and alternatively the metaphysical mystery of death that encircles life. Her three eyes represent omniscience, her voluptuous breasts both sexual lust and nurturance. Her nakedness simultaneously represents carnality and purity. Her necklace of severed heads and girdle of severed arms signifies her killing rage but are also tantric metaphors for creative power and severance from the bonds of karma and accumulated deeds. Even her stance is imbued with dual meaning. The respectable, right handed path of Tantra (Dakshinamarga) is emphasised by her right foot forward stance, while the infamous left-handed path (Vamamarga) followed by "degenerate" Tantric practitioners such as the Aghori is down-played. While her right hands are generally associated with positive gestures, her left hands hold weaponry – depending on the number of arms she is portrayed as having, a bloodied sword or trident, a freshly severed head and a skull cup to catch the blood. However, even these are symbols of greater purpose. The sword symbolises higher knowledge, the head the human ego that must be severed in order to exit from the cycle of life and rebirth."[123]

In Nepal spiritual forces are considered real and everywhere penetrating in to daily life in both positive and negative ways, from demons such as the Nyen from Himalayan Nepal bringing sickness, to deities such as Durga or Kali rewarding those who sacrifice animals to them. These views are the opposite of my own secular culture where sickness is caused by bacteria or viruses not demons, and committing an animal sacrifice would bring prosecution in the courts. All religions make reference to some kind of selection from a cast of angels, demons, holy beings, sacred figures and deities. Either the world is more than it seems, and spiritual forces have reality, or they don't, and all religion and spirituality is mere superstition. Both those opposite alternatives have their drawbacks. My own culture reflects faith in materialism and reason but it pays the price of spiritual sterility, whereas Nepal has faith that spiritual forces determine just about everything but pays the price of rampant superstition. It has been a long climb from the witchhunts and burnings of the Middle Ages, where devils and demons were lurking everywhere and religion totally controlled people's lives. That was a grim reality. Can a path be negotiated between the two polarities of a spiritually dead world and a world dominated by religion, fear and superstition? Is it possible for spirituality to be reconciled with reason and for it to exist in a way that does not slide in to magic and superstition? These are all questions that spring to mind as we return from Khokana to the urban sprawl of Patan.

Patan, once known as Lalitpur, is now engulfed by Kathmandhu but has a proud history as one of the three great kingdoms of the Kathmandu valley. There is evidence that the Mauryan Buddhist King Ashoka from India visited the Kathmandu valley in the third century BCE, leaving pillars and inscriptions behind, and Patan's history may stretch back to that time. The existing town was mainly built during Malla rule between the 14th and 18th centuries and is a well preserved example of Newari architecture despite the earthquake damage of 2015. The Durbar square in Patan is perhaps the most impressive of them all, with strong Hindu and Buddhist influences. I stunned by the variety, artistry, and history of this place and as we walk we try to take in Buddhist vajra's, Hindu temples, secret back lanes leading to surprising open spaces called chowks, often with a shrine or temple of some kind at their centre. This place could not be invented by Hollywood even if it were so ambitious as to try.

We start our tour at Durbar Square and a beautiful stone building, the Krishna Mandir, built in 1663, is immediately recognizable as the location for one of Rob's photographs from his time here in the early 1970's. He was a professional photographer and took many fine images of Nepal, India, and Afghanistan. His photograph of the Krishna Mandir is a close up of a long grey-haired man lying asleep outstretched between the stone columns of a colonnaded area at its base. He is wearing the robes typical of a sadhu so perhaps he is a holy man. It is a favourite from Rob's pictures and part of what lured me to Nepal all these years later, the face of the resting man showing great calm as the camera of a man from far away captures him. I often look at that photograph, a moment in time with the picture outliving both men, the taker and the taken. An image on a fragile piece of paper can and often does outlast the flesh and blood person who is the subject, and the same is true of books, of houses, of paintings, of most things that are not alive: they will outlast us because it is only that which lives that dies. Everything, particularly life, is impermanent, and Nepal constantly reminds that we all pass through both birth and death, and according to samsara, back in to rebirth.

The Durbar Square has lived through many generations and dealt with earthquakes, pollution and change. The repair work from the 2015 earthquake is clearly in progress but much remains to do. We enter the door of the Sundari Chowk originally constructed in 1623, into an open square with an elaborate pool, the Tushahiti stepped well, at its centre. The gilt bronze spout in to the fountain is decorated with an image of Laksmi-Narayan on a Garuda, a bird figure revered in Hinduism as the mount of Vishnu. The walls are surrounded by deities in niches, Krishna at the main axis and a Naga or serpent surrounding the top of the well encircling it. To describe it as extraordinary is an understatement. We explore the astonishing collection of temples, chowks and sculptures, all of them inspired by religion combined with worldly power and artistic brilliance. Our next destination north of the Durbar Square is the so called Golden Temple or Hiranyavana Mahavira, built in 1409 as a Buddhist monastery. Inside the courtyards are the most beautiful shrines and statues of Boddhisattvas and Sakyamuni Buddha. We then wander west and south towards the home of the Kumari, or living Goddess, of Patan. These are prepubescent young girls worshipped as incarnations of Durga, or Telaju as she is often known in Nepal. The girls always come from a Buddhist Newari family but Durga is a Hindu Goddess, the syncretism between Buddhism and Hinduism being one of the most interesting aspects of religion in Nepal. The Kumari are regarded as vessels of sacred power and protection and surrounded by many secret rituals until such time as their first menstruation when another girl replaces them. It is a tradition of great antiquity shrouded in secrecy, with Kathmandu and Bhaktapur also having Kumaris. We have missed the time when she is available to receive visitors so we return to Durbar Square, immersed in a place where nothing matches the familiar world. It is impossible to know if religious traditions such as the Kumari will survive in the twenty first century.

We leave Patan smitten with Nepal, its heritage and its people. Walking the broken streets of Thamel late at night we never feel afraid or threatened despite the grinding poverty and struggle for survival so obvious all around. A couple of times struggling with obscure writing on rupee banknotes gets too much with my reading glasses lying buried at the bottom of my bag, so I open my wallet and the shopkeeper or waitress plucks out the appropriate notes. On a number of occasions someone insists I have given them the wrong and too large denomination bank note and ask to exchange it for a smaller one, their honesty and lack of resentment of someone who has the luxury of being a tourist, remarkable. Idealizing and romanticizing is naïve, there is so much that an outsider cannot know and will never know, and the dynamics of poverty, corruption, caste, superstition, abuse of women and ignorance still loom large. It is a place where spirituality is soaked in to every aspect of life presenting a rich awareness of forces and dimensions outside of the material world completely absent in my own dry bland culture but bringing with it rituals such as animal sacrifice in the name of religion, and hefty doses of what is labelled 'magical thinking'.

The intense all pervasive spirituality is also accompanied by a shadow side of superstition, magic, and abuse or murder of women accused of being practitioners of black magic, and shockingly, cases of ritual murder. There are many cases of women being accused of being witches, usually coming from lower status backgrounds, who are subjected to terrible punishments such as beatings and being forced to eat excrement. If a local healer or shaman fails to bring about the intended result, or there is an unexplained illness or death in a village, the blame is often shifted to someone accused of being a witch, who then suffers awful retribution. In 2015 two Nepalese women were convicted of ritual child sacrifice, evidence being given at the trial that these kinds of events are not uncommon, particularly in southern Nepal. The perpetrator Mahadevi Yadav admitted in court: "My teacher Chhabilal Raya asked me to find a child, kill it and offer its fresh blood to honor the gods. I had to do it to learn witchcraft. I only murdered a child. There are many people who practice witchcraft and even killed because their teachers say that if they do not kill a child and extract the fresh blood, they cannot have complete knowledge."[124] Similar incidents in India offer insight in to this dark aspect of religion in Nepal and the potential for Tantra to be employed for evil purposes. The following account from **The Guardian Online** describes a ritual killing in Dhurja, a poor and isolated rural region of Uttar Pradesh, India, that reflects the ritual killings in Nepal.

A village woman beset by poverty and problems "....consulted a tantrik, a travelling 'holy man' who came to the village occasionally, dispensing advice and putrid medicines from the rusty amulets around his neck. His guidance to Sumitra was to slaughter a chicken at the entrance to her home and offer the blood and remains to the goddess. She did so but the nightmares continued and she began waking up screaming in the heat of the night and returned to the priest. 'For the sake of your family,' he told her, 'you must sacrifice another, a boy from your village.' Ten days ago Sumitra and her two sons crept to their neighbour's home and abducted three-year-old Aakash Singh as he slept. They dragged him into their home and the eldest son performed a puja ceremony, reciting a mantra and waving incense. Sumitra smeared sandalwood paste and globules of ghee over the terrified child's body. The two men then used a knife to slice off the child's nose, ears and hands before laying him, bleeding, in front of Kali's image. In the morning Sumitra told villagers she had found Aakash's body outside her house. But they attacked and beat her sons who allegedly confessed. 'I killed the boy so my mother could be safe,' Sanjay screamed. All three are now in prison, having escaped lynch mob justice. The tantrik has yet to be found. Police in Khurja say dozens of sacrifices have been made over the past six months. Last month, in a village near Barha, a woman hacked her neighbour's three-year-old to death after a tantrik promised unlimited riches. In another case, a couple desperate for a son had a six-year-old kidnapped and then, as the tantrik chanted mantras, mutilated the child. The woman completed the ritual by washing in the child's blood. 'It's because of blind superstitions and rampant illiteracy that this woman sacrificed this boy,' said Khurja police officer AK Singh. 'It's happened before and will happen again but there is little we can do to stop it…. This has been going on for centuries; these people are living in the dark ages.' According to an unofficial tally by the local newspaper, there have been twenty-eight human sacrifices in western Uttar Pradesh in the last four months. Four tantrik priests have been jailed and scores of others forced to flee."[125]

A search of Google will bring up numerous such horrifying cases in both India and Nepal, where a child has been sacrificed to Kali. It is terrible to contemplate that in a twenty first century world ritual killings remain commonplace in sub-Saharan Africa, body parts harvested from victims or cemeteries for use in sorcery, ceremonies and potions. It is not difficult to be an atheist with the abuses of religion and superstition so blatant and appalling. A desperate desire to gain some control over the brutal realities of poverty, lack of education or lack of medical care, often drives these kinds of practices, and whoever performs the rituals offers hope for a means to overcome the suffering of illness, inequality and hardship that manifest in samsara, often in unjust or arbitrary ways. Personal hatreds, hopes and desires also drive people to magic and witchcraft to achieve their ends, and that can and does sometimes result in tragic outcomes such as the ritual murder described. The world is often an unpredictable place where cruel things happen, and that combination of powerlessness, superstition, religion, belief, despair and hope to overcome cruel realities, provides impetus for dark practices such as black magic and ritual killings.

I am grateful at times to be without belief as that provides a powerful, if illusory, refuge from supernatural forces, even if their existence or non-existence is in no way dependent on belief or lack of belief. Supernatural dimensions either exist, or they don't, and belief neither creates them nor eliminates them. Is it at all possible that what is described by Lama Anagarika Govinda in **Land of The White Cloud** reflects something real? "... invisible forces, whether we call them Gods or spirits, divine or demoniacal powers, that influence the human mind, are not merely abstractions...but realities with which every religion and psychology has to cope. I could very well understand now the type of forces which Padmasambhava had to fight, and that such forces could only be conquered or subdued by calling up counterforces in the human mind, which is exactly the function of ritualistic magic...We are dealing here with spiritual realities, not with theories, with actual forces, and not with religious doctrines."[126] That is what places like Nepal do: they oblige contemplation of the existence of spiritual dimensions and forces not previously acknowledged, and recognition that what appear as random events or circumstances might be woven through with meaning. Those are uneasy possibilities to consider.

The powerful ever present spirituality of Nepal forces contemplation of questions easy to ignore in more materially focussed societies. The extraordinary truth, that the subatomic world is patterns of energy in some way interacting with the consciousness of the observer, is veiled from awareness by the mask created by everyday material reality. We are often so utterly immersed in that mask we are oblivious to the underlying mystery of our existence as conscious beings, and the emphasis of Western societies serves to reinforce this. In everyday life in the neat suburbs of Australia spirituality is all but invisible, its presence hinted at by occasional churches but there is no sense of a real spiritual presence permeating every aspect of the world, it being easy to be atheist or agnostic and dismiss belief in spiritual forces as nothing but superstition. Nepal challenges this, the veil is thinner and the numinous seeps through to stir awareness obscured in less spiritually saturated cultures. Perhaps the experiences offered by psychedelic substances do something similar, by rendering the veil more porous and opening the "doors of perception". Mystical experiences that arise from meditation, or psychedelics, or spirituality, perhaps all point in the same direction towards a reality that transcends the boundaries of any particular religion. Perhaps all religion is a groping towards a divine mystery that lies just beyond the borders of everyday experience?

Despite finding dark aspects to religion in Nepal, we both feel changed by our time there, privileged to have experienced such a place and understanding why Rob loved it so much. My thoughts about religion remain highly sceptical: there is just too much baggage of some kind or another in all of them that obscures rather than reveals the face of spiritual truth. That might be self-righteous belief that one's God or belief is the only true path and those that fall outside of it are doomed to eternal damnation by a 'loving' God, or discrimination against those of a different caste, the repellent aspects of Tantric practices in Hinduism and Buddhism, animal sacrifices, or at the extreme end of the spectrum witch hunts or horrific cases of ritual murder, all of those having their roots in the baggage of religion. But Nepal unveils much that is astounding, inspiring and mysterious, revealing that the world is nowhere near as straightforward as it appears from a place like Australia, where spirituality disappears from view in its individualistic, pragmatic, secular, consumerist, competitive, materialistic culture. In Nepal, and later Bali and India, samsara and spirituality appear like figures emerging from the mist, wraith like but visible and recognizable as central to what we might be, and where we may be going, and that has felt like a gift, even if a somewhat problematic gift. It is time to go home.

CHAPTER SEVEN
BALI

The journey triggered by Rob's death is not finished by the trip to Nepal and I am not ready to settle in to my life without him until they are done. The new online business dreamed up in the back street of Bhaktapur is also in need of stock to get it going so thoughts turn to where next and settle on Bali, a tiny island in Indonesia. Travel there is easy from Australia, the place is beautiful, the culture extraordinary and its unique form of Hinduism creates a powerful spiritual presence. Having been to Bali as a student in the early seventies, and with Rob in more recent years, it is time to return to this hothouse of religion and artistic brilliance with its exquisite architecture, food, music, art, handcrafts, traditional clothing, dance, ceremonies and ritual. Nepal presented many challenges and Bali intensifies that process. As in Nepal the Balinese perceive the universe as woven through with invisible supernatural forces humans must placate, worship or fear. The material world is not inert and separate but entwined with consciousness, charged with dimensions, energies and entities that impact on every aspect of life. In both cultures the ideas of rebirth and samsara are understood and accepted without question: that is what life is. According to that view we are spiritual beings immersed in samsara by birth, depart from it at death and resume our journey by repeated rebirths on its ever turning wheel.

Bali possesses the only indigenous form of Hinduism away from the shores of India. Most Balinese are follower of Agama Tirta, or "water religion" a unique Shaivite Tantric form of Hinduism taken to Bali from India many centuries ago where it blended with pre-existing beliefs and practices. Its distinct features draw from animism, ancestor worship and Tantric Buddhism preceding the arrival of Hinduism brought by the Majahapit royal court fleeing the spread of Islam in Java during the fifteenth century. Balinese Hinduism is still the dominant religion, particularly in the East and South, continuing to determine every aspect of daily and village life and the thinking of those that live within it. There are a variety of sects and details of ritual and belief may differ, often slightly from one village to another, but the broad characteristics are consistent across the island and Tantric in nature. Pre-Hindu groups remain in Bali in places such as Kintimani and Bali Aga villages, speaking an older different language and worshipping nature gods and spirits. Animism and the practice of magic lie hidden beneath and embedded in religious life across Indonesia, both Islamic and Hindu. I remember a ceremony at Parangatritis in Muslim Java, where the entire village was on the beach worshipping and performing rituals to the sea Goddess asking for her protection, and placing lighted candles on to the water, thus revealing old beliefs and practices predating Islam continue to flourish. My parents' discussions of the folk religion of Malaya were fascinating as a child. It was syncretic, influenced by Hinduism, Buddhism, and Islam and involving traditional healers and magic much like Indonesia, and the practice and fear of magic remains widespread across Indonesia particularly in Bali.

The perception in Bali and Nepal that nature is alive with spiritual forces is a powerful antidote to the dry rationalism of Western societies. The implication of perceiving every aspect of the world as seething with spiritual energies is potentially terrifying and goes a long way to explaining the fear of magic and evil spirits so strong in Bali. According to the animist view everything in nature, from rocks and trees to animals, is alive with supernatural power that must be constantly appeased, controlled, guarded against or invoked according to a complex system of rituals and rules. If those rituals and rules are not properly performed then the balance of good and bad forces is broken with negative outcomes. Balinese religion is not one of church and God on Sundays: there is no division between the sacred and the secular, the spiritual and the material, nature and consciousness, all of them are inseparably intertwined.

Islam is the dominant religion of much of Indonesia and the Muslim population of Bali is increasing. Although simmering tensions between the two religions have been thus far contained the rise of Islamic fundamentalism and extremism in Indonesia will inevitably impact on Bali. Whether it can and will continue to show acceptance of floods of scantily clad Western tourists lounging on beaches in bikinis is unknown. The bombing by Islamic extremists of Paddy's Bar and the Sari Club at Kuta Beach in 2002, which killed two hundred and two people, has left deep scars. Beneath the surface of a tropical paradise Bali's history has many dark chapters including the mass killings during the mid 1960's in a vicious purge of those associated with communism. The violence and bloodshed raged across Indonesia but at its most virulent in Bali where many were murdered not because of their communism, but because of old hatreds and divisions, political conflict being used as an opportunity to settle old scores.

Complex currents and undertows lurk below the surface of this most extraordinary of islands, and at the core of those lies religion. It was easy to be oblivious to this on earlier visits being content to lie on beaches and ride the island on motorbikes, the crowds of tourists just a relative trickle at that time in the early seventies. Ugly modern development in places like Ubud, Denpasar, Sanur, and Kuta Beach was yet to come. That trip in the 1970's revealed small winding roads leading through dense forest, valleys of emerald green terraced rice fields dropping to exquisite river gorges, groves of lush bamboo with the volcanic mountain, Gunung Agung, serenely gazing over its island jewel, when it wasn't erupting with the anger of the Gods as it periodically does. And everywhere temples, so many temples. On a number of occasions my then boyfriend and I chanced upon processions of people dressed in exquisite traditional clothes, the women carrying what appeared to be elaborate offerings on their heads as they walked with incredible grace down the road towards a nearby village, hypnotic gamelan music playing in the distance, the colour, music and rich clothing dazzling. There was not a tourist in sight, and we had no idea what was happening but clearly this island was like nowhere else on earth. No wonder multitudes of artists from the wider world have been drawn to Bali from the early twentieth century, entranced by its beauty, its people and its culture.

Temples such as 17th century Pura Ulun Danu on the shore of Lake Bratan were then quiet and pristine without shanty complexes of shops, carparks and hawkers as they are now. I am surprised to see on this trip a small town of buildings have appeared to the rear of Pura Ulun Danu, the dome of a mosque clearly visible behind the temple and busloads of tourists being disgorged in to the nearby carpark. During earlier trips villages appeared as much temple as places to live, and religion was clearly important, but it was easy to be oblivious to the extent of its reach in to every aspect of life. The flood of foreigners to Bali for the sun, sand, surf, bars and nightlife, continues to grow, but many will be unaware of its complex layers. There is much about Balinese spirituality that the Balinese are not keen to reveal to outsiders and is easy to miss.

The first inkling there was much more going on came during a flight in the mid 2000's with Rob. Our seats were next to a woman reading **Trance and Possession in Bali.**[127] As we talked she opened up a whole new perspective, suggesting reading the book during the flight and she would finish it later. It brought remarkable revelations of a spiritual world pervaded by belief in demons, evil forces, occult power, spiritual danger, mysticism and possession by spirits requiring exorcism or control by priests or healers. It was reminiscent of the fear of witches and possession in Europe in the Middle Ages when many (estimates vary from hundreds of thousands to millions) were persecuted, put to death or became victims to the Inquisition. The **Malleus Malificarum,** ("hammer on the anvil of witches") an Inquisition guide from 1486 to sniffing out witchcraft in Christian Europe where the Catholic Church ruled absolute, is testament to the terror of unseen dark powers. Much of it is extremely bizarre with accounts of witches collecting testicles in the dead of night and putting them in bird's nests. Parts of the text read like a twisted fantasy of sexual repression and dread of women, women being the main victims of the medieval witch hunts. It also reveals obsessive terror of magic, demons, and possession by evil spirits, and it was astounding to find similar ideas persisting at the start of the twenty first century in cultures so far removed from medieval Europe as Bali.

That trip revealed something very different from the tourist paradise Bali with its attractive temple architecture visitors admire for its artistry. The endless small offerings lying on the footpaths in the mornings, with a collection of fruit, flowers and food artistically arranged in a palm leaf basket, or canang, had hitherto seemed a charming if quirky custom. It became clear that these are not offerings to benevolent Gods but are on the footpaths, or cemetery, or at places of danger like an intersection or road, to appease demons and keep forces of good and evil in balance in a world where those are in constant struggle and destructive forces always lurking. Everywhere are small shrines with offerings to please the gods and to placate and appease the demons: in luxury hotels, in markets, in homes, on street corners, restaurants, in the airport, literally everywhere.

To the Balinese every aspect of the world is governed by antagonistic opposites, or rwa-bendida, and without proper attention to ritual they are always threatening disorder, this applying to the planet, nature, individual lives, families, villages and nations. According to Balinese Hinduism the cosmos shows order, or dharma, simultaneously with adharma or disorder, and the aim is always maintaining balance so as the forces of adharma do not gain the upper hand. The aim is not the eradication of evil or demons, they are woven in to the fabric of reality, but maintaining harmony and balance. The dualistic tension between good and evil, darkness and light, is represented by the black and white checked fabric, poleng, often wrapped around statues, a tree, at the post of a bridge, worn as clothing, or any place where spiritual forces are present, that being in the Balinese view pretty much everywhere.

During an earlier trip a taxi driver explained that particular trees wrapped in the poleng fabric are repositories of spiritual power and if injured or destroyed they will have revenge in some way, perhaps the perpetrator meeting with an accident. This was such an astounding concept it seemed he must be joking, but he was absolutely not joking and many Balinese have total conviction that the world is permeated and controlled by the interplay of supernatural energies manifesting in natural phenomenon. Buta kala, or demonic spirits, gather at crossroads bridges, rivers, graveyards, some trees, and where birth, death or accidents have occurred. These buta kala are used by Balinese magicians, either 'white' or 'black,' to hurt or to heal, and offerings are made daily to those spirits in households and temples to appease their destructive potential.

Fear of witchcraft, black magic, and evil spirits is widespread in Bali and the term sekala niskala, visible-invisible, sums up the belief that the spiritual world and physical world interpenetrate each other, the invisible being as real and as powerful as the visible. Every Balinese Hindu home has a house temple, or merajan, and daily offerings to the Gods are made for protection and to the demons to placate them. Every morning the roads and footpaths will be dotted with canang offerings to keep the demons content, and scrupulous care is taken not to accidentally tread on them as to do so would risk an evil spirit attaching itself. We had encountered similar ideas in Nepal, where gods deliver earthquakes and floods, demons manifest in illnesses or crop failures, and spiritual forces are alive in every aspect of life, death and nature. These ideas are the opposite to the materialistic views common in Western culture, where everyday perception is that the material world is inert, neutral, and indifferent to human affairs, not alive with spiritual power, gods or demons. If a tree branch breaks in heavy winds and injures someone it is believed to be an unfortunate accident caused by impartial natural forces. In Bali, nature possesses consciousness that interacts with other living beings including humans, they are all reflections of an inseparable whole. To the Balinese the material world is a living system of energies and powers that must constantly be propitiated to keep destruction at bay. Trees, rivers, mountains and seas are perceived as imbued with spirits that can act in destructive ways if humans offend them, or don't seek the protection of gods, or fail to keep the spirits appeased with offerings and rituals. The tree branch falling and causing harm would, from a traditional Balinese perspective, be caused by an angry demon or spirit that had not been sufficiently controlled through offerings and rituals, or perhaps is the work of a curse or black magic. Someone told me a story that someone had told them, about a Western business man residing in Bali who cut down a tree blocking his view. Some days later he met with a road accident that was viewed by many Balinese as punishment for his heedless destruction of the tree, the spirits of the tree being believed to have caused his accident.

Despite great cultural differences perhaps there is more in common than is initially obvious between all religions, because whatever their faith believers accept that unseen supernatural forces are real and at work in the world and life. This expresses itself in many ways such as prayer, worship, fear of the devil, belief in angels, gods or demons, and innumerable rituals and practices. In Australia people do sometimes pray for God's intervention in to nature, such as for rain, perhaps not so utterly different from the small temple at Swayambhunath Nepal where Shantikaracharya, an 8th century mystic, is believed to remain in deep meditation controlling the weather of the Kathmandu valley. People also pray for healing of an illness for themselves and others, this being labelled as miracle if it succeeds in defiance of usual natural processes. The shrine of the Virgin Mary at Lourdes in France springs to mind: interestingly holy water as a vehicle of spiritual power plays a central role in Lourdes as it does in Bali.

Turning to supernatural forces for healing of illness is the norm in Bali as illness is regarded as a result of adharma, or imbalance brought about by some neglect of proper religious observation, a demon, or perhaps black magic. Church congregations, prayer groups and prayer websites in the West also offer recourse to divine intervention to overcome illness, not so different from what happens in Bali as might at first appear. Websites abound in the United States claiming God solves financial problems in response to prayer. That parallels the petitions to Ganesha in Nepal, as the overcomer of obstacles in commerce as well as everything else. It is the cultural context of these appeals to the supernatural that make them appear more different from each other than perhaps they really are. Many Christians also believe in the devil as a real actual being, not dissimilar to the belief in dark forces and demons so prevalent in Nepal and Bali. It was surprising to notice the Catholic Herald announce the following in relation to the devil in its April 2018 issue: "In his new apostolic exhortation, "Gaudete et Exsultate" ("Rejoice and Be Glad"), released by the Vatican April 9, the Pope urged Christians not to think of the devil as an intangible construct but rather 'a personal being who assails us. We should not think of the devil as a myth, a representation, a symbol, a figure of speech or an idea,'…. 'This mistake would leave us to let down our guard, to grow careless and end up more vulnerable…. The path to holiness does not involve wrestling with some abstract boogeyman, but involves a 'constant struggle against the devil, the prince of evil,' Pope Francis said."

How Christianity manages to reconcile certainty as to the omnipotence and benevolence of God, with acceptance of an independent devil outside of control of that God, is puzzling as they seem contradictory. Sri Aurobindo's comments as to Brahman, the ultimate reality and consciousness underlying the universe gives pause for thought: " Brahman is indivisible in all things and whatever is willed in the world has been ultimately willed by Brahman. It is only our relative consciousness, alarmed or baffled by the phenomena of evil, ignorance and pain in the cosmos, that seeks to deliver the Brahmans form responsibility for Itself and its workings by erecting some opposite principle, Maya or Mara, conscious Devil or self-existent principle of evil. There is one Lord and Self and the many are only His representations and becomings."[128] Aurobindo is asserting that Brahman, as the all knowing all powerful source of the whole universe, embraces what we categorize as evil and project on to a devil, as well as all that is good. Brahman contains all opposites and polarities in the same way as Shiva, an aspect of Brahman, represents both destruction and creation, and the dark goddess Kali represents both death and the divine mother.

That humans believe that evil is a real personal force out to deceive and ensnare is astounding in the twenty first century, leading straight back to the fear of the devil and witchcraft that haunted the Middle Ages before the scientific revolution replaced those with alternative explanations for natural events and human behaviour. Christian churches still perform exorcisms that are premised on belief in evil supernatural forces, and perhaps that is closer to the fear of demons and witches typical of the Middle Ages than we like to think in the supposedly enlightened contemporary world. Acceptance of an unseen spiritual world of real malevolent powers is shared across diverse cultures and religions, be those devils, demons, or punishing deities. Being an atheist has advantages as it rids the world of tricky spiritual energies that must be accounted for and managed, but on its down side leaves nothing but an indifferent material world in which we unaccountably find ourselves. Our lives are then devoid of intrinsic meaning as they result from blind evolutionary processes with no greater purpose and death is nothing but absolute extinction. It is ironic that being a believer or an atheist are both unsatisfactory in some way or another, and we humans must choose between them. For many that is an impossible choice, so they opt like me to sit on the fence as agnostics, unsure of belief or disbelief. If a third path could be found outside of those opposites of a "demon-haunted world," as Carl Sagan[129] describes it, and a universe utterly devoid of a numinous or transcendent dimension, could that offer a way forward between equally unpalatable alternatives?

Balinese Hinduism designates one supreme God, Sang Hyang Widhi (or Acintya) who is similar to Brahman from Indian Hinduism, and this means that Balinese Hinduism is able to fit within the Indonesian social ideal of Panchsila that has as a central principle belief in one God. Similar to Indian Hinduism the aim is purification of the atman, or soul, to eventually achieve liberation from endless rebirths in samsara and blissful reunification with God. According to Balinese Hinduism there are three levels to the cosmos: heaven or suarga home of the Gods, buwah the world, and bhur or an underworld, home of demons and a place of punishment for bad deeds. For the first two hundred and ten days after birth a baby's feet are not to touch the ground where bad spirits are closest, and the daily offerings left on the ground are to placate those spirits. A newborn baby is regarded as a pure being newly incarnated from heaven and must be fiercely protected from demonic energies or black magic with amulets and protective objects.

Priests are very important as they possess knowledge, ritual authority, and spiritual power over supernatural forces. At the highest level are the Pedanda High Priests from the Brahmana caste who can understand and speak the old Javanese Kawi language derived from Sanskrit, and who provide the Balinese with holy water because they know the correct rituals and methods. Then there are temple priests or Pemangku who organize temple affairs, processions and ceremonies and oversee offerings. The final group is an assortment of mediums, healers and magicians known as Balians who deliver, sometimes in a state of trance, messages from the gods, find out the cause of illness or who has reincarnated in to a family. The Balians vary greatly in their methods, their background and the areas of treatment they offer. Some specialize in spell and curse removal, others in physical healing, others in trance channelling information and are known as Ketakson. Some have studied for many years ancient texts known as lontars in the Kawi script that contain knowledge about meditation, yoga, Tantra, medicinal herbs, and treatments. Others have been chosen to be Balians by the spirits or have realized they are Balians through a personal discovery or revelation. Some become Balians after a particularly severe sickness where they discover the spirit that has either caused their illness or healed them. Balians also study and practice magic which can be complicated because that which separates white from black magic, or right hand path from the left hand path, is the intention of the practitioner. A Balian Putih who practices white magic is often called upon to remove the spells cast by a Balian Hitam who practices black magic.

It is believed by most Balinese Hindus that bad fortune, accidents or illness are all the work of either karma, over which one has little control, spirits, or the practice of some form of magic, and for the latter a Balian is seen as the remedy. Balians are consulted by most Balinese and every village will have at least one. The path of being a Balian is regarded as one of great danger as it involves penetration and utilization of spiritual realms and energies with tremendous power for both good or ill. People hold Balians in both respect and fear it being considered most unwise to cross one. A Balian will be consulted after the birth of a baby to discover the identity of the returning soul. Balinese Hinduism has very clear ideas as to the mechanisms and protocols of rebirth and karma and how those determine a person's rebirth in samsara, it being believed that babies are reborn in to families.

A fascinating account of this is described in **Bali Now** magazine: "People often say, Ancestors are "water" (yeh). And to incarnate is to come down as "titis", or as "drops" of water from the "old country", the ancestors' abode high above the mountains. Souls normally incarnate again only once they are ready, i.e. after they fully have paid for their sins in "the field of sorrow" (tegal penyangsaran) or purgatory, where they have been tortured by Yama's demons. Those which try to leave purgatory before their due time unavoidably end up in an abortion or in a child's death and thus find themselves back to square one, in the field of sorrow they have just left. People say that those souls tried to cheat and have to be punished. To have a child in proper condition is to pay proper attention to its soul's incarnation…. Another thing is that it is not just anyone that is incarnating. It has to be an ancestor's soul… But in order to have the right soul coming down, all should be well prepared, including the right offerings and the right prayers. And one should address one's request at the right place. …a sign (pawisik) will tell your wife that she is pregnant: this means the soul has found a place to come down through the meeting of the "white desire" (kama petak) with the "red desire" (kama bang). From that time on, the ancestor is there, waiting to come out in birth. When he/she does so, he/she is called as a "dewa" – an incarnating god. The most interesting, and what makes people most anxious is: who is incarnating? No need to overly speculate. There are mediums (balian) whose job is to intercede with the "invisible" world (niskala). If you find a good one, he/she will find out for you, which is usually done on the 12th day after birth. "Ding-ding-dingding-dingding," the priest's bell jingle jingles for a long-long time while he mutters mantras addressed to the Lords of the three worlds. The smoke of the burning incense is wafting over the nearby altar, offering "stairs" to the gods and ancestors to come down and "sit" (napak) on the requesting shaman (balian). Two women helpers are coming and going with offerings. But Nyoman Kemprot does not pay attention: he is holding in his hands a baby girl a few days old, and he, as well as all his relatives present, want to know who it is indeed who has thus come down from the ancestral abode, and whether he/she wants to be given something in particular for the upcoming otonan (first anniversary in Balinese 210 day calendar). But he does not have to wonder too long. His mantras become a jumble of inaudible sounds he shudders and his eyes turn white."[130]

To the Balinese it is ancestors and family who return to samsara to continue their pilgrimage with the same souls with whom they share a karmic history. The idea is disconcerting that all the people I know, my friends, my children, my family, are ancient souls that have been taking the endless journey in samsara wearing different roles, genders and personalities, incarnating with me in this life as one of an endless series of lives we have shared together. It is an astonishing possibility to contemplate. According to this understanding my parents have perhaps in another life, in another time, in another place, been my sister, or brother, or daughter, or son, or friend, or uncle, or aunt, and my children have been perhaps my mother, or my sister, and I their son or daughter, and so on in innumerable combinations. Those ever changing roles are like suits of clothing, put on and taken off according to the needs of the soul and the dictates of karma echoing the words of Krishna to Arjuna in the **Bhagavad Gita** "As a human being puts on new garments, giving up old ones, the soul similarly accepts new material bodies, giving up the old and useless ones."

This is all to the Balinese not a matter of conjecture but certainty. I remember a strange split second moment immediately after one of my children was born when he gazed straight in to my eyes with a look of what I could only interpret as recognition, an experience I could make no sense of at the time. It was over in an instant but I have never forgotten it. To a Balinese that experience was simply a greeting of each other as souls that have travelled many incarnations together. An observation by Carl Jung in the prologue to **Memories, Dreams, Reflections**, suggests something similar: that when we first meet someone we recognize them if they are to be important to us, the implication being we know them already from a previous life: "Similarly other people are established inalienably in my memories only if their names were entered the scrolls of my destiny from the beginning, so that encountering them was at the same time a kind of recollection."[131]

In many contemporary non-Balinese accounts by people undergoing past life regressions that same idea arises, that the people who they have strong connections with in this life have been significant to them in previous lives, often having made some kind of agreement to incarnate together to work out karma. They also often mention that family members have played the role of other family members in previous lives, for example a daughter might have been the person's grandfather in an earlier incarnation. Individuals experiencing past life regressions frequently describe the significant people in their current life as being brought into their life by powerful karmic connections stretching back in to ancient time. The Balinese understanding of reincarnation is very fixed, with rebirth following prescribed protocols that owe as much to tradition as the likelihood of fact.

Nevertheless the fundamental concept of the reappearance in our lives of people significant for karmic reasons, is common across cultural and religious boundaries, so perhaps it is a case of spiritual truth jumbled up with cultural constructions. Distinguishing where one ends and the other begins is the hard part.

As in India caste is central to Balinese Hinduism and linked to the doctrine of rebirth. Rebirth is viewed as being determined by one's past deeds (karma phala) and that sanctions the Balinese caste (wangsa) system. It is believed a person is born in to samsara with a particular caste status due to the actions of their past life, and their next life caste status can be improved by proper fulfilment of religious and social obligations. The caste system of Balinese Hinduism somewhat resembles that of India: the highest caste of Brahmanas deal with sacred texts and religion, the Satrias (warriors or rulers), the Wesias (merchants), and the Sudras as farmers and craftsmen who constitute the vast majority of the population.

The Balinese language reflects these social divisions and exhibits different levels of politeness as low Balinese, medium Balinese, high Balinese, and sacred Balinese known only to some Brahmanas. Balinese is a different language to to the official language of Indonesia, Bahasa Indonesia, which is a form of Malay and not an indigenous language for many Indonesians. There is also a sacred language of Kawi originating in Java that is predominantly Sanskrit only used by Brahmana priests. In modern Bali old caste distinctions are breaking down with a Brahmana street vendor perhaps serving a wealthy Sudra, and many people marry without consideration of caste status. That said a Balinese will know their caste position and those of a higher caste will be offered special honour at religious ceremonies. It is troubling that in Bali, as in India, karma becomes the explanation for the hereditary social inequalities of caste that cause much suffering, particularly in India, to the lower and untouchable castes. That does not invalidate the concept of samsara or karma, but teasing those out from religious and cultural baggage is tricky as they are deeply enmeshed with religion but also transcend it. In accounts of individuals who have experienced past life memories a consistent theme is rebirth being shaped by past life events and the need of the soul for particular experiences that bring about growth. Interestingly many of those people have no religious belief of any kind and cross religious, gender, cultural, and social boundaries from one incarnation to the next, so as to serve the purposes of the soul. Social structures such as caste, or previous religious affiliation, played no role in any of their recollected experiences of rebirths.

The concepts of karma and rebirth can also be used in other troubling ways. Recently a friend mentioned to me that when their child had a serious car accident causing permanent brain damage someone had remarked that it was the child's karma, the accident being 'chosen' by them before they incarnated. Another friend described to me that someone had informed them that prosecuting in the courts their child's sexual abuser would incur 'bad karma,' and that they needed to 'forgive' rather than take legal action. Both of these incidents caused much distress and turned karma and rebirth in to weapons of judgment and justification in a way that says more about human nature than it reveals about spiritual truth.

So what do Indian Hindu scriptures have to say about reincarnation? The **Bhagavad Gita** describes rebirth "As a person puts on new garments, giving up old ones, the soul similarly accepts new material bodies, giving up the old and useless ones," making no reference to caste or religion. The **Brihadaranyaka Upanishad** describes rebirth in samsara:

"As a person acts, so he becomes in this life. Those
who do good become good; those who do
harm become bad. Good deeds make one
pure; bad deeds make one impure. So we are
said to be what our desire is. As our desire is
so is our will. As our will is, so are our acts,
As we act, so we become.
We live in accordance with our deep, driving
desire. It is this desire at the time of death that
determines what our next life is to be. We will
come back to earth to work out the satisfaction
of that desire."

What karma and rebirth mean in practice at the coalface of samsara is ambiguous, giving religions traction to interpret and harden those ideas in to religious formulations that become instruments for some humans to judge other humans or dominate them through social structures such as caste. That does not make the essential core of the concepts wrong, but it does mean they are heavily contaminated with tendencies of human nature and ideas created by culture. The practice of religion is inevitably entangled with cultural tradition and the challenge is to identify and hold on to what is of central universal value and let go that which is not. That presents a dilemma in relation to samsara as the concept seems to have a foot in both camps: it speaks universal truths about life, suffering, death and rebirth that are not specific to any particular religion, place, or time, but at the same time it is deeply entwined with religion and culture.

Rituals and ceremony are very important dimensions of Balinese Hinduism and those occur for just about every facet of life and death, tourists often being dazzled by processions and cremation rituals. Hotels will sometimes inform foreign guests of the location of a cremation and they stand around on the fringes of those looking strangely awkward and yet entranced by what is unfolding around them. Rob and I attended several cremation ceremonies including one that involved around fifty simultaneous cremations attended by thousands of people. The bodies were burned in ornate sarcohphagi, the corpses becoming visible and alight as the ceremony reached its end. As one of the burning bodies revealed itself to be clearly that of a young child I gasped in horror, my Western death denying background making me totally unprepared for that sight.

Rob hustled me away from the burning corpse of the child as grief is considered a terrible thing to show at a cremation because it drags the spirit of the dead person back to the world rather than releasing it to the next stage of the soul's journey. That journey might involve time in either heaven or hell, but will eventually bring the dead person back in to samsara as a baby, or possibly as an animal, according to their karma. The body is regarded as a mere shell, the casing of the soul, and what matters is the atman or spirit which must be appropriately released and farewelled from this life to prepare for return to samsara in the next life. If the required ceremonies and rituals are not properly performed it is thought that the spirit of the deceased can create all sorts of disturbances for the living so great care is taken in these matters. There are pre-cremation ceremonies, cremation ceremonies and post-cremation ceremonies, and we accidentally stumble upon the latter at a small temple beside the beach at Sanur. The ashes of the corpse are being washed and then a great celebration is held for the returning spirit. Family and friends are gathered in their beautiful traditional clothes, gamelan music plays continually from a small group of men under a nearby tree, and offerings are piled up on a huge table, as the soul is welcomed back in to another round of samsara. Nobody displays grief but rather joy that the soul will be re-entering the world. I wish I could share that certainty and joy as to what has become of Rob after death. All that can be done is hope that his journey after death has brought him release and peace after his years of suffering. When his ashes were scattered in Nepal there was a quiet certainty that all was now well with him, and I have held on to that despite lack of any idea as to where if anywhere he might be. Has he taken on another body in samsara, or is he in some kind of afterlife, or is he nowhere at all? It is impossible to know where Rob is now but the peace that came as his ashes were scattered has remained.

Religion in Bali defines every aspect of family and village life. Family compounds are entered through a small door in a gate with a wall, the aling aling, designed to prevent demons from entering. The family compound will have its own shrine or temple, every village multiple temples, and one person can belong to several temples they will attend for important ceremonies. Temple entrances feature carvings of fierce fanged demons to scare away evil spirits. The time involved with fulfilling religious obligations is demanding and for many Balinese difficult to reconcile with running businesses or working in jobs that require regular attendance away from their village, such as a hotel or office. Offerings will be made daily at family and village temples to gods, demons and spirits. Traditional Balinese villages are orientated along a mountain sea axis and will have three or more temples: a pura puseh or temple of origins, a pura desa where the particular deity associated with the village is worshipped, and a pura dalem or temple of the dead. There are also clan temples, market temples, temples to nature gods, and temples of former kingdoms, adding up to hundreds of thousands of temples on one small island.

It is believed that Balinese Hindu deities enter the effigies in the temple shrines during sacred ceremonies and a parasol is displayed to indicate the living presence of the god. The temples usually contain consistent architectural features including tall Meru towers representing the holy Mt Meru in the Himalayas, abode of the gods and mythological and sacred centre of the universe for Hindus, Buddhists and Jains, and the Candi Bentar which is a large split entrance gate representing the opposing forces of good and evil. The Padmasana shrine in the most sacred part of every temple with an empty chair at the top for Sang Hyang Widhi, the supreme being who is the source of the universe and everything in it. Statues that are considered charged with magic forces are wrapped in the same black and white checked poleng fabric as significant trees, bridges, or rocks, to symbolize the dualistic nature of those magic forces. At times of religious ceremony the temples come alive with traditional Balinese gamelan music, offerings and dance, each village having its own set of gamelan instruments some of which are regarded as sacred. Every temple will have an annual Odalan ceremony to celebrate the anniversary of its dedication, the date determined by one of two traditional Balinese calendars, the Saka or lunar calendar or the Pawukon a two hundred and ten day ceremonial calendar, rather than the Gregorian calendar used in the West. They are a great event with many ceremonies, dances and music performances inviting the gods to come down from the world of the unseen (niskala) in to the world of the seen (sekala), in the form of temple effigies and shrines. It is also an opportunity for temple renovations and the whole village will participate.

According to the Balinese there is no boundary between the physical and the spiritual: invisible spiritual energies, gods and demons are inextricably woven through the material world. Consciousness also has no boundaries as everything is seen as an expression of consciousness, similar to Indian Hinduism where everything is a manifestation of Brahman or the Self. Two examples of sekala and niskala, (seen and unseen) are the huge importance of holy water, and the sacred Keris dagger of Malaysia and Indonesia. Holy water is regarded as charged with spiritual power and can ward of evil or demonic forces to purify and strengthen. Not all holy water is equal, and its mystical power and importance varies according to who makes it, where it comes from and what mantras have been said over it. Holy water is central to all rituals, and priests sprinkle it over participants in ceremonies to purify and bless. The collection and distribution of holy water is subject to a complex system of rules that must be observed along with all the other myriad restrictions and requirements the observation of religion brings for Balinese Hindus. The most powerful holy water is made by Pedanda priests early in the morning in a ceremony known as maweda, involving mantras, mudras (hand gestures) and a bell. There is holy water to purify the body, pangelukatan pabersihan, there is holy water, prayascita, to purify one's thoughts, and holy water, tirtha giu kawonen, to repel dark thoughts. The lay priests or pemangkus also make holy water as can others such as the puppet master, or dalang from the Wayang Kulit puppet shows, or various other individuals under certain circumstances. Holy water is always treated with great respect and handled and stored carefully as it represents the presence of unseen energies present in a material form. It assumes that matter and energy are essentially identical which is an assumption that subatomic physics has essentially confirmed. Holy water is not just water and is regarded utterly differently from ordinary water.

The Keris is another example of a material item being a repository of spiritual power that must to be treated with great care and respect, so as to not invite destructive consequences. The blades of Keris are often in a distinctive wavy curved shape although some are straight. They are considered charged with supernatural energies, prayers and mantras being said over them while they are hand forged from nickel and iron layers creating beautiful patterns, by members of a special caste group, the Pandes. Once the appropriate rituals and offerings have been completed the newly created Keris becomes a visible vehicle for invisible forces, as in the case of holy water reflecting the interpenetration of matter and energy. Some Keris are considered so powerfully charged with occult forces that they must be kept in a special shrine, and some are considered to be extremely dangerous in the wrong hands. Keris are chosen according to an esoteric formula of how they match the hand measurements of their owners and the wrong Keris can bring bad luck or disaster. Once females reach the age of menstruation they are forbidden to touch the Keris, and can only do so once they are post menopause.

Menstruating women are also forbidden from entering temples. On previous trips I was irritated by what appeared as simple sexist discrimination, and amused by the English of signs stating "It is forbidden to enter menstruating women in this temple," as several did. Since that time, reading anthropologist Mary Douglas's **Purity and Danger: An Analysis of Concepts of Pollution and Taboo**[132] and **The Dangerous Sex**[133] by HR Hays has revealed this is typical of a widespread anxiety about women and female bodily functions that manifests in many cultures and through time. Some Christian orthodox churches still forbid menstruating women from attending church as does traditional Jewish law that forbids them entering the synagogue. Leviticus in the Torah or Old Testament gives great detail why a menstruating woman is spiritually polluting and outlines rules for her behaviour and purification. The ancient Romans believed if women handled food while menstruating then it would putrify. Women in Nepal are still subject to chaupadi, where they are banned from the house while spiritually 'unclean' with menstruation. Whether the ban on menstruating women entering temples in Bali is to keep them out because they are ritually polluting, or to protect them from harm that blood in a temple could bring upon them, is a moot point, and both seem to be involved. The ban on menstruating women also extends to anyone with blood from a wound, so clearly blood itself is feared as it provokes a state of 'unseen impurity', cuntaka in Sanskrit, or sebel or leteh in Balinese. There is a long list of restrictions and conditions in relation to ritual impurity including people in mourning or associated with a death in the family or village, breast feeding women and people who are sick or afflicted in some way. For a person in mourning purification ceremonies with holy water must be performed before they can once more be ritually pure and able to attend the temple.

Because it is believed all visible phenomena are expressions of invisible spiritual energies people with deformities are seen as ritually unclean and not permitted to enter temples during some ceremonies. It is troubling that a person with a deformity, disability or illness is forbidden access to a spiritual event because of belief that their condition is indicative of bad karma or spiritual impurity. In Australia that would provoke outrage and be hauled before the courts as a case of blatant discrimination. It is reminiscent of the world of Jesus healing the sick and making the lame walk by casting out demons held responsible for those conditions. In earlier centuries in Europe mental illness was treated by a hole being screwed in to the top of the person's head to let out the demons. In Bali demons and negative spiritual forces, rather than viruses and bacteria, are still believed to be the source of sickness and Balians are usually consulted in precedence to modern medicine. It is shocking to discover that people suffering from mental illnesses frequently receive no treatment other than a Balian because the illness is believed to be caused by demons or curses, this situation being compounded by poverty and lack of modern treatment facilities or psychiatrists. Many of those afflicted are locked up by their family and live in filth and isolation in what is called pasung. Some have chains around their ankles, others have their feet secured through a hole in a heavy wooden log or are shackled to a wall, but all are confined. It is estimated there are over 18,000 people in pasung in Indonesia and many of them are in Bali, a dark side of tourist paradise and a dark facet of Balinese religion.[134]

It is examples such as the latter why it is important to not embrace uncritically the reality of spiritual dimensions or abandon evidence based examination of those. It is not possible to intellectualize a way to spiritual realization, that is the wrong key for the wrong lock, but equally to abandon rational examination of what is labelled spiritual is a folly that could easily lead to wild superstition best left in the Middle-Ages. Finding a path between rational analysis and spiritual realities is daunting and maybe no such path exists. And if there is no alternative way between those then it becomes a choice between mutually exclusive opposites. That is an absolutist position impossible to adopt so sitting on the agnostic fence, sceptical but curious, fascinated but wary, remains the least impossible place to be.

In his excellent study of Balinese religion **Sekala and Niskala: Religion, Ritual and Art**, Fred Eiseman JR expresses this dilemma beautifully if somewhat enigmatically. He adopted Balinese Hinduism so his perspective is from the inside, but he was also, as an American, deeply aware of alternative explanations in no way reconcilable with the Balinese view. He describes many examples of Balinese in states of trance who are believed to be possessed by gods or spirits. During this trance possession they may moan, writhe on the ground, or in the case of the men turn their Keris against their chests and try to stab themselves. They may speak in a voice not their own as the spirit possesses them and afterwards have no recollection as to what has happened, somewhat resembling the Oracles of Tibetan Buddhism who deliver messages from supernatural entities in a state of trance possession. If, as occasionally happens, a Balinese man is hurt by the Keris during his trance self-stabbing it is considered it is because he was in some way not properly ritually protected.

At the end of his discussion on trance Eiseman puts forward explanations from Western psychology as to dissociative states, hysteria or multiple personality disorder, and gives examples of trance states from other religious traditions such as Pentecostals speaking in tongues. He then concludes the chapter with the following comments: "Thus the trance phenomena that have been described are not without precedent. Which explanation should one accept? Whichever one you feel fits your own ideas and makes you feel comfortable. I will not suggest the superiority of one over the other. I was trained in science, yet I have lived in Bali for a long time. I know how real the feelings of the Balinese are about these matters, and I respect them. That is as far as I care to pursue the matter." [135]He is clearly unable, or unwilling, to reveal what side of the fence he is positioned, or whether he is sitting on top of the fence having a bet each way, although he does hint that he accepts the Balinese view that supernatural energies are indeed involved in the examples of trance possession he describes. He also hints that the Keris used by the trance possessed self-stabbers are not sharp, so unlikely to produce injury, so what he actually believes is not clear. Fred Eiseman died in 2013 and his ashes have been returned to Bali. It would be great to be able to ask him what he discovered after death and whether he has reincarnated in to another round of existence in samsara, but death being what it is that is unfortunately not possible.

An interesting example of trance possession on a mass scale is the religious ceremony described by Eiseman held every two hundred and ten days at the Pengerebongan temple in the village of Kesiman to the east of Denpasar. Many devotees stream in to the temple to make offerings to God to protect the human race from evil and avert disaster. Everyone is dressed in their best ceremonial clothes, sacred fires are burning, and gamelan music plays continuously. The women wear a white lacy kebaya or top with a sarong, and the men a white jacket and sarong with the traditional udeng or head-dress. What is known as the

Ngerebong ceremony begins after a ritual shedding of blood in a cockfight. In an open hall near the temple hundreds of men gather who have fallen in to a trance and have begun stabbing themselves with their Keris daggers believed to possess sacred power. Sanghyang is a sacred trance state where Hyangs (deities), or helpful spirits, or spirits of ancestors temporarily occupy the bodies of those in trance and its purpose is to restore spiritual balance with what is a kind of exorcism. The trance seems to be induced by religious fervour combined with hypnotic music and dancing creating an altered state of consciousness with similarities to those created by mind altering substances. The men in trance are led around by other men who support them while they plunge the point of the Keris in to their bodies without injury. It is believed that sacred powers are providing protection and no harm will come to them whilst in a state of possession by the gods. Women also fall in to a trance and scream and cry while making strange unchoreographed dance movements. Barong and Rangda masked figures are also present in what is a scene of religious frenzy.

The Balinese are usually a controlled and dignified people and unleashing of usually well-hidden intense emotions is part of the ceremony. There is a phenomena that occurs in Malaysia and Indonesia called running amok where "an individual (often male), having shown no previous sign of anger or any inclination to violence, will acquire a weapon (traditionally a sword or dagger, but present any of a variety of weapons) and in a sudden frenzy, will attempt to kill or seriously injure anyone he encounters and himself. Amok typically takes place in a well populated or crowded area. Amok episodes of this kind normally end with the attacker being killed by bystanders, or committing suicide, eliciting theories that amok may be a form of intentional suicide in cultures where suicide is heavily stigmatized. Those who do not commit suicide and are not killed, typically lose consciousness, and upon regaining consciousness, claim amnesia."[136] According to religious lore running amok is the result of possession by a demon or spirit such as a tiger spirit, or can be triggered by the power of a Keris. Western psychiatric literature of course perceives the phenomena through an entirely different lens, and once again a stark choice is presented between two opposite and incompatible explanations based on radically contrasting assumptions about the nature of reality.

Many years earlier Rob and I attended a dance that involved many men in a state of trance possession, thrusting the Balinese dagger or Keris against their bare chests and drawing no blood. We were sceptical that the dancers were in a trance providing spiritual protection from injury, and presumed it was all just a show for the tourists. The men in the dance were in a kind of frenzy, and the point of the Keris appeared to be being pushed hard against their skin, but I could not suspend my disbelief sufficiently to believe that they were really protected from injury by spiritual energies. However on the way in to the dance venue we peered over a temple wall and watched a priest performing a very serious ceremony with the dancers away from the eyes of tourists. Clearly both the dancers and the priest believed that spiritual forces were being invoked and the dance was not merely a performance to entertain foreigners. Bali is famous for its extraordinary dances often involving masks, walking across burning fires, and trances, that are closely connected with religion and ritual. Some have been adapted for tourists but many are still performed in villages in the most sacred part of the temple for spiritual purposes not foreigners. Dances involving the Barong and the Rangda, portrayed by masked dancers, exemplifies the Balinese division of the world in to opposing forces in constant tension. The Barong somewhat resembles a Chinese dragon figure with the face of a lion. He represents good. The Rangda is a fearsome witch figure portrayed by a terrifying mask reminiscent of Durga or Kali, with the same coloured iconography of black, red and white. Her tongue is lolling out with a necklace of skulls around her neck, her naked pendulous breasts dangling and her fangs bared she is the personification of evil, an eater of babies in perpetual conflict with the Barong. Each village will have its own Barong and Rangda masks and they are regarded as possessing sacred power, the Rangda mask being kept in a village's temple to the dead. There is no clear winner in the ongoing duel between good and evil, the Rangda being always ready and waiting for another round of conflict with the Barong. The aim is not to eradicate evil but bring about balance so as evil forces do not become out of control. To complicate matters in some parts of Bali the Rangda is also seen as a protective figure similar to Kali or Durga.

Rangda is the queen of a unique Balinese phenomenon, the leyak, a practitioner of black magic who has studied the lontars or sacred texts but uses them to aquire supernatural powers to cause harm to others for their own advantage. During the day a leyak looks like a normal person, but at night his or her spirit transforms in to another form where it can fly and can kill, poison food, insert foreign objects in to the body, cause illness or accidents, or any of a long list of dark outcomes, and feed on the blood of its victims. Midnight is seen as a very dangerous hour as that is when leyaks are most active and their favourite haunts are graveyards and crossroads. People are most vulnerable to the assaults of leyaks when ill, injured, or a new-born baby, and are often surrounded by amulets to give them protection. A slice of raw onion will sometimes be placed on the fontanel of a new baby to protect it from the entry of a leyak. Balians are often consulted about protection from leyaks and they will provide magical mantras, amulets or objects to offer protection. If there has been a death the Balian may hold a kind of séance to identify the spirit responsible but taking vengeance is strongly discouraged. Terror of leyaks is why Balinese are very fearful of being outside late at night as that is when leyaks are active. At our hotel the foreign owner told me that no Balinese would walk along the path across the paddy field to the house at night because of that.

A fascinating aspect of Bali is how it manages to straddle two completely different worlds that co-exist in the same physical space whilst occupying opposite mental universes. One world is that of foreign tourism, bars, hotels, restaurants, theme parks, beaches, sun bathing, scuba diving, river rafting, cooking classes, mountain trekking, and whatever other activities visitors from elsewhere like to divert themselves with. The other world of traditional Balinese beliefs, rituals, religion, and customs, are often impenetrable to foreigners. An example of the two parallel worlds is the paradox that while so much of Bali's tourist economy is based on beaches and the sea, to traditional Balinese the sea is where dangerous spirits live and not to be trusted. Traditional Balinese culture such as gamelan music or dances are marketed as entertainment to tourists who are often oblivious to the rich and complex religious beliefs lying behind the dance and music performances. They are also mostly unaware that the pretty little offering canangs dotted on the footpaths every morning are to appease demons and the small offerings placed on the dashboards of cars are to protect from supernatural powers. It is almost impossible for a Westerner to understand the extent recognition of magical forces, kasaktian, plays in the lives and perceptions of the Balinese. The word kasaktian is rarely used and not discussed as even mentioning it can attract the attention of those dangerous forces which are everywhere, at all times, penetrating every aspect of life and the world.

We spend weeks in Ubud that has mushroomed from a quiet village to a busy town and tourist hub. Discovered in the 1930's by foreign artists and writers it has become a centre of cultural tourism and traditional Balinese arts, craft, music, painting and dance. The streets are increasingly busy with shops, art galleries, and restaurants ranging from Mexican and Pizza to traditional Balinese. The shops abound with the lovely and the tacky, the expensive and the cheap, the latter mostly mass produced in China. Much of the development has a random thrown together quality with shoddy looking store fronts tacked on to the front of old family compounds, with most of them catering entirely to tourists who wander up and down the warren of streets. We count numerous Ralph Lauren Polo shops selling the usual identical ware that could be bought in any city anywhere, from shoddily constructed premises that do little to promote the goods inside. I am shocked how much development had occurred since my last visit and how little planning appeared to be involved in the ever expanding sprawl of Ubud in to the surrounding villages and countryside.

The pristine quality of Bali has been much eroded by large scale tourism but every now and again the intense green of rice paddies and bamboo groves hovering down steep hillsides in to deep forested gorges still takes the breath away. When travelling by car vistas of exquisite Balinese countryside pop in to view through the strips of buildings strung along the roads. We visit artisans weaving lovely fabrics in a tiny village beneath the foot of the sacred Mt Agung. The cotton thread is hand dyed and stretched in the sun to dry before being hand woven in to traditional Ikat designs on ancient rickety looms at the back of a family workshop. It is a form of production millennia old and the artisan's skill and dedication to their craft is inspiring. The artistry of Balinese people is legendary be it wood or stone carving, cloth weaving, shell or egg painting, bone carving, furniture making, batik fabrics, jewellery, or Balinese style painting on canvas created by local artists. The paintings have become increasingly eclectic in style and subject matter embracing everything from Che Guevara, to Lady Gaga or Donald Duck, often in lurid colours, while the exquisitely subtle traditional works seen on earlier trips are harder to find. In the region surrounding Ubud virtually every village displays some kind of creative skill as well as extraordinary architecture and design expressed in the endless temples. Walking through Ubud offers glimpses through traditional Balinese gates of walled compounds in to exquisite gardens, raised pavilions, lotus ponds, and poleng clad statues just behind the façade of ugly shops and development. Once again Bali gives that odd sensation of two parallel worlds overlapping but not intrinsically the same, with Ubud the busy tourist town overlaying an ancient culture where spiritual forces swirl just below the surface of a bustling centre for foreigners. Ironically much of Ubud's new found wealth is spent on religious ceremonies that reflect a way of understanding the world utterly removed from that of the foreign tourists who are the source of that wealth.

Our hotel in Ubud provides a window below the surface dynamics of Bali that leaves me, as someone without spiritual framework, both curious and somewhat unnerved. The owners are a family half European and half Balinese. The story told of black magic, death, sickness, intrigue, and rivalry over property is chilling, and the other Bali of demons, sorcery, possession, and spirits peers out from below the pretty, happy, tourist paradise. This is a Bali where people live with the constant effort of controlling dark disruptive energies by religious vigilance, and walking at night brings threat from demons and spirits lurking everywhere. It is astonishing to learn that a main centre for black magic on Bali is the beachside tourist area Sanur where we will be spending our final time on the island and where Rob and I had stayed on previous occasions. It is a pleasant beachside village with a long strip of hotels mostly populated by foreign tourists lying around beautiful swimming pools, or strolling along its beachside paths enjoying the restaurants, totally unaware that Sanur is tenget, a place of great and dangerous supernatural power. It is difficult to know as an outsider what to make of this other Bali, but conversations with various foreigners who live there impress on us that it is indeed a mysterious island with dimensions beyond an outsider's understanding. Their experiences left them questioning their previous assumptions and uneasily veering towards acceptance that perhaps there are supernatural realities at work that cannot be explained.

A particularly interesting example of this are the Balians. Their activities are outside of anything I have ever known or could imagine, leaving me intrigued and a little apprehensive. I have no idea what to make of them. Spiritual tourism has become very big business in Bali and undoubtedly many foreigners are unaware of the spiritual forces they might be exposing themselves to. A visit to a Balian has become popular since the publication of **Eat, Pray, Love** and the release of the movie starring Julia Roberts, but the complexity and diversity of what they do is not explored in either the book or the film that have been described as reflecting New Age spiritual naivety. Whether the Balian falls in the category of white or black magic practitioner is very much determined by context and intention and extremely difficult for an outsider to distinguish the difference. Avoiding them altogether seems like a good idea given our ignorance and naivety as to what they represent. One European resident of Bali we spoke to was adamant that there were many examples of naïve Western tourists experiencing strange and negative consequences after dabbling with Balinese healers, Balians or magic that they were not equipped to manage because they represent a dimension utterly outside of their experience. Perhaps it is a little like Benny Shannon and ayahuasca which cast him adrift from everything he thought he knew with no spiritual framework to make sense of where he had been cast adrift to.

Conversations with a friend who had lived in Bali for over twenty years, revealed much that is unfathomable and best not messed with. The idea of demons and supernatural forces lurking in the shadows of Balinese spirituality is confronting and not something to invite close exposure to. Are those spiritual forces real or mere superstition? I have no idea, but erring on the side of caution seems like a good idea. It is easy to dismiss belief in spirits and magic as superstition but Bali has the capacity to undermine assumptions and challenge the certainties of people from Western rationalist, materialistic, science based societies, leaving me utterly floundering. Do spiritual forces actually exist or is the entire range of religion, spirits and magic on Bali just a case of superstition in a "demon haunted world," as are all religions and beliefs in supernatural realities everywhere? Those are questions without clear conclusions but the words of Hamlet regarding the vision he had seen of his father's ghost springs to mind: "There is more in heaven and earth than dreamed of in your philosophy Horatio." It is not possible to be absolutely sure that supernatural realities don't exist and exposing oneself to potentially unknown and unknowable forces seems foolish. It would be like opening Pandora's box, unleashing energies best kept at a distance.

We visit many temples some of which were missed on previous Bali trips. As always they are both beautiful and mysterious, and the sight of the people in them deeply absorbed in making offerings or prayers is moving. They are approaching something that I have no way to approach and have no certainty even exists. We aim to reach Pura Besakih the mother temple of Bali and its most sacred space high on the slopes of Gunung Agung, Bali's sacred mountain and an active volcano that has been rumbling and spewing ash and smoke for months, many villages at its base having been evacuated. The journey leads through spectacular scenery, wild forest, deep ravines, and lush rice paddies in varying shades of intense luminous green. Dotted across the landscape are small shrines to Dewi Sri the rice goddess seeking her aid for plentiful rice harvests. Sarong clad figures with large eyed small Balinese cattle wander past as the vehicle speeds through scenes of village life that could have been from a thousand years ago except for the cars, motorbikes and little warungs with fridges full of coca cola. A group of men are gathering a short distance from the road and the driver informs us it is a village cock fight, a tajeng, in progress. He pulls over so we can see for ourselves this event that despite being banned still goes on across Bali with the authorities usually content to ignore them.

These fights have a long history as a religious event called tabuh rah or "the spilling of blood" to propitiate demon spirits, but are now mostly opportunities for gambling and male contests of pride in their "cocks", the double meaning of the word being applicable in Bali as elsewhere. Hundreds of men shout bets in a scene of pure chaos, their roosters crowing raucously from woven bamboo baskets. A long thin steel blade is strapped to one of each bird's legs and a series of fights unfold in the middle of the crowd as the gamblers wager and yell and money is exchanged. The birds are thrust in to a dual to the death that is fast and efficient, the winning bird a source of much pride to its owner, the losing birds being not wasted but presented to the winner's owner and taken home to eat. In Nepal the animal sacrifices at Dakshinkali Temple had stirred up conflicting responses to practices such as this, and I knew I must be careful as a person who eats chicken not to reach easy judgments. The death of the fighting rooster is perhaps better, and certainly not worse, than that which awaits a chicken carted off to mass slaughter ending up on a plastic tray in a supermarket, having most probably lived a miserable life in a cage in a commercial chicken farm where they can't walk let alone enjoy a life. I am acutely aware of my own hypocrisies as a meat eater who really doesn't want to see the truth of what they are eating: the flesh of a once living creature that would have experienced terror at the moment of its death. In Australia chickens are slaughtered by being hung upside down on a conveyor belt, passed through an electric current to stun them, and then have their throats cut by a machine. On balance perhaps the fighting cocks have a better deal of it than commercially farmed chickens because they lead a good life of freedom and indulgence from their adoring owners, and their death is usually fast, clean and not more terrifying than being hung upside down on a death machine conveyor belt. Recently a friend who had lived in Timor described how cocks that fail to perform are sometimes beaten to death with a stick by their enraged owner, as he had personally witnessed, so once again drawing any kind of conclusion becomes a quagmire of contradictions.

Animal sacrifice is an important dimension of Balinese Hinduism, more so than in India where the teaching of ahimsa, or do no harm to any living being, is strong. Balinese Hinduism holds the deities of Siwa (Shiva) and Durga as central, and its Hinduism is a strongly Tantric form associated with animal sacrifices, as it also is in Nepal. Balinese and Nepalese Hinduism are closer to each other in many respects than either of them are to the Hinduism of India. So how does animal sacrifice express itself in Bali? Fred Eiseman, Jr., explains animal sacrifice, or caru, in **Bali: Sekala and Niskala**: "In the Hindu faith, one must take the bad with the good, and while the Gods must be worshiped, the demons—in respect for their great power—must be placated. And the demons, the leering and fanged bhutas and kalas, have great and gross appetites. Caru range from a fairly simple offering requiring the sacrifice of a single chicken, to elaborate ceremonies involving the slaughter of dozens of animals." Rajiv Malik in **Hinduism Today**[137] explores Balinese animal sacrifice explaining the practice of Buta Yadnya: "We follow Durga and Siva, who are two sides of the same coin. We worship Durga if we want something magical. She is extremely popular in Bali, and every home worships Her every fifteen days with animal sacrifice. Every hundred years we have to perform the Ekadasa Rudra festival in which more than 200 kinds of animals are offered. Though most people I interviewed avoided this question, I gathered that a family may typically offer between five and two dozen animals per year in various ceremonies, according to its means..." **Hinduism Today** goes on to recount the experiences of an Indian born restaurant owner in Bali's capital Denpasar: "Animal sacrifice is done in a big way here, close to the culture prevailing in Bengal. When we opened our restaurant, Balinese Hindu priests conducted the ceremony, which began with killing and burying a dog out in front. Then a pig was roasted, grilled, worshiped and buried. They killed fifty chickens, burying them in the various corners of the building. I had requested all of this not be done, but I was told it had to be done according to the local traditions, that animal sacrifice is an integral part of any big ceremony. We had to follow the customs; we were told that if we did not, and something untoward were to happen later on, we would be blamed for it." Bangbungkem puppies, which have browny-orange fur, are sacrificed in Mecaru Balik Sumpah ceremonies to cleanse the surroundings of bad spirits, it being believed that the sacrificed dog will be reincarnated as a human. This is also the case in Nepal as it is believed sacrificed animals will have a better incarnation in their next life in samsara, perhaps as a human rather than an animal, a human birth bringing with it the possibility of escape from rebirth in samsara.

The journey to Besakih begins to feel a big mistake as we pass deserted villages, their residents moved out of harm's way from the potentially erupting Gunung Agung. Our driver's cheerful reassurances are of little comfort as we pull in to the entrance area of the Besakih temple complex and most of the shops are closed with almost no one there. The volcano rears up behind the temple and plumes of smoke and ash can be seen spurting out, the smoke gathering at its crater creating a strange atmosphere of simmering power ready to explode at any moment. Gunung Agung is Bali's most sacred mountain and regarded as the home of Mahadewa, a manifestation of Shiva, every village and temple in Bali being built on an axis between Gunung Agung and the sea. Gunung Agung has erupted many times the first known event being in 89 AD. In 1963 it erupted with devastating consequences killing thousands of people, and at the time of our visit an eruption had been expected for months. All over Bali people are praying, asking for forgiveness and making offerings to calm the wrath of the gods believed responsible for volcanic eruptions. It is possible to climb it with a guide who will pray to the gods for protection before starting. Some claim Gunung Agung is angry and ready to explode because tourists have been having sex on its slopes during their trek to the summit.

Visiting so close to a volcano that could erupt at any time is undoubtedly stupid, but the enormous Besakih Temple complex of twenty-three temples is an incredible sight I'm glad we do not miss. Pura Besakih has been a sacred place for over a thousand years and some parts of the oldest temples date back to the fifth century. We wander around Besakih for hours, glancing up at Gunung Agung and its cap of smoke and ash against a brilliant blue sky, pondering the Balinese view that this holy mountain is the home of gods who if angered will rain destruction on Bali and its people, just like many Nepalese believe the gods punished them with earthquakes. Christian leaders, such as Bishop Jensen in Australia, stated that the Asian Tsunami of 2004 was a punishment from God for human sinfulness so the idea that natural disasters are the product of spiritual forces exists across cultures and religions. Does it come down to either the world is in the hands of sometimes vengeful gods, or a world where there are no gods at all? Neither of those seems appealing and the old conundrum remains.

Are we all journeying round on the wheel of samsara according to karma, governed by maya or illusion, as spiritual beings in a spiritual reality masquerading as a material reality, where unseen forces are suffused through every aspect of that material world? Or do we, and all life, inexplicably find ourselves in an entirely material world where there are no spiritual realities and any belief to the contrary is nothing but superstition? It would be wonderful to find a middle path, or is that attempting to have a bet each way on two mutually exclusive alternatives? Bali and its all pervading spirituality, as in Nepal, makes very obvious the stark nature of those opposites and the choice between them.

The last week in Bali is busy, picking up products and visiting more temples and archeological sites. It is the festival of Shivaratri, Shiva's birthday, and celebrations are happening in Ubud. A friend remarks that attendance at these events is dropping, and that particularly young people are not observing their religious obligations to the same extent as previous generations as they become caught up in global changes from the widespread use of internet and cell phone technology. Wherever we go people are utterly absorbed in their phones. One witty restaurant advertises its wifi availability with a sign "We have wifi so you don't have to talk to each other." It is common to see groups of people in the temples clearly there for religious reasons, as they are dressed in traditional clothes, but sitting on the edge of a wall or raised pavilion focused on their cell phones, just as people everywhere are. It is hard to know how this will pan out in Bali as religion and belief in supernatural dimensions, are so strong. Life in samsara is changing fast and the extent the old beliefs and practices will survive is unknowable, just as it is anywhere that traditional cultures have been swamped by new technologies and the ways of thinking that come with them.

Our last day is spent visiting Pura Tirta Empul, a very beautiful temple with holy water bathing pools for ritual cleansing. It is crowded with worshippers for the Shivaratri celebrations, its large pools filled with long lines of people making offerings and bathing under the stone spouts through which holy water from a spring up the valley is pouring through. It is a purification ceremony known as melukat to purify sickness and bad karma from present and past lives. A couple of European tourists are in the line of people passing through the sacred pool and I wonder what the Balinese make of that. I wonder what the tourists make of it too. They seem sincere, respectful, and clearly longing to participate in a ritual that is satisfying a dimension of life they probably cannot access in their own culture. That is what Bali offers. A completely different way of understanding that infuses every moment and aspect of life in the material world with a transcendent spiritual dimension woven in to everything and everyone. Bali is a mysterious place where the numinous is everyday reality and everyday reality is suffused with the presence of spiritual forces. A spirituality such as possessed by the Balinese is both a blessing, and perhaps also something of a curse as there is no escape from the unseen presence of supernatural dimensions, constant effort and vigilance being required to prevent spiritual forces of disorder from destroying order. The aim is always to keep those in balance and harmony for the good of the world and all life passing through it in samsara.

There is profound gratitude that places such as Bali exist to remind twenty first century humans of what we have forgotten we don't know, and to invite awareness of the presence of the unseen as well as the seen. Spending time in cultures such as Nepal and Bali has opened other perspectives and eroded easy certainties. If, as quantum physics suggests and mystics have long claimed, consciousness is a field that gives rise to everything, including life as the experiencer of those, then the Balinese view of the world as full of vibrant forces and energies, good and bad, with which we interact through the medium of consciousness, does not appear so utterly impossible. That is a disconcerting idea for someone like me from a culture like mine and without any spiritual framework of belief. It is easy to understand why Benny Shanon felt so disconcerted by his experiences with ayahuasca in the Amazon: they forced him to face possibilities that contradicted his faith in rational and materialistic interpretations of the world. I'm not sure whether to be glad of the possibilities that cultures like Nepal and Bali suggest, or afraid of letting go convictions that matter and our awareness are utterly separate, and belief in demons, deities, and spiritual forces pure fantasy. We leave this magical island stranger than anywhere Disneyworld could dream up with many more questions than answers but determined to return. The next step will be to Cambodia, and then finally to India, the place where ideas surrounding rebirth and samsara were born.

"Where there are humans
You'll find flies,
and Buddhas"
Issa

CHAPTER EIGHT
CAMBODIA

The traumatic past of Cambodia looms large as the flight descends through heavy cloud over broad swathes of the Mekong River spreading across the plains near Phnom Penh. The airport is new and surprisingly smart and the visa processing system efficient and brisk. The immigration officials are surly and vaguely hostile, to be expected considering the history of European interactions in Cambodia, first appropriated by French Imperialism and then bombed relentlessly by the Americans during the war in Vietnam, President Nixon remarking that the US would "bomb Cambodia back to the stone age". This generated forces of nationalism and resistance to French rule and against American bombing, offering hope for an independent and fair Cambodia but instead unleashing the horrors of the Cambodian genocide perpetuated by the Khmer Rouge. Most Cambodians are Theravadan Buddhists acutely aware of the unsatisfactory nature of samsara brutally apparent in a country where so much slaughter has taken place and the reality of impermanence and suffering inescapable and obvious. In Australia it is easy and tempting to avoid acknowledging the ubiquity of suffering but that is impossible in Cambodia.

Phnom Penh has the chaotic air of many Asian cities but with a harder edge than most, the obvious poverty in glaring contrast to those whizzing by in Range Rovers and Lexus, the streets a jumble of motorbikes often with whole families aboard and not a helmet amongst them, motorbike Tuk Tuks, cars, bicycles, pedestrians, skinny dogs, people sitting on broken pavements, fruit, soft drink and street food vendors wheeling their wares through it all. We are met at the airport by the brother in law of a friend who delivers us to our small and pretty hotel half a block from the National Museum where we hide for an hour or two. The heat is overwhelming and like many from wealthy countries we are happy to escape to the comfort of the hotel away from the chaos just over the top of it's high razor wired wall, the swimming pool we take such pleasure in being a luxury beyond imagining to the vast majority of Cambodians. Coca Colonization is everywhere and its bottles and tins clog the gutters. We buy two bottles for one US dollar each reflecting on the fact that a third of Cambodians live on around three dollars a day, less than the cost of a small local beer or three Cokes.

It seems beyond the powers of government to provide for the poorest Cambodians or provide garbage collection of any kind. Awful piles of festering litter are scattered everywhere, plastic bottles, bags, food, food containers, plastic spoons, straws, stinking nappies, no one seeming to have any idea where to put rubbish but dump it in a pile or drop it where they stand. Individual homes and businesses are often immaculately swept and the garbage is then transferred to the drain next door or the gutter in front. This is more of the same we see continually on our travels, garbage garbage everywhere, mostly plastic. If it is collected then it's dumped in a river, or an empty bit of land, or behind a wall, or piled together in small garbage mountains that no one knows what to do with so they just keep growing. I watched several times in Nepal a truck backing up to a small river then proceeding to offload its entire load of collected waste straight in to the river to flow on downstream, clogging up the waterways and eventually ending up in the ocean before finally breaking down in to toxic micro plastics.

Phnom Penh is a city of little charm, that being utterly unsurprising given Cambodia is one of the poorest nations on earth with a turbulent, brutal, twentieth century history. The legacy of this is disturbingly apparent with unexploded landmines still maiming and killing many Cambodians every year, and it's political situation continuing fraught with problems. The leader for over thirty years, Hun Sen, is an ex Khmer Rouge cadre and the elections of 2018, that reinstated him for another term were regarded as a complete sham, involving brutal repression, intimidation and extreme corruption. Cambodia is in practice a one party state, without tolerance of dissent or a free uncensored press, so the oppression of the Cambodian people continues in the twenty-first century.

The land that is now Cambodia has shown evidence of occupation since the seventh millennium BCE. Great kingdoms such as Funan ruled most of Indochina from Vietnam through much of Thailand up until the sixth century. The time of Cambodia's greatest achievements were under the Khmers from the 8th until the 14th centuries, reaching its pinnacle under the Khmer rulers based at Angkor near Siem Reap. The incredible artistic, cultural and architectural legacy they left behind includes some of the greatest architectural masterpieces ever created, and Angkor Wat remains the largest religious structure on earth. The remarkable achievements of the Khmers have shaped the history and culture of much of South East Asia leaving a legacy that continues to the present day. We hope at a later date to visit the ruins of the great Khmer temple complexes of Angkor but our first concern is finding our way in the strange street numbering system of Phnom Penh and getting some sleep after the all night flight. Later that evening we take a tuk tuk to Sisowath Quay, expecting a gracious legacy of French Colonial rule but finding a depressing ugly strip along the edge of the rubbish strewn Mekong River, with gelati bars and Mexican food outlets promoting themselves alongside tawdry shops selling cheap trinkets and plastic goods from China. At a local night market we perch on mats on the ground picking at some not very appetizing dishes served with cheerful good humour. Music is playing by a small band of land mine victims and their children never letting us forget for a moment what these people and this city have been through. Cambodia is a constant assault on one's faith in any possibility of divine providence, or the goodness of human nature, with so much evidence to the contrary everywhere to be seen.

The forty degrees plus temperatures are extremely challenging and we are exhausted. There are meetings planned with producers of Cambodian handcrafts and this brings us face to face with the brutal realities of Cambodia's past as we visit workshops supporting and employing land mine victims and street kids. Land mines and unexploded bombs remain a devastating legacy of war both from the American bombing during the Vietnam War and the Khmer Rouge, and each year thousands are maimed or killed by explosion of these still lurking in vast numbers. We visit one workshop managed by a woman who lost her leg aged twelve when collecting wood for her family in the forest. Her friend who was with her was killed in the explosion. She points proudly to a photograph of herself with Princess Diana during the latter's campaign against land mines. Her artificial leg and foot are made from carved timber, as are the artificial limbs of the other disabled workers in the workshop. Her courage and her optimism are extraordinary and inspiring in circumstances that are a product of the worst of human behaviour and history that she, and countless others, were caught up in circumstances utterly beyond their control. I would have liked to talk over the question of karma with the Cambodian Buddhist monk who was walking past the workshop, but unfortunately there was no opportunity to do so. We purchase beautiful silk bags and wallets made by people in home made wheel chairs still at work late in the day yet able to greet us with warmth and friendliness. No one seems to bear me any ill will for being Australian, a country that participated in the Vietnam War with the United States and so indirectly implicated in the devastation of Cambodia. Film footage of the Vietnam War played on the news channels during the early seventies broadcast scenes of destruction and death in to living rooms throughout Australia while young men were compulsorily 'called up' to fight in Vietnam according to a lottery based on their date of birth. The image of a young Vietnamese girl running alone down a road seared with napalm was one the whole nation recoiled to in horror that this was something our country was participating in. Australia had weighed in to that war as an ally of the United States, "all the way with LBJ" (Linden Basil Johnson), under the leadership of Prime Minister Robert Menzies in 1962, and many young men lost their lives, were injured, or suffered a life time of psychological fallout and PTSD as a result.

Years ago I purchased **The Sorrow of War**, on the streets of Hanoi, written by an ex-soldier of the North Vietnamese 'enemy,' and the shock and guilt he described mirrors that of soldiers on the other side for whom equal trauma unfolded. He was a devout Buddhist and believed himself to have incurred much bad karma for killing American and other soldiers. At that time feelings and divisions ran deep in Australian society as to participation in that war and I remember with shame how little understanding I had of the plight of a young conscript forcibly sent to fight in a country many of them would have barely known where it was. Later, when at the land mine museum near Siem Reap, the full horror of land mines and the American bombing of Cambodia and the Khmer Rouge rule is graphically demonstrated. It dawns on me how clueless I was during the Vietnam War, and then in the late 70's under the Khmer Rouge regime, about the enormity of what was going on in Cambodia.

There are many people who have arrived from outside Cambodia keen to help and they are doing so in great numbers. Sadly there are also those who see the poverty of Cambodia, and the vulnerability of its people, as opportunities to exploit. Our hotel features a small brass plate at the entrance stating "sex travellers not welcome here," a clear reference to the gritty realities of sexual exploitation in a poor and highly disorganized country where corruption is rife. Young kids are commonly trafficked in to the sex trade, their poverty and lack of education making them easy prey. I notice two men at our hotel, Australians by the sound of their accents, sitting at breakfast with two heavily made up very young looking women. At a guess they are prostitutes they have purchased for the night. The next morning they are there with another two, and the morning after with yet another pair. The girls look embarrassed and ashamed and keep their heads down, the Cambodian staff clearly uncomfortable with their presence. I finally can restrain myself no longer and speak with one of the men who confirms they are prostitutes and that's why they are in Cambodia. This is such a contrast to those who are trying to rescue girls from the clutches of an ugly prostitution trade and its consequences, many of them sold in to prostitution as children. Cambodia has a very high HIV infection rate and prostitutes suffer much abuse, violence and misery.

As humans travel through samsara the disparities between advantage and disadvantage, poverty and plenty, comfort and misery appear randomly and unfairly allocated seemingly without justice or logic. Why are some destined to live much harder lives and carry the heaviest burden of suffering and others not, simply because of accident of birth? Life backs people in to many corners of circumstances beyond their control, casting them to a life of suffering, poverty or deprivation that appears randomly allocated, but if the law of karma is true then our lives, including suffering, are not random or accidents. That disgusts me to think about as those wealthy selfish men disappear from the hotel lobby with their parade of sold women bought with their white skinned, rich country, privilege. A place like Cambodia brings out the absolute worst and best in human behaviour and both are on graphic display.

It is in Cambodia we see the absolute horrors of the killing fields and Khmer Rouge torture centres, but also meet modest self-effacing saints working hard to do their bit to release sentient beings from samsara's ocean of suffering. The determination to alleviate the pain of others, apparent in the many inspiring people we meet in Cambodia who are trying to counteract despair, parallels the Mahayana Buddhist path of Bodhicitta:

" May I be an isle for those who yearn for land,
A lamp for those who long for light;
For all who need a resting place, a bed;
For those who need a servant, may I be their slave."
Śhāntideva, **The Way of the Bodhisattva**.

As an example an Australian woman walking down a street in Phnom Penh heard a screaming little girl calling out for help from a small lane. With incredible courage she went to her aid as the child was being sold to a group of men intending to sexually abuse her, a not uncommon story. That woman could not turn her back and went on to found Daughters of Cambodia to assist families and young women to avoid the horrors of rampant prostitution in a country where extreme poverty drives the realities of survival for so many, particularly children. We feel overcome by the intensity of the problems so obvious in the city but also filled with hope and gratitude for the people who face that with determination to help in positive ways. Cambodia is a rollercoaster of opposites. Returning to the hotel at the end of each day dripping in sweat and eager to escape the heat and chaos, we are aware what privileges the air-conditioning and swimming pool are. Places like Cambodia stir guilt because people such as us take for granted eating well and living in comfort, never obliged to sell our bodies to feed ourselves or our families. We can escape the poverty, garbage and chaos simply because of economic advantage that most Cambodians do not possess, and justifying that by "its karma" seems a terrible glib cop out, a blaming of the victims and an evasion from active concern about social justice.

The following few days are spent touring more workshops that create beautiful objects from recycled waste materials that are innovative and imaginative. We find ourselves in the showroom of an Italian man who had come to Cambodia fourteen years earlier to adopt a Cambodian child and never left. He has used his skills as a jeweller to set up the organization Education For The Future, where young homeless Cambodians receive an education and learn skills to recycle brass bomb casings in to necklaces, bracelets and earrings. Creating this beautiful jewellery provides young people with a chance to escape the vicious cycle of poverty and prostitution. The products are gorgeous, and bomb casings are a material in great abundance in Cambodia as a legacy of both the American bombing and the Khmer Rouge, the countryside remaining littered with unexploded ordinance. The bombs are gathered and detonated by licenced army teams so as to prevent local people trying to collect them and risk their lives to sell the brass. We take photographs of earrings lying on the top of an exploded land mine with bomb-shells piled around them, shocked at the realities behind his work and awed by his response to them. There is something about people like this that defies easy description, a quality of goodness that they emanate in their response to dire need with some positive concrete action to help and this Italian jeweller is one of them.

In the corner on the floor is a small shrine. Buddhist shrines are common in houses, shops, or gardens, with incense and offerings lovingly placed. But this particular shrine contains not Buddhist figures but those illustrating the life of Jesus and the Virgin Mary with a tiny nativity scene at the back. Clearly this man possesses a faith that sustains him in his endless effort to overcome evil with good as he lives a simple life, in a modest home, in a back alley, in a poor part of Phnom Penh. The twenty first century is an age where the Catholic Church has lost so much credibility amidst revelations of widespread child sexual abuse, cover ups, misuse of church power and funds, and disgust that it still prohibits contraception to prevent unwanted pregnancies. In countries like Columbia the power of the

Catholic Church and clergy remains strong and one of the commonest causes of death for young women is botched abortion. How dare an organization controlled by a male Pope and a male only priesthood, see fit to condemn women to uncontrolled pregnancies and the reality of STD's such as HIV because condoms are not permitted. But despite all the faults of the Catholic church as an institution many of its priests, monks, nuns and laity give service to educate and work to alleviate suffering and poverty and this Italian man is one of them.

Everywhere children are working, serving customers in markets, begging, clearly not attending school. We tour the enormous complex known as The Russian Market and watch young girls perched on the concrete floor spending their days cutting heads off fish in suffocating heat and smells. Young boys are loading whole cooked pigs on the the back of a tuk tuk their skins stained a dark glistening brown from being roasted with some kind of soy sauce glaze, flies gathering around as they are readied for transport to destinations unknown. So many of Cambodia's people are young. The generation older than early forties is conspicuously underrepresented having been caught up in the Khmer Rouge genocide that only finished in 1979 when the Vietnamese entered Cambodia and took over. Anghkar, as the Khmer Rouge called their regime, controlled every aspect of life in Cambodia as millions were forcibly sent to work in rural communes. When the Khmer Rouge entered Phnom Penh in 1975 they were welcomed as liberators who would free Cambodia from the scourge of French colonialism and American bombing. Very quickly the truth emerged that the wholesale re-shaping of Cambodian society would be forcibly implemented, and anyone who was an intellectual or seen as collaborating with the French or Americans, or perceived as privileged, was stripped of their property and forced in to rural labour. Millions were murdered by the Khmer Rouge with estimates that as many as one third of the population was killed. Even wearing glasses was enough to trigger murder at their hands. Buddhist monks were a particular target in Anghkar's drive to eliminate those they regarded as parasites and representatives of religion, that being seen as an obstruction to the creation of a perfect communist state.

Despite the many inspiring individuals to be found in Phnom Penh the city is deeply shocking. Feeling the need for a break we book a couple of nights at an Eco lodge on the Tatai River in south-western Cambodia, close to the border with Thailand. We decide to leave visiting the killing fields and the S21 torture centre at Tuol Sleng until we return to Phom Penh. The Tatai is a remote region of dense jungle in the wild unspoiled Cardamom Mountains, having been preserved, ironically, by ongoing conflict with remnants of the Khmer Rouge. For years after the Vietnamese deposed Pol Pot in 1979 the Khmer Rouge continued to occupy and fight from this remote area so it was a no go zone until recent years. We leave our Phnom Penh hotel tired and ill humoured at five am and try in vain to explain to the tuk tuk driver where the bus station for our bus to Koh Kong departs from. We lurch wildly around the early morning streets, already chaotic and crowded trying desperately to navigate him on MapsMe, a great little app that works offline. He rose to the occasion and after a few wrong turns screeches to a halt in front of our bus that is just beginning to pull away. The driver is not pleased to see us as he has apparently sold our tickets purchased online to someone else and there is no seat for us. A stiff conversation ensues and finally our seats are returned to us.

The bus is old and shabby and the shiny fluoro pink satin window treatment faded and torn with large brown stains, but at least we are on our way. The drive through the outer fringes of Phnom Penh takes us from wide tree lined boulevards that looked like a legacy of French rule, to increasingly shabby and ugly streets strewn with garbage and evidence of great poverty. I fall asleep and probably snore to the amusement of other passengers. The air conditioning is barely limping along and the heat unbearable: how we will survive nearly six hours of this is hard to imagine. The temptation to grumble is great and we do so freely to each other until progressively silenced as more and more people keep boarding the bus and sit quietly, with no complaints and great dignity, on the floor. It puts us, and our sense of tourist entitlement, in a very bad light that these people can smile graciously through what we find an ordeal. The bus lurches on through a dusty landscape desiccated by the late dry season intense heat. Scrawny cattle wander the roads trailing ropes and grumpy looking water buffalo scratch themselves in the empty ricefields, beautiful white birds like egrets often perching on their backs.

Many of the village homes strung along the roadsides are once charming structures, built high above the ground with long staircases to the first floor. Some are timber with lovely shuttered windows and pitched roof-lines attractively roofed in palm leaf thatching. Unfortunately many have been brutally altered with ugly concrete fill-ins downstairs, and large tin rooves thrust out from the original building to accommodate a car or motorbikes. Some of the homes look immaculately clean but many do not, and some are overwhelmingly filthy with garbage piled everywhere right to the front door. The problem of waste disposal in a society that offers no disposal solutions is extremely pressing and the curse of plastic trash glaringly obvious. There are some villages in which every home contains an area of depressed ground at the front completely filled with garbage, some with sad looking, half dead, lotus plants fighting their way through the plastic bags and bottles. It is a depressing sight and must be depressing for the people living amongst it. I found myself fighting with my privileged Western self yet again to not make easy and wrong judgments as to the filth and rubbish everywhere.

On a couple of occasions I drop trash just like everyone else because there are no alternative way of disposing of it. I vainly search for rubbish bins but they are never anywhere to be found except for tourist attractions like the National Museum. I soon realize that if I lived in the shoes of the residents of these villages I would be doing exactly the same as they do, just dumping rubbish in whatever hole or pile or corner that can be found, a massive amount of waste being produced by a culture of disposable plastic in poor country which has no system in place to get rid of it. The roads themselves are surprisingly good as this is a relatively new road built only after the final end of Khmer Rouge resistance. Traffic rules are virtually non-existent and the bus hurtles along dodging motorbikes, food vendors, tuk tuks, pedestrians, buffalos and dogs with great skill. The journey is broken a few times for toilet and food stops. The piles of meat and food sweltering in the heat alive with flies do not look appetizing, and nor do the boiled eggs with what appear to be fully formed chicks popping out of them. A large bowl on the corner of a food table contains a glistening pile of enormous cooked cockroaches, good protein for sure but my stomach turns as I look at them. We find people selling green mangoes and guavas and a small round sourish fruit that comes with a dipping mix of chilli, salt and sugar. It is surprisingly delicious and sustaining. The toilet is another major challenge but necessity is the mother of invention in that as in all things. Finally late in the sweltering afternoon heat the bus pulls in to a small bus station in the middle of nowhere.

This is it, Koh Kong, the launching point for our eco-lodge experience. Something is clearly wrong. The eco lodge explains by phone that we must get to the settlement of Tatai Bridge. Eventually a tuk tuk driver is located to take us the fifteen kilometres to the Tatai River Bridge where the eco lodge will send a boat. A smiling gracious pair of lodge employees arrives and bundles us in to the open wooden boat for the journey upstream. We pass a stunning pristine jungle landscape of towering bamboo, wild lush forest, coconut palms and dense mangroves lining the river banks. The trip feels more like the Amazon, or a journey in to Joseph Conrad's heart of darkness.[138]Savage but beautiful. The Eco Lodge is superb, constructed of tents and bamboo structures floating on the river. Bamboo ramps lead from each little hut straight in to the water that is limpidly warm, and we are assured, crocodile free. Nothing except jungle and river is visible apart from the occasional boat heading up river taking loads of Buddhist monks to some destination unknown.

We take a trip upstream the following day to an amazing complex of waterfalls busy with picnicking families bathing in pools at the top of the falls. It is also the destination of the groups of Buddhist monks who we had seen passing the day before. Walking along the jungle path large piles of plastic and garbage are accumulating to the side, little mounds of human excrement stinking in the sweltering heat. The falls are spectacular and we enjoy a couple of hours sitting with relatives of the boat driver who share their lunch and beers with warmth and generosity. One woman, who looks exhausted, tells us this is her first day off in months and her sharing her food with us so lovingly and acceptingly is a great lesson that somehow erases my disgust at the piles of garbage scattered everywhere. Happy laughing Buddhist monks pose with us for photos then clamber back in to their boat and are gone.

Thinking to take a little dip I swim out towards deeper water at the edge of the falls and am dragged in to the ferocious current taking me straight for a sheer drop that will undoubtedly bring death. It is a terrifying moment and nothing brings home the preciousness of life until you are about to lose it. Suddenly the boat driver lurches from a rock and grabs me, hauling me back to safety behind the rocks. He saves my life and risks his own to do so without hesitation. These people are teaching me lessons every day and they are lessons I very much needed to learn. I pause at a little Buddhist shrine set up near the falls and say thank you for both the lessons being given to me and my life being saved by a total stranger far braver than me. I have no idea exactly who or what I am saying thank you to, but nonetheless I feel gratitude for the blessings I am being given by whoever or whatever is giving them. I later discover several tourists have died at the falls doing exactly the same stupid thing but they were not so lucky as to have that wonderful boat driver.

Marck and a large group of Cambodian men, including the boat driver, entertain themselves by jumping from high rocks in to the swirling waters at the base of the falls. Having neither the courage nor the inclination to enter that raging current after a near miss with death, I watch from the bank. It is remarkable how little we think about the only certain fact of our lives, death, until we have a near brush with it and are shocked in to intense awareness of mortality. Perhaps that is part of why Tibetan Buddhists practice chod rituals in charnel grounds amongst corpses and Aghori sadhus choose to live in cremation grounds, cover themselves in human ash and keep human skulls as their company: to remind themselves of the inescapable truth that the human body will decay and die, as is the fate of all living beings, and denial is of no use whatsoever. I shudder, death has glanced at me, and Yama forgets no-one. I would much prefer to not think about that at all, except of course that kind of wilful denial is not possible and even less so after Rob's death. After leaving the falls the boat driver takes us up another absolutely secluded branch of the Tatai river deep in to the foothills of the Cardamom Mountains. We swim for hours in that wildly lovely spot, with not a shred of plastic waste to be seen anywhere, before returning to the Eco lodge tired but deeply content in the present moment and satisfied with our day. Perhaps my near brush with drowning has awakened an appreciation of each moment that is easy to lose in the maelstrom of life. The Eco lodge is a shining example of sensitive tourism development that leaves no footprint on the land creating a very special place of harmony and beauty. It is a wonderful escape from Phonm Penh and provides fortification to return and confront the awful truth of Cambodia's past.

Nothing can prepare anyone for places like the S21 Tuol Sleng Genocide Museum on the outskirts of Phnom Penh, one of an estimated one hundred and ninety torture centres across Cambodia. This is where massive numbers of prisoners were tortured between 1976 and 1979 before being sent to extermination in one of Cambodia's three hundred and thirty killing fields all over the country. At any one time it contained around fifteen hundred prisoners. We are tempted not to visit this place but that would be an act of cowardice denying the truth of what happened in this country and that is the worst insult the world can pay the Cambodians: to pretend their past didn't happen and not want to know. My father used to say that those who are ignorant of history are condemned to repeat it so there is no choice: this is somewhere that must be visited. Every Cambodian we speak to at the torture centre and the killing fields thanks us for coming and being willing to share with them what they have experienced. It clearly helps a little that people from outside see the truth of what happened in their country.

That humans are capable of what was done at places such as these is an awful fact to face, but they are and have been throughout time, history being written in blood and conflict. Samsara is often brutal and cruel as humans travel its treadmill of births and deaths. War after war, killing after killing, genocide after genocide, hatred after hatred, injustice after injustice, oppression and exploitation a constant story. Apparently there is more slavery now in the modern world than there has ever been but this is a fact obscured from general awareness. Twiggy Forest, the head of Australian mining corporation Fortescue Metals, has written extensively about modern slavery in all its awful forms, and full credit to him for doing so, it is much too easy to adopt wilful blindness to horrible truths. The S21 torture centre is a confrontation with the most cruel, vicious, fanatical acts humans are capable of, all done in the name of political liberation to create a future utopia. The Buddhist teachings about the three poisons of ignorance, attachment and hate tossing us all across "the sea of samsara" in an endless chain of karma, rebirths, suffering and deaths become graphically revealed stepping through the razor wire fence into a torture centre that was once Chao Ponhea Yat High School. As a teacher this is a stomach turning realization only made worse to discover that the superintendent of the torture centre, Kaing kek lew, or Duch, was a high school maths teacher. When S21 first opened those associated with the previous Lon Nol regime were arrested and tortured and confessions extracted, friends and family who were named were in turn arrested and tortured before being murdered. Soldiers, political leaders, intellectuals, Buddhist monks, anyone with an education, were rounded up as threats to the Khmer Rouge regime. Later when paranoia set in regarding political rivals, extensive purges of senior Khmer Rouge officials began much like as in Stalin's Russia or Mao's China. The place was finally exposed and closed in 1979 when the Vietnamese invaded and ousted the Khmer Rouge.

Upon arrival at S21 the prisoner would be photographed, stripped of all belongings and shackled by iron chains to the walls or floors with no bedding or blankets. Photographs of many of those prisoners are displayed in the museum, their eyes haunted by that terrible look that comes with falling victim to such evil. It is chilling. These were real people enduring the unendurable. Most of them would have been Buddhists, hopefully that might have been of some help to them even if any expression of religion was viciously repressed. Brutal beatings were continual and food consisted of four small spoons of thin rice gruel twice a day. Punishments included the forced eating of human excrement or urine. Prisoners would be interrogated within days of arrival at Tuol Sleng where they would be drilled in the ten rules that are displayed on a sign there now, not well translated from the original Khmer.

1. You must answer accordingly to my question. Don't turn them away.

2. Don't try to hide the facts by making pretexts this and that, you are strictly prohibited to contest me.

3. Don't be a fool for you are a chap who dare to thwart the revolution.

4. You must immediately answer my questions without wasting time to reflect.

5. Don't tell me either about your immoralities or the essence of the revolution.

6. While getting lashes or electrification you must not cry at all.

7. Do nothing, sit still and wait for my orders. If there is no order, keep quiet. When I ask you to do something, you must do it right away without protesting.

8. Don't make pretext about <u>Kampuchea Krom</u> in order to hide your secret or traitor.

9. If you don't follow all the above rules, you shall get many lashes of electric wire.

10. If you disobey any point of my regulations you shall get either ten lashes or five shocks of electric discharge.

The aim was to make prisoners confess to whatever crimes they were accused of and that was implemented with vicious beatings, electric shocks, burning with hot metal instruments, hanging and torture from various horrendous devices on display in the museum. Prisoners were cut with knives, suffocated with bags, or their fingernails pulled out with alcohol poured over the wounds, their heads held under water, or waterboarding, a torture technique adopted by the Americans at the Abu Graigh prison in Iraq. Although many prisoners died killing them was avoided since the Khmer Rouge were seeking confessions and the names of others who might be opposed to the Khmer Rouge or Pol Pot. Seeing the various torture instruments displayed in the museum is deeply shocking: they are the actual devices that have been used on real people.

The "Medical Unit" inflicted experiments on prisoners such as bleeding them to death to see how long it took and organ removal with no anaesthetic. These medical experiments parallel those inflicted by the Nazis on their prisoners in extermination camps during WWII. It is unimaginable how doctors trained to save and heal can bring themselves to participate in such horrors, but they did. Prisoners at S21 would often name hundreds of people as a result of these 'confessions' extracted by torture and then those people would be arrested for interrogation, the atmosphere of terror, suspicion and paranoia increasing towards the end of the Khmer Rouge regime. Many admitted under torture to collaborating with the CIA, the KGB or Vietnam, almost all of them innocent. As George Orwell shows in his novel 1984 a prisoner such as O'Brien, being tortured by rats eating his face in room 101, will betray anyone, as O'Brien betrays Julia, and is willing to admit to anything including that he loves Big Brother.

The vast majority of those tortured at S21 were Cambodian but also at least four hundred and eighty eight Vietnamese and seventy nine other foreign nationals including French, British, Canadian, American and two Australians. Some were captured sailing off the coast of Cambodia by sea patrols, having drifted in to Cambodian waters, taken to S21 and murdered. There were only twelve known survivors of S21, two of them children who died shortly after the Vietnamese took over Phnom Penh in 1979. Walking through S21 is a journey through what was a hell. Visitors and tourists silently contemplate the torture instruments, the cells where the shackles still lie on the floor, the glass cabinets full of skulls, the photographs of the damned displayed throughout. It is so disturbing no one can speak and room after room unfolds with yet more atrocities. When we finally complete our visit we are numb with shock at what we have seen and what humans are capable of.

The final place we visit is in many ways even worse than the S21 Tuol Sleng Genocide Museum, but we cannot leave Cambodia without also facing what happened there. After interrogation and torture at places such as S21 prisoners were then sent to mass extermination centres, 'killing fields,' scattered throughout Cambodia. Bodies of the murdered were buried in over twenty thousand mass graves discovered all over the country, with estimates ranging from 1.7 million to 2.5 million killed out of a total population of less than 8 million. UNICEF estimates the number murdered was closer to 3 million. The killing fields were depicted in the film of the same name covering this gruesome part of Cambodia's history.

Choeung Ek was the largest killing field, seventeen kilometres south of Phnom Penh in what was once a former orchard, becoming an extermination centre between 1975 and 1979 for perceived enemies of Angkar, the Khmer Rouge regime. People were sent for "re-education", which meant near-certain death or encouraged to confess to Angkar their "pre-revolutionary lifestyles and crimes," those being any contact with the outside world, foreigners, missionaries, international relief organizations, being educated, or land or business owners. They were told that Angkar would forgive their past but instead were taken to places such as Tuol Sleng or Choeung Ek to be tortured, murdered and buried in mass graves which are now visible as a series of huge pits once full of skeletons. To save ammunition poison, shovels, farming implements, steel bars, or sharpened bamboo sticks were used to kill the victims. One notice board at Choeung Ek describes how razor sharp fronds from a particular tree were used to cut prisoner's throats. There is a large tree on one side of the pits where children and infants were murdered by having their heads bashed against its trunk before they were thrown in the pits with their parent's bodies. As the murders were carried out at Choeung Ek a large loudspeaker high in a tree played loud music celebrating the Khmer Rouge regime, so as to mask the sound of screaming of victims as they were executed. Some victims were required to dig their own graves, others were made to kneel their wrists bound behind their backs as they were clubbed to death and then thrown in to the pit. This place is like entering an unimaginable hell. Everyone looks stunned as they walk around the site and read the various information boards beside the mass graves.

We find ourselves beside a large stupa with a huge glass core and walk up its steps. Inside the glassed centre of the stupa is an enormous collection of skulls, eight thousand of them dug up from the pits that have been opened at Choung Ek. Many of the skulls show sign of massive trauma from being bashed with iron bars or farming implements or bullet holes. This is a horrifying form of tourism but necessary if the truth is not to be ignored or forgotten. Humans forget what they are capable of at their peril. To ignore or not remember this this would be an unforgiveable insult to the suffering of the Cambodian people, so it is as important people visit these places as it is to celebrate Cambodia's incredible past in places like Angkor, capital of the great Khmer Kingdoms. We exit the gates of Choeung Ek desperate to sit for a few moments and reflect, ordering cokes as we make our way to a table. A man is sitting there and asks us about our visit. We find it difficult to know what to say. He then starts to tell his story. He is a volunteer at the Choeung Ek centre who comes here to feel close to his parents and siblings who were all murdered there in the late 1970's. As he spoke tears were pouring down his face and his voice breaking with emotion. He then thanked us for coming and told us how much it meant to him and all the other survivors of the Khmer Rouge that their story is remembered.

It is not only just a few rotten apples in the barrel that are able to commit the monstrosities that happened at S21, Choeung Ek, or Auschwitz, or the massacres of indigenous peoples during European colonialism, or the genocide in Rwanda, or the Armenians in Turkey, or the dungeons of the Spanish Inquisition, or the village of My Lai during the Vietnam War, where a whole village of civilians was murdered by a bunch of American soldiers from good middle class boy next door families. Given certain combinations of ideology, belief, power, and circumstances, ordinary decent people become capable of doing terrible things. It is Golding's **Lord Of The Flies** writ large, where sweet English choirboys degenerate in to violent murderers when isolated from social order and control. Eugene Gericault's painting in the Louvre, "Raft Of The Medusa" depicts a small raft adrift on the sea where the survivors ate each other one by one. The wreck of the Dutch vessel, the "Batavia," off the NW coast of Western Australia, reveals the same awful truth that humans can degenerate alarmingly easily into the worst kind of savagery, including cannibalism. A museum in Fremantle near Perth displays the remains of the "Batavia," a number of skeletons clearly showing axe marks on their skulls from their brutal murder. Perhaps one of the most shocking aspects of the holocaust is that nice middle class German families with children, went about their daily lives of socializing and birthday parties only a short distance from where Jewish people were being mass murdered in gas chambers and burned in places like Auschwitz, the smoke from the crematorium chimneys no doubt wafting over their homes as good Christian husbands, wives and children played together in the gardens.

Those terrible places, S21 and Choeung Ek, will haunt us and all those that visit them for the rest of our lives, but ignorance is not bliss and denial is not the solution to the potential for evil in the hearts of everyone that passes through samsara. We know that there is no going back to a naïve ignorance of the truths that Cambodia reveals. It is critical places such as S21, Choeung Ek, or Auschwitz, or the holocaust museum, are visited if Homo sapiens sapiens as a species is to have any hope of not repeating the same tragic mistakes over and over again, out of ignorance as to what they are capable of.

Perhaps political philosopher Thomas Hobbes was right when he asserted that the state of nature is a state of "all against all" a brutal fight for dominance and survival.[139] David Attenborough, in his TV documentary series **Life of Mammals,** reveals groups of chimpanzees in Uganda, our close relatives with whom we share 99.8% of our DNA, hunting each other in packs, ripping each other apart in the fight for dominance and hunting monkeys to eat them. Nearly all the perpetrators are male. In an interview Attenborough was asked what was the most distressing thing he had ever seen in animal behaviour to which he replied "Seeing chimpanzees kill monkeys, they do this to eat them. They chase them, set an ambush, catch them, and tear them apart."[140]It is so shocking that the film footage was not screened when the series was first shown and it raises very disturbing questions about human behaviour with it's thin veneer of civilization coating much more primal potentialities. As C.P. Snow put it "Civilisation is hideously fragile and there's not much between us and the horrors underneath, just a coat of varnish."[141] Novels can powerfully illustrate what can emerge in human behaviour under dictatorships or circumstances of isolation, conflict and social breakdown. **Brave New World, 1984, Oryx and Krake, Heart of Darkness, Lord Of The Flies,** the list is endless. Cormac McCarthy's **The Road** is a particularly horrifying account of what humans do to each other when reduced to a desperate need for survival in a post-apocalyptic world.

Experiments such as the controversial Milgram experiment shockingly exposed under controlled scientific conditions, what humans are capable of when instructed by an authority figure. It was run by Stanley Milgram of Yale University shortly after the Nazi war crimes trial of Adolf Eichman in 1961. It showed that a very high proportion of participants would be prepared to administer increasingly severe electric shocks to another person when instructed to, including lethal electric shocks.[142] The experiments demonstrated that ordinary people have a capacity for cruelty and a willingness to inflict pain on others, particularly when obeying orders of from an accepted source of authority, in places like S21 and Choeung Ek, or Auschwitz and Treblinka.

Samsara is where we experience and must deal with much that is dark in ourselves, and in the world, as the Tuol Sleng Genocide Museum and Choeung Ek killing fields graphically demonstrate. Buddhism makes no comment as to how and why samsara and humans are like they are, being silent as to the existence of a creator God. Hinduism suggests our experiences in samsara are about karma, learning and growth. We must experience both good and evil in ourselves, and others, and work through our karma as we move towards increased spiritual awareness, eventually reuniting with our source, Brahman, to realize bliss in moksha and liberation from samsara. Both Hinduism and Buddhism recognize that much of the pain of samsara has its roots in the tendencies of our own minds. This is described by the **Bhagavad Gita**: "For him who has conquered the mind, the mind is the best of friends; but for one who has failed to do so, his mind will remain the greatest enemy." The Dalai Lama expresses a similar understanding "…negative thoughts and emotions, the inner enemy, will always remain the enemy. They are your enemy today, they have been your enemy in the past, and they will remain your enemy in the future as long as they reside within your mental continuum. Therefore, Shantideva says that negative thoughts and emotions are the real enemy, and this enemy is within."[143]

Christianity talks of 'original sin' and 'the fall' in the garden of Eden, interestingly blamed on Eve as the instigator, a classic case of misogyny and woman blaming. Sociobiology, and the behaviour of chimpanzees shown in Attenborough's film suggest it is biologically hard wired in to us: territoriality is expressed as war and nation state conflict, sexual dominance as sexism and misogyny, and violence is a primal instinct. All of these perspectives are depressing in their views of human nature. Perhaps our best hope is awareness of that which is dark in ourselves and our world so as to be able to steer our way through those. Carl Jung talked much of the importance of recognizing and integrating our shadow, both personally and at the level of what he called the collective unconscious. Much effort is invested in taking groups of younger Cambodians through the museum at S21 so that their country's past is never forgotten, and a vital warning is given as to what humans are capable of and what must never be allowed to happen again.

Cambodia cuts very deep and there is no going back from what has been shown by S21 and Choeung Ek. Samsara is often a journey of extremes, as these places of such horror and suffering have made very clear. I am at a total loss how to process what we have seen and what unfolded here less than forty years ago, and ashamed of my ignorance of Cambodia's history before coming to this country. While the Khmer Rouge regime was happening I was travelling the world, studying at university, getting married, renovating a house, having parties, and living life almost oblivious to what was going on here. There were occasional mentions of Kampuchea and Pol Pot in the media, and the Vietnamese takeover in 1979 was briefly covered. **The Killing Fields** movie was released in 1985 but I didn't view it until years later. During Rob and my trip to Cambodia in 2008 we did not visit anywhere except the tourist mecca of Angkor, a selfish desire to escape dealing with Cambodia's dark past and indulge our own tourist pleasure keeping us busy exploring the magnificent temples. Rob had by that time received the results of a DNA test confirming he would develop the hereditary dementia that had afflicted his mother and grandmother, so shielding him from more horror than was already facing him down the track of his own life meant we both avoided the terrible truth of Cambodia and its history. But of course, as is the way of samsara, no amount of avoidance would delay or prevent the inevitable progression of the illness that was already stalking him. What a blindly privileged life I have led and the truth of how the pain of losing Rob and people dear to me is only one tiny drop in the endless ocean of suffering experienced by all sentient beings in samsara, becomes blindingly real. Cambodia shows the enormity of suffering as it really is, and Shantideva was right, Bodhicitta is medicine for a sick world. Understanding the truth about our human selves and the world are essential if we are to make any progress at all.

We leave Phnom Penh and try to turn our minds to another very different dimension of Cambodia's past: the extraordinary complex of temples and architecture covering hundreds of square kilometres at Angkor, capital of the ancient kingdom of the Khmers. We are haunted by what we have seen in Phnom Penh and Siem Reap near Angkor also had its killing fields and torture centres, but these are not shown to tourists. As a small child, a friend of my parents had described the monuments she had seen on a visit to Angkor in the 1920's as dazzling beyond compare. When in Siem Reap with Rob in 2008 we toured the

most famous temples and were stunned by the architectural achievements of the
Khmer people so many centuries ago. I had not thought to consider the tremendous
loss of life and suffering the construction of these massive stone buildings would
have meant for the labourers, and the constant power struggles between rivals that
were their back story. They are the "immortality projects" of great rulers defying
impermanence and death as much as monuments dedicated to Hindu Gods or
Buddhism. In **"Pyramis or House of Ascent"** Australian poet A D Hope describes
the building of the Egyptian pyramids as an "immortality project". The words of
the poem could equally well describe the monuments of Angkor:

"This is their image: the desert and the wild,
A lone man digging, a nation piling stones
Under the lash in fear, in sweat, in haste:
Image of those demonic minds who build
To outlast time, spend life to house old bones-
This pyramid rising squarely in the waste!

I think of the great work, its secret lost;
The solid, blind, invincible masonry
Still challenges the heart. Neglect and greed
Fret it away; yet, all fortetold, I see
The builder answering:"Let the work proceed!"
I think of how the work was hurried on:
Those terrible souls, the Pharoahs, those great Kings
Taking, like genius, their prerogative
Of blood, mind, treasure: "Tomorrow I shall be gone:
If you lack slaves, make war! The measure of things
Is man, and I of men. By this you live

No act of time limits the procreant will
And to subdue men seems a little thing,
Seeing that in another world than this
The Gods themselves unwilling await him still
And must be overcome; for thus the King
Takes, for all men, his apotheosis.

I think of other pyramids, not in stone,
The great, incredible monuments of art,
And of their builders, men who put aside
Consideration, dared, and stood alone,

Strengthening those powers that fence the failing heart;
Intemperate will and incorruptible pride."

Angkor on the hot plains of North-West Cambodia was the political heart of ancient Khmer kingdoms from 802 until 1431 CE, covering around two hundred square kilometres. The scale of construction and magnificence of the temple complexes, moats, and waterways is one of the wonders of human achievement, even if much of it has vanished in to dust. What remains are the temples, bridges, sculptures and waterworks built of stone, the enormous timber palaces and cities of timber long rotted in to oblivion. The crumbling edifices of stone emerge from the jungle and new discoveries continue to be made. Percy Bysshe Shelley's 1818 poem **"Ozymandias"** captures both the grandeur and the tragedy that places like the pyramids or Angkor display, as they bear testament to people and cultures vanquished by decay and impermanence, the inescapable truths of samsara:

"I met a traveller from an antique land
Who said—"Two vast and trunkless legs of stone
Stand in the desert. . . . Near them, on the sand,
Half sunk a shattered visage lies, whose frown,
And wrinkled lip, and sneer of cold command,
Tell that its sculptor well those passions read
Which yet survive, stamped on these lifeless things,
The hand that mocked them, and the heart that fed;
And on the pedestal, these words appear:
My name is Ozymandias, King of Kings;
Look on my Works, ye Mighty, and despair!
Nothing beside remains. Round the decay
Of that colossal Wreck, boundless and bare
The lone and level sands stretch far away."

Everything, the greatest buildings, greatest empires, and all living beings, come in to existence then dissolve and pass, undone by time and change. The dancing Nataraja Shiva expresses that reality as he dances the dance of creation and destruction on the prostrate form of ignorance within a circle of flame representing samsara. Alone among living beings humans struggle against this and seek permanence in their lives through the buildings they create, the dynasties of rule they establish, wherever and however they can. The enormous edifices of stone at Angkor built to honour the Gods and Buddhas, are crumbling gently in to the ground and in a thousand years will most probably be entirely gone, as perhaps too will humans if they keep treating the planet with disrespect and global warming is not halted. Or maybe a world nuclear war will obliterate most of us and humans will start again climbing their way in to a new history.

At the mysterious and evocative temple of Ta Prohm massive tree roots entwine their way through what remains of the building, a powerful image of nature reclaiming her ground. It is the location of the Hollywood movie **Tomb Raider** starring Angelina Jolie. Ta Prohm was built as a Buddhist temple monastery during the reign of King Jayavarman VII (1181-1218) and the colonial French left the massive banyan, strangler fig, and silk-cotton trees in place, creating an atmosphere resembling the experiences of 19th century explorers. Ironically the trees are simultaneously agents of preservation, as without them the buildings would totally collapse, and also destruction, as their roots and weight break apart the masonry. If the tree dies so will the building it grows on. It is huge, beautiful and sad, a metaphor of power and impermanence, it's poignant carved deities such as Prajnaparamita shaped to resemble the long dead mother of the long dead King who ordered Ta Prohm built. Exquisite stone figures of devatas and apsaras are visible amongst the massive tree roots and on Gopura 111 is the most peculiar image of what appears to be a stegosauras dinosaur that no one has managed to successfully explain.

From Ta Prohm we move on to Angkor Wat, the largest and most overwhelming of the Angkor temple complexes. Built during the 12th century by Suryavarman II it was originally dedicated to the Hindu God Vishnu, the preserver and its layout is the form of a mandala representing the Hindu cosmos. At its centre are five huge towers to represent Mt Meru as centre of the cosmos and mythical place of the gods. Surrounding this largest religious building in the world is a huge artificial moat of water symbolizing the cosmic ocean. At some time during the 14th or 15th centuries the complex was converted to Theravadan Buddhist worship and alterations were made to the original building, Buddhist sacred figures being added to the pre-existing Hindu deities. The whole complex covers almost 200 hectares and the outer walls of the actual building encompass 82 hectares. The day is searingly hot, and walking across the enormous stone entrance causeways across the moat leaves me giddy with exhaustion and the grandeur of this place. We walk on through hall after hall, mostly well preserved, astonished by what is here. The rooves of the hallways are constructed in stone carved to imitate large tiles, many of the window openings being blocked by stone rails carved to imitate wood.

The most remarkable part of the temple is the approximately six hundred metres of bas-relief carvings two metres high covering the outside walls of the third enclosure. Most of the subject matter is Hindu from the Ramayana and Mahabharata epics although depictions of the processions of the ruler who built Angkor Wat, Suryavarman II, heavens and hells, also appear. The scale beauty and precision of these carvings and the details they reveal of the Khmer people, the power of their empire and rulers, their lifestyle, and their religious beliefs, are astounding. Life in samsara in 12th century Angkor is graphically depicted and all that is now left of that world is these monuments in stone that have outlasted the Khmer empire, its rulers and its people, by over eight hundred years. In eight hundred years will people from a future time wander through what remains of the grand monuments and buildings of the twenty first century speculating about the lives and beliefs of those who lived then and built them? The absolute transience of all power and all types of society, of everything and everyone, all mowed down by time, is graphically demonstrated by a place such as Angkor Wat. Our individual lives are just the merest little blip on the radar of history, bringing to mind the comment of Allan Watts about being "a brief light that flashes but once in all the aeons of time — a rare, complicated, and all-too-delicate organism on the fringe of biological evolution, where the wave of life bursts into individual, sparkling, and multi-coloured drops that gleam for a moment... only to vanish forever."[144]

Somehow I become separated from Marck and start to wander alone through Angkor Wat's maze of galleries, halls, and courtyards. Searching fruitlessly for an exit the heat becomes increasingly unbearable with no clues where to go. Being lost in in this massive structure in such temperatures is frightening, particularly without water. Various passers by indicate the way to get out and none of them turn out to be right. Perhaps they are also lost, the building is so huge.

Eventually a German tourist points and gesticulates towards an exit even if it is not the one we came in by. Being very close to collapse I make my way straight for a row of trees to the side of the building where a woman comes rushing from a small stall, takes my arm and leads me to a plastic chair in the shade and brings a cold drink. That kindness and care from someone who has probably worked since early in the morning, making a tiny income from selling snacks, is moving. I thank her, pay her for the drink and go searching for Marck who is standing where we first entered from the causeway across the water. He has been faithfully standing there for hours, understandably not happy at having to wait in the appalling heat. How people like rickshaw drivers and labourers survive doing hard physical work in the heat is a mystery, samsara certainly gives some people particularly tough life assignments.

After the exhausting debacle of the afternoon as Angkor Wat we return to our Siem Reap hotel to rest before a big night out for the Khmer New Year celebrated in April. In the centre of Siem Reap is a scene of joyous chaos filling the streets. Many thousands of mostly young people are dancing to heavy pounding music issuing from speakers wired up to poles and verandahs. Food stalls abound and alcohol is flowing freely but we see no signs of serious drunkenness or misbehaviour that is common in the streets of Australia on New Year's Eve. The really surprising part of the party is the talcum powder throwing and spraying from massive water pistols happening all around. Everyone is covered in powder and absolutely drenched which is perfect in the heat. It is great fun and the sincere happiness of the crowd is infectious.

There are a few sodden looking tourists too and the Cambodians give shy and sweet grins as they douse us in powder and squirt us with water, the girls giggling loudly. Police officers with massive machine guns stand gossiping and accepting talcum powder and water sprays with good humour, their guns an incongruous sight sprinkled in baby powder and doused by exuberant youths with water pistols. It continues long after midnight but by then we have called it a night, glad to have shared such a cheerful event with people whose recent history has offered so much trauma. This continue for several days and on the final night we travel back to Angkor for night dancing and festivities at various temples, celebrating the heritage of the Khmer people along with the New Year. Angkor Wat is lit up, its tall towers reflected in the huge moat, shimmering lights of candles in peoples hands and floating with offerings on the water. Families out together enjoying the evening is a real joy to watch, the power and beauty of Angkor's past still resonating so many centuries later.

We visit many more temples each astounding in it's own way. Some of them offer amusing sights such as the Buddhist monk preoccupied with operating his selfie stick and taking endless photos of himself as he wanders through the temple. Some temples are primarily Hindu, some Buddhist, and many are combinations of both, reflecting changes in dominant religious beliefs during the centuries of Khmer rule. The buildings themselves are a metaphor for samsara. Everything that manifests in the material world is impermanent and will return to the dust from which it came, including the massive monuments we are viewing, and us as the viewers. One of the most startling is the Bayon constructed from the late 12th to the late 13th centuries during the reigns of Jayarvarman II and Jayarvarman VIII. It is an enigmatic and puzzling structure with a maze like quality that began as Hindu and transitioned to Buddhist. It is comprised of a mass of towers carved with faces to create a kind of ascending stone mountain arising from the jumble of towers. Inside are shrines to Vishnu and Siva, Siva linghams, and a huge 3.6 metre tall Buddha seated in meditation that was reconstructed from pieces found at the bottom of a well, probably thrown there during one of the periods of struggle between Hinduism and Buddhism for dominance. Scenes of armies and battles with armies from the neighbouring Cham dynasty are portrayed on the bas-relief carvings in the outer galleries. In one carving a buffalo is tied up about to be sacrificed, as still happens in Nepal. Another bas-relief depicts men betting as a cockfight is about to begin, a tradition still common in Bali. Many representations of every day life are interspersed between battle scenes and scenes from Hindu mythology. It is a fascinating if confusing building, defying conventional logic and graphically illustrating the transience of daily life and the ubiquity of change and decay yet expressing the underlying commonalities of human experience. Love, family, friendship, cooking, eating, fighting, playing, power, war, jealousy, loss, joy, and hate, are carved in depictions that are both culture specific and universal across time and place.

Our final visit is to Banteay Srei, a small and exquisite temple twenty kilometres north of Angkor, built in the second half of the tenth century under the reign of Rajendravarman. The drive through the countryside brings glimpses of children playing, chickens scratching, buffalo grazing, people seeking out the shade and chatting. Large signs beside the road in English shockingly proclaim that if the sexual abuse of a child is suspected please phone the number given on the sign. One sign announces that any one caught sexually abusing a child in Cambodia will face prosecution in their home country. Those signs graphically underline the enormity of this horrible reality across Cambodia, and how immensely vulnerable economic inequality makes people's lives, particularly children and those trapped in unrelenting poverty. A child may be sold in to prostitution because a parent is desperately ill and there is no money for medicines or treatments, or for food to feed the remainder of a family. I cannot imagine the horror of the circumstances that could prompt something like this to happen or the baseness of the person who purchases children for an evil moment of entertainment.

How is it people who appear to be models of goodness and light, such as priests or scout masters, can hide in their shadow selves dark acts of sexual abuse? It was shocking to discover that St John of God, a Brazilian mystic and healer attracting many thousands of followers from around the world to his centre of healing near Brasilia, has been accused by hundreds of people, including his own daughter, of rape and sexual abuse. Australia's highest representative to the Vatican, Cardinal Pell, has finally been called to trial for alleged sexual abuse from decades earlier. On and on the same awful story repeats itself of the evils humans are capable of and their willingness to adopt pretence and deceit to hide them. It is as if the higher humans aspire the lower they fall, and the more they display the outer forms of religion the less the inner meaning of it is present, all of which reinforces distrust of religion in any of its forms.

We pass a small building with a sign in English describing itself as the Landmine Museum and make a mental note to stop there on the way back from Banteay Srei. A string of roadside villages display small stands selling home-made palm sugar and large pots of brown liquid bubble on open fires nearby. Women are seated beside enormous piles of palm fruits that are whitish, sweet, and not particularly pleasant, but are processed in to the delicious palm sugar much loved from childhood in Malaya. We buy a plastic jar of round palm sugar tablets and munch them as our journey continues. Banteay Srei is unique in many ways. It was not discovered by Europeans until 1914 and its stone apsaras were pillaged by the French in much the same way as the English helped themselves to marble friezes from the Parthenon in Athens, but in the case of Banteay Srei the missing carvings were recovered. The Greek government is still unsuccessfully seeking the return of the carvings looted by Lord Elgin from Athens. The building is constructed from a pretty pink sandstone that has proved remarkably hard wearing so the sharpness of the carving is well preserved, and beautiful apsaras, celestial singers and dancers, in exotic costumes laden in jewellery, spring from the wall in a gorgeous thousand year old scene. Stories from Hindu epics such as the Ramayana and Hindu deities, are carved in superb detail, many of them the same tales performed in the sacred dances of Bali. Imposing stone guardian lions guard the temple as they do many of Angkor's buildings, resembling the lion statues common in Nepal. It is a very small temple in comparison to the massive Angkor Wat, or Bayon, or Ta Prohm, but in detail, design and execution it is exquisite, often described as the jewel of Khmer art.

We reluctantly leave Banteay Srei so as to get to the Landmine Museum before it closes. This is to prove another of those lurching journeys from beauty to horror from evil to the possibilities of goodness that Cambodia provides in abundance. This country does not allow for banal superficialities or disguise of the opposites inherent to samsara, there is simply no escape from them. Even at Banteay Srei this is evident as young children are working selling postcards to tourists to help their family's economic survival rather than being in school where they might get a chance to escape the cycle of poverty. The Landmine Museum, was previously near the ticket booth for Angkor Wat but that closed in 2006. A Canadian charity, the Cambodian Landmine Museum Relief Fund, raised money and donations from around the world to build the new museum near Banteay Srei, opened in 2007. The Landmine Museum and Relief Facility began with Aki Ra, an ex-child soldier from the Khmer Rouge regime. He was ten when captured to fight for them along with many other children, armed with AK-47's and M-16 rifles and set to work to kill and plant landmines. After the end of the Khmer Rouge and Vietnamese occupation he returned to the villages where he had laid thousands of mines as a child soldier and began manually removing them, defusing them with homemade tools. This led to displaying the mines to tourists and the one dollar he charged was used to support children of land mine victims, or orphaned or maimed children he was caring for, many of whom had been abandoned by families unable to look after them. This eventually resulted in the establishment of the Museum in 1997. Now the base of the Museum facility has broadened and houses and educates children in need from a variety of situations from villages all over Cambodia. The Facility has its own school and teaching staff and volunteers from around the world come to help teach English, work in the Museum and assist in the office. It also funds the establishment of schools in the poorest areas of Cambodia having started twenty-two schools teaching thousands of children who would not otherwise have received an education.

In 2008 Aki Ra worked with the US based Landmine Relief Fund to set up a formal demining NGO, Cambodian Self Help Demining (CSHD), and they expertly and safely clear landmines throughout the country. Landmines and unexploded ordnance still litter the countryside with dozens of people killed or maimed every year, and it is likely this will continue for decades. This is the result of many years of bitter conflict from American bombing during the war in Vietnam, a brutal civil war, the horrors of Khmer Rouge rule between 1975 and 1979, followed by the Vietnamese invasion in 1979. The aim of the Landmine Museum is to promote awareness and gather support to overcome the terrible legacy of landmines and war. Visiting it is a shocking but inspiring as so many good people work tirelessly to alleviate the suffering that has been caused. We pass exhibit after exhibit telling the story of landmines and unexploded bombs in Cambodia and around the world. One large panel displays a map of Cambodia almost completely filled with red dots on the Eastern half of the country. Each dot represents a village or target area during the over 60,000 bombing missions flown by the Americans between 1965 and 1973, where around 540,000 tons of bombs were dropped on Cambodia. It began in 1965 when President Lyndon Johnson ordered the bombing of the Ho Chi Minh trail, a supply line for weapons and soldiers that ran from North Vietnam through Laos and Cambodia. Approximately 600,000 civilians died during American "carpet bombing" missions, many of the bombs being cluster bombs released from the air. They often failed to detonate on impact and so explode many years down the track when a farmer or child accidentally disturbs them. I was aware Cambodia and Laos were bombed but had no idea of its enormous extent and the devastating consequences of land mines and cluster bombs across the globe. That is the problem with ignorance: one has no idea what one doesn't know and so these terrible realities can be swept under the carpet of history out of sight out of mind. After a visit to this Museum that is no longer possible.

We notice at many of the larger temples groups of musicians, many missing limbs, who explain on a simple poster that they are land mine victims supporting their communities through music performances. One elderly man missing a leg from above the knee smiles with great grace as I place a twenty dollar note in the collection tin, knowing how pathetically little it is costing me to relieve a little of the guilt that comes with the unfairness of samsara. In my wallet is many more dollars and my ticket home to a relatively easy life, whereas for him there is no escape from poverty or earning a hard living by playing all day in the heat and dust for people from somewhere else, most Cambodians being unable to afford to visit Angkor. Cambodia annihilates easy and comfortable complacency about human history or human nature and the extremes of experiences in samsara are graphically revealed. Knowledge of this is both liberating and devastating: liberating because it is the truth and devastating because of the nature of that truth. The Buddhist and Hindu understanding of samsara as a deeply unsatisfactory place of inevitable suffering seems sadly accurate as we contemplate the realities demonstrated by the S21 torture centre, Choeung Ek, the Landmine Museum or the disabled temple musicians.

We head back to the hotel in a sombre frame of mind. We are leaving Cambodia the following day having seen so much that cannot be come to terms with or understood. This country will trouble us for the rest of our days. It will be strange to return home to Australia and all the first world problems that preoccupy so much time and energy, they seem utterly irrelevant from the perspective of Cambodia. We are deeply grateful for all the truths it has taught us about samsara, from its darkest dimensions to the incredible courage and dedication shown by those like the Italian jeweller and countless others who confront those dark dimensions with love and goodness. The latter are present day Bodhisattvas, although they would not think of themselves in those terms, providing endless inspiration and tireless service. They quietly affirm the message, be it delivered by Shantideva, Buddha, Krishna, or Jesus, that it is through compassion or karuna, and loving kindness or maîtri, that truth and hope are to be found as humans take their ever repeating journeys around the wheel of samsara.

Cambodia has been a powerful lesson about the fragility of human life and civilization. Permanence and certainty are illusions in a constantly changing world where the dark strands of human nature lurk in subterranean haunts in the depths of the human psyche. Being Buddhists Cambodians understand the nature of impermanence, the power of karma and the poisons of anger, craving and ignorance that drive both individual lives and the history of nations, but that does not make those any less painful. It will be odd going home to a quiet suburban life where the horrors of the killing fields are at first glance unthinkable. The truth is however that appalling crimes of murder and dispossession have occurred throughout time everywhere and took place in Australia to its indigenous people, its prosperity being founded on realities often wilfully forgotten and swept under the rug of the unremembered past.

"As a caterpillar, having come to the end of one blade of grass, draws itself together and reaches for the next, so the Self, having come to the end of one life and dispelled all ignorance, gathers in his faculties and reaches out from the old body to a new"
Brihadaranyaka Upanishad

CHAPTER NINE
INDIA

The final step of our travels is to the birthplace of the concept of samsara and the religions that embrace it: India. India endlessly fascinates in its diversity, landscape, art, music, architecture, history, cultures, people and spirituality. Four of the world's religions, Hinduism, Sikhism, Jainism and Buddhism, have their origins here, and after the long and winding road through Nepal, Bali and Cambodia it is like following rivers to their source to be on India's sacred soil. As in Nepal and Bali a pervasive spirituality hovers over every aspect of life saturating the very air. The concepts of rebirth and samsara are central to all faiths born here, so if anywhere can give insight in to those perhaps this is it. Rob lived in Goa for two years in the seventies, along with hordes of other curious Westerners exploring the beaches, the culture, the mysticism, and the ganga, so once more I'm following his footsteps back to that period in his youth. Before his illness we travelled to north India together, our journey from Delhi to the Thar desert of Rajasthan taking us through such fabled cities as Jaipur, Jodhpur, Udaipur, and Jaisalmer, visiting temples towns and architectural sites on our way. This visit now without Rob in an utterly changed life ten years on will be to India's south. I wish so much he was coming with me to a country he greatly loved.

India has a long history of drawing outsiders to taste its spirituality for themselves. Since time immemorial India has been perceived as a land of mystics, saints, rishis, seers, sadhus, gurus, holy men and women seeking direct knowledge of divinity. Its focus on mystical experience of the inner world of the spirit is in marked contrast to the dominant ideas and religious traditions of the West. Indian spirituality has been attracting outsiders since before the British Empire. British Orientalist Sir William Jones learned Sanskrit and awakened interest in the culture and philosophy of India in the late 18th century. Another European, who made Indian mysticism accessible to the West in the early twentieth century, was Sir John Woodroffe (1865-1936), an English judge on the High Court of India during British colonial rule. He studied Sanskrit, Indian philosophy and Tantra, writing and translating sacred texts in to English both under his own name and as Arthur Avalon. His 1919 **The Serpent Power – The Secrets of Tantric and Shaktic Yoga**, introduced the chakras, kundalini yoga and Tantra to the West. He was said to be an initiated adept of Tantra who meditated on his rooftop in Calcutta in the evenings after court.

India's saints, mystics, gurus and spiritual teachers have attracted large followings around the world since the nineteenth century. It is worth a brief reference to a few of those as illustration of the extraordinary contribution India has made to spirituality that belongs to humanity not just India. Although their spiritual roots are in Hinduism these spiritual teachers point towards a universal spirituality without reference to any particular religion, way of life or cultural identity. The willingness of India to share its spiritual knowledge with the outside world has been its great gift to humanity, producing multitudes of teachers and gurus of whom the following are only a few examples. These gurus and teachers have not been immune to the personal flaws and frailties of the rest of humanity but they have opened doors to spiritual possibilities in a way unique to India.

Sri Aurobindo, born in 1872, inspired a global following, and his ideas are at the centre of the international community of Auroville near Pondicherry. His understanding of karma, rebirth and samsara are of particular interest and we hope to visit the Sri Aurobindo ashram, and Auroville, down the track. His teaching of Integral Yoga and evolutionary rebirth counter the pessimistic premise of both Hinduism and Buddhism that life in samsara is a state of suffering and illusion with the only desirable end being escape by ending rebirth. Krishnamurti, born in 1895 near modern day Chennai, was proclaimed by the Theosophical Society to be the new "World Teacher" and raised within those expectations. However he eventually rejected that mantle and Theosophy itself declaring himself without religion, caste, or belief, describing his ideas as the teachings rather than as his teachings. He points to a way forward between a spiritual morass and a spiritual desert that being ironic given offering a way forward was the very thing he was keen to avoid: " I maintain that truth is a pathless land, and you cannot approach it by any path whatsoever, by any religion, by any sect. That is my point of view, and I adhere to that absolutely and unconditionally. Truth, being limitless, unconditioned, unapproachable by any path whatsoever, cannot be organized; nor should any organization be formed to lead or coerce people along a particular path. ... This is no magnificent deed, because I do not want followers, and I mean this. The moment you follow someone you cease to follow Truth. I am not concerned whether you pay attention to what I say or not. I want to do a certain thing in the world and I am going to do it with unwavering concentration. I am concerning myself with only one essential thing: to set man free. I desire to free him from all cages, from all fears, and not to found religions, new sects, nor to establish new theories and new philosophies."[145] So perhaps no path is the path? Krishnamurti settled in the United States and formed deep friendships with people such as Aldous Huxley, physicist David Bohm, and Fritjof Capra author of **The Tao of Physics**, and his legacy has been enduring.

Another significant figure was Paramahansa Yogananda, born in 1893 in Uttar Pradesh. At seventeen he met his guru Swami Yuketswar and began his life's journey to "know God" as described in **Autobiography of A Yogi**. That has been widely read in the West and provided access to Indian spirituality for millions. Like Krishnamurti he too eventually ended up in the United States where he taught meditation, Kriya yoga and the unity of spiritual truth, founding a strong global following that continues to this day as the Self Realization Fellowship. The Indian saint and mystic, Ramakrishna born in 1836, along with his disciple Swami Vivekananda, also had a profound influence both within and beyond India. He too taught the universality of religion: "Many are the names of God and infinite the forms that lead us to know him, in whatever name or form you desire to call him in that very form and name you will see him". God could be approached from many paths: "As one can ascend to the top of a house by means of a ladder or a bamboo, or a staircase, or a rope, so diverse also are the ways and means to approach God, and every religion and every religion in the world shows one of those ways." That is an understanding of God that makes much more sense than numerous competing religions all claiming they alone have the correct path.

His student, Swami Vivekananda born in 1863, took Indian spirituality to the United States and Europe at the end of the nineteenth century and was a great influence on figures such as Ghandi and Nikola Tesla. He met the latter in the 1890's while Vivekananda was on a lecture tour, and they both agreed that everything in the universe, including matter, was composed of energy or prana, a term Tesla adopted. In 1895 Vivekananda wrote in a letter to a friend: "Mr. Tesla thinks he can demonstrate mathematically that force and matter are reducible to potential energy.[prana].... In that case the Vedantic cosmology will be placed on the surest of foundations. I am working a good deal now upon the cosmology and eschatology of the Vedanta. I clearly see their perfect union with modern science, and the elucidation of the one will be followed by that of the other."[146]The friendship between Tesla and Vivekananda helped the continuing development of these ideas in our own time, and both men sought the reconciliation of spiritual and scientific truth. Vivekenanda's comments regarding prana are confirmed by modern physics that everything in the universe at the smallest level is comprised of subatomic particles that are vortices of energy whose intense forces give the appearance of solid matter. Vivekananda also sought universal spiritual truths that would liberate rather than imprison in religion. "Each soul is potentially divine. The goal is to manifest this Divinity within.... Do this either by work, or worship, or mental discipline, or philosophy – by one or more or all of these – and be free. This is the whole of religion. Doctrines, or dogmas, or rituals, or books, or temples, or forms, are but secondary details." [147]

The legacy of Indian spirituality from Ramakrishna, Krishnamurti, Vivekenanda, Yogananda, and Sri Aurobindo is their recognition of the unity of spiritual truth independent of religion and providing guides to meditation and spiritual realization to seekers from across cultures or creeds. Since those teachers there have been a multitude of twentieth century Indian spiritual figures, including the Maharishi beloved of pop stars and founder of Transcendental Meditation, Guru Maharaj Ji now known as Prem Rawat, Swami Satyananda founder of a worldwide yoga network and the Bihar School of Yoga, and a host of others. There have also been a few against whom serious accusations have been made, Indian spiritual figures being as vulnerable as those of any other spiritual tradition to the dark shadows that often haunt them. Innumerable seekers, hippies, and the just plain curious, have flocked to India to find a guru and maybe a little ganja, and they continue to do so. YouTube is a veritable twenty first century shopping centre for Indian gurus such as Sadhguru who continue to attract the spiritually thirsty in droves. Westerners such as Ram Dass and Bede Griffiths journeyed to India for spiritual inspiration. The French monk working with Bede Griffiths, Henri Le Saux, came bringing Christianity and end up immersed in Indian spirituality as Swami Abhishiktananda. Arundhati Roy in her novel set in Kerala, **The God of Small Things**, creates the character of a European Christian cleric arriving to convert the natives but ending up a swami, not a totally unknown path for Westerners. Some have even become sadhus: apparently at the huge Hindu religious festival, the Kumbh Mela, they can be seen and it will be fascinating to discover those when and if travel to a Kumbh Mela happens. Over thirty million people attend in one day and it is the greatest gathering of people on earth. Some gurus and godmen have been accused of being charlatans, or worse, none being exempt from human flaws and frailties and a few are plain criminal, but nonetheless India's contributions to human spiritual endeavours have been huge and enduring.

India is a huge sprawling country of over a billion people so full of contradictions it is hard to know where to begin or what to make of it. Astounding architectural brilliance and history, great technological and social achievements, a robust democracy despite it's torrid history after independence from British colonial rule, a staggeringly diverse range of people, languages, customs, beliefs, and practices are all its faces. Alongside this is much that remains deeply troubling. Poverty, superstition, caste divisions, pollution, lack of gender equality, and huge social problems, remain dark faces of modern India. Technological sophistication is simultaneous with many villages not having running water or toilets, mobile phones are everywhere but emails are still delivered by bullock cart to very remote rural areas. Human existence in the cycle of samara is becoming ever more complex and contradictory as India graphically displays.

The Bill and Melinda Gates Foundation have partnered with the Indian government in the "Reinvent the Toilet" campaign, to bring decent and dignified sanitation, something the vast majority of its people have never had. Defecation in the open has now been overcome in over fifteen percent of Indian villages whereas in 2015 only eight percent had the privilege of toilets, so progress is happening but it is slow and much more needs to be done. When my eldest son visited India in the 1990's on a school trip to Auroville and to dig wells in a remote village, two things stuck in his mind. The first was the incredible generosity, kindness, and hospitality of the Indian people, and the second was going to the toilet at the edge of a field early in the morning along with the rest of the village. He took several rolls of toilet paper with him as he had been told it was hard to get, only to discover that there was absolutely no toilet in the village so the toilet paper was an irrelevance. These paradoxes of India, fast modernizing but with one foot simultaneously in an ancient past, are everywhere. A snake charmer with a cobra in a basket might plan his next venue by a cell phone hidden in his turban, probably navigating there by Google maps if he can get the often temperamental Indian internet to work. Somehow in the midst of all its chaos, diversity, and contradictions, India holds together as a nation. Busy highways are likely to have cows wandering along amidst the anarchy of trucks, cars, motorbikes, buses, pedestrians, and motor rickshaws, where road rules appear non-existent and there is an accident rate of horrific proportions.

Tolerance of religious diversity co-exists with religious hatred flaring in places like Kashmir. India has a long history of religious conflict, particularly between Hindus and Muslims, and riots continue to intermittently break out. For example in Gujarat in 2002 approximately 1044 people died, 2500 were wounded, and 223 declared missing, when the Municipal Council decided to move a Muslim shrine. At the time of India's partition following independence from British Rule in 1947, it has been estimated millions died in religious conflict. Hindus fleeing to India from West Pakistan and East Pakistan (Bangladesh), and Muslims fleeing India to those two newly created countries, slaughtered each other at train stations and in villages. Neighbour turned on neighbour and sectarian divisions swept the country in to a bloodbath. Salman Rushdie's novel **Midnight's Children** powerfully captures that turbulent flow of India's twentieth century history.

Beautiful, disturbing, inspiring, shocking, vibrant and confronting, all at the same time, are my earlier memories of India and probably little will have changed. My mother gave grim accounts from the time in early childhood when our family was in Calcutta, of carts collecting those that died during the night on the streets. Massive slums abound in India's cities, the dark joke about Mumbai as Slumbai evident on an earlier trip when Rob and I flew in to the airport over enormous slums cobbled together from plastic, old bags and tins. Around forty percent of Mumbai residents live in one of its many slums, and its largest, Dharavi, has a population of over a million people, many having no access to safe drinking water or sanitation. Yet these places are hives of industry and are fascinating social worlds that are now marketed to tourists to take 'slum tours'. Kevin McCloud's 2010 documentary "Slumming It" portrays a vibrant but confronting portrait of Dharavi, simultaneously rich in community, kindness, hard work, courage, and happiness, but extremely poor in terms of plumbing, sewerage, hygiene, comfort, facilities and safety from marauding rats and disease pathogens in its open drains. Anawaddi slum in Mumbai demonstrates the contradictions of modern India where elegant hotels surround a busy international airport adjacent to the slum, its inhabitants struggling for survival by collecting the trash left behind by rich hotels and the airport. The deeply precarious nature of life and survival for so many in India is played out in the lives of its inhabitants most of whom are swept along by global economic forces over which they have no control. Reading Katherine Boo's account of the Anawaddi slum, **Behind The Beautiful Forevers,** while visiting Mumbai in 2010 revealed tragedy, hope and an incredible ability to adapt and survive. India is a place difficult to remain neutral about and old responses of love and loathing will no doubt resurface.

We arrive in Chennai to the usual hurdles of finding a taxi and getting local currency. Chennai is absolutely unknown to both of us, a relatively new city founded as Madras by merchants from the time of the British East India Company. Driving from the airport the concrete freeways and relative order and cleanliness is not the India from memory, but the closer we get to the city that impression of order and cleanliness rapidly wears off. New buildings for expensive consumer goods or luxury car dealers have sprouted up in the middle of chaotic streets, where the usual garbage, mangy dogs and street vendors ply their trade. As we cross a small bridge a glimpse is offered, past a sleek new building, of a canal choked with garbage, men sitting on the bank in lunghis in startling contrast to the suited business men emerging from nearby offices. Our hotel is large, ugly and relatively modern, with the strangely Indian phenomenon of staff appearing to outnumber customers, the end result being neither efficient nor easy to navigate but at least many are employed in the process. There is evidence of technology everywhere, laptops appear on many desks and everyone is poring over a cell phone, but the phone lines aren't working which explains why our airport transfer did not happen. The most fascinating array of lurid looking cakes striped like the gay pride rainbow are in the display cabinet in the lobby entrance. They look toxic in the almost fluorescent intensity of their blue, pink, green, red, aqua and yellow layers but perhaps they might taste good. I settle for the most boring on offer, a chocolate layer cake that is pleasant if bland.

The hotel has a swimming pool, welcome in the intense heat. Men are swimming and young children are taking swimming lessons with male teachers and fathers but not a single woman enters the water except me. The women all sit demurely near the pool in saris waiting for their children to acquire the swimming skills they no doubt don't possess. The pool is large and clean but the surrounds are bare concrete with nowhere to sit except dirty and torn vinyl seats. The wall backing the swimming pool area is filthy, the paint peeling and rubbish collecting in the corners. At the end is a small lawn area dotted with ornate ironwork gazebos, a few straggling yellow flowered creepers and a table at the centre, but not a chair or anywhere to sit to be seen. It is a completely useless space. Several men who look like employees hover so I enquire where the towels are kept. This brings a response of incomprehension and then one returns with a tiny, dirty, grey square of worn towel about fifty centimetres long and hands it over with a radiant smile, it being better to focus on the smile rather than the towel. This is to be our experience of India everywhere. Much effort is invested in something that is poorly maintained and or filthy like the clean hotel swimming pool with zero aesthetic appeal surrounded by stained walls and garbage. This is a marked contrast to Bali where the pools are often truly beautiful, surrounded by lush vegetation and comfortable chairs. Garbage and poverty abound in Bali beyond the artificial cacoon of luxurious hotels but many of those hotels are masterpieces of artistry and design. I feel disgust at my negative judgements already surfacing based on such trivial and selfish criteria as the aesthetics of a swimming pool in a country where so many still live in tremendous poverty, without proper housing, running water, sanitation, health care, or secure work.

There is much talk of the 'new India' and there is evidence everywhere of this with shiny cars clogging broken roads that have no useable footpaths, the ubiquitous cell phones, ATM's and advertisements for sophisticated medical or business services. But the old India remains close to the surface apparent not just in its huge slums but everywhere. Luxury hotels back on to an ancient potholed laneway where cows graze on dust, plastic bags, and a few shreds of stringy grass, where people sleep on the bare earth at the edge of the road as often there are no footpaths, their bodies and clothes caked in dirt, the luxury of a shower unimaginable. The Indian middle class has dramatically expanded but along with the success stories remain tough realities of survival for so many. It is overwhelming to contemplate and a powerful reminder of privileges so easily taken for granted by those that have them such as me.

It has been claimed that Hindu beliefs that the world is an illusion, the important goal being to escape rebirth in samsara, and that destiny is determined by karma, act to paralyse the inclination and capacity for social progress. In the pursuit of the inner life and release from samsara have the religions of India generated indifference to realities of the material world such as poverty and lack of toilets? That is the polar opposite of Western societies that are so intensely grounded in the outer world they have neglected the inner world of the spirit. Is there truth in those assertions about Indian religion? Does that mean ideas such as maya, karma, rebirth and samsara carry some responsibility for inhibiting social progress in India? Sri Aurobindo points to this in **The Life Divine**, expressing hope for a middle way that embraces the best of what the East and West have to offer: "In Europe and in India, respectively, the negation of the materialist and the refusal of the ascetic have sought to assert themselves as the sole truth and to dominate the conception of Life. In India, if the result has been a great heaping up of the treasures of the Spirit, - or of some of them,- it has also been a great bankruptcy of Life; in Europe, the fullness of riches and the triumphant mastery of this world's powers and possessions have progressed towards and equal bankruptcy in the things of the Spirit."[148]

We take a ride from the hotel in an auto-rickshaw ending up at T Nagar shopping area. Every few steps someone selling shabby plastic trinkets offers goods with that pleading desperation born of grinding poverty. Men materialize everywhere as uninvited "guides" offering to lead the way to some shop or other where most likely they will receive a few rupees for bringing customers. They are persistent and saying no feels rude and is mostly ignored, so I find myself lying and promise to return to their shop, "later" knowing that of course that will never happen. White skinned tourists are regarded as a gold mine of business opportunity and the price of services such as an auto-rickshaw ride is inflated many times because they are assumed to be possessors of relative great wealth. Skin colour is oddly paradoxical for pale skinned visitors and there is a shocking kind of religious sanctioned preference for pale skin embedded in Indian society associated with high caste status. Non-Hindu foreigners are people without caste or place in the Hindu social system at the bottom of the religious status pile and yet pale skin and blonde hair are highly prized. It is disconcerting at tourist attractions to be approached by Indian families for joint photographs for no other reason than possessing blonde hair. I become acutely and uncomfortably aware of my own whiteness and how it shapes my experiences in Asia. Skin colour is a prominent aspect of marriage advertisements and possessing a "wheatish complexion" is proudly advertised as it designates higher social and caste status. This also drives massive sales of whitening creams such as "Fair And Beautiful" in Nepal and India. The untouchable caste, the Dalits, are the darkest skinned, and continue to suffer all sorts of prejudices and discrimination being allocated the worst and most undignified jobs like cleaning toilets. There are over a hundred million untouchables in India and discrimination against and murder of Dalits remains common, the number being difficult to exactly quantify as many deaths are passed off as 'accidents'. Some Dalits seek to escape caste by converting to Christianity, Buddhism or Islam, but that usually does nothing to improve their living standards or reduce prejudice. For city dwelling educated Indians caste has become less dominant than previous generations, but out of the cities it still drives social relationships. Most powerful and educated people in India still come from the higher paler skinned castes.

The streets of India are not places for the fainthearted and many tourists retreat to their luxury hotels shocked and dazzled by the polar opposite of the sanitized bland world many of them come from. Mange ridden, skinny, dogs, often suckling puppies hidden in a broken drain, trot the streets joining the endless throng of sari clad women, ancient barefooted men in filthy dhotis, smart looking men in business shirts, jeans clad young men, lovely schoolgirls with kurta uniforms and long plaited hair, and maybe an occasional sadhu, all of them awash on the "sea of samsara" in their own particular way. It is a place of intense vibrancy, of life, real and present, parading through samsara in the shimmering heat in an infinite variety of guises of body, dress, sex, age, occupation, social status, circumstances and experience. We make our way through the crowd in need of rupees. Invariably the ATM cubicles have broken doors, the glass caked in grime with litter all around the entrance, the steps broken. Frequently the ATM's do not accept foreign cards, a problem we have not experienced anywhere else, and obtaining cash is a race around lanes and streets in an auto-rickshaw trying to find a machine that works. The internet services in India are consistently the worst by far of anywhere we have yet seen in our travels which is surprising given India's supposed technological miracles. The internet was faster, more reliable and more widely available in hotels and restaurants all through Nepal, Cambodia and Bali, whereas in India it is frequently slow unreliable and unavailable outside the more expensive hotels.

Impressive medical facilities announce themselves behind high walls separated from a street where vendors are selling food on broken rubbish strewn pavements, cows and dogs wandering or dozing in the heat. One such facility proclaims its offerings of diabetology and many kinds of surgery. Down the face of this building are power cords dangling, some cut with no insulation and the side face of the building unfinished and beginning to collapse, the paintwork peeling and stained and the usual accumulation of garbage near its entrance. It does not inspire confidence in India's medical services and reading the **Indian Times** at the train station in Kumbokorum a few days later does little to help. The newspaper reported that every patient at a prominent Indian hospital had contracted either hepatitis B or C because of cross contamination from poorly maintained and cleaned dialysis machines. A documentary came to mind from twenty years earlier revealing that HIV infection in India was spread in hospitals by the recycling of one syringe to as many as five hundred patients without sterilization and from blood donations. Blood donors were selling their blood, unofficially of course, in the carparks of the hospitals, often infected with HIV because the equipment used to take their blood was not sterile. So HIV infection spread to the blood donors from the medical system itself was passed on to the blood recipient. How much has changed since that time? Hopefully we will not need to avail ourselves of a blood transfusion because whatever might be said about the new India the old India is glaringly present. HIV is spreading fast in India but is associated with great shame and fear and is little talked about because association with the illness makes a whole family social outcasts.

We make our way from the T Nagar district eventually stumbling on the Pondy Bazaar. Outside the bazaar a young man dressed in the orange robes of a sannyasin, or renunciate, has set up a footpath bookshop. He has a selection of works by Bhaktivedanta Swami Prabhupada, founder of the International Society for Krishna Consciousness. Is this the Hare Krishnas common on the streets of Melbourne in the 1970's with bands of devotees in orange robes chanting the Maha Mantra?

"Hare Krishna Hare Krishna
Krishna Krishna Hare Hare
Hare Rama Hare Rama
Rama Rama Hare Hare"

Whatever happened to the Hare Krishnas? They don't seem to be the noticeable street presence they once were and their story is an interesting one. They represent a good example of organized religion that polarizes people between true believers and ardent haters revealing the harm religion can cause even with the best of intentions. Every religion has its shadow side, perhaps that is inevitable in any human organization. Indian spiritual ideas, and practices such as yoga and meditation, have made an overwhelmingly positive contribution across the world creating tolerant more spiritually aware followers. The Hare Krishnas are an exception to that with a fervent missionary bent not typical of Indian spirituality, creating mixed outcomes as a consequence. The young man is indeed from that group, the International Society for Krishna Consciousness, now known as Iskon. Rob talked of when a poverty stricken student in Sydney he would eat free vegetarian food provided by the local Hare Krishna group who lived in the upmarket suburb of Double Bay. Iskon has its roots in the Vaishavite (followers of Vishnu) and Bhakti Yoga tradition of Hinduism but has sought to establish a movement that transcends its Hindu origins. Bhakti Yoga is the yoga of loving devotion to the divine in the form of Krishna who is worshipped as the 'Supreme Personality of Godhead'. Texts such as the **Bhagavad Gita** portray Krishna as the divine master who reveals to Arjuna sacred knowledge.

Iskon was born in New York City in 1966. At sixty-nine Bhaktivedanta Swami Prabhupada took 'God consciousness' to what he considered the spiritually dead and lost society of the United States. It had a zealous prozyletizing purpose of bringing salvation in the form of surrender to the Supreme Personality of God, Krishna, a marked contrast to the generally non-evangelical habits of Hinduism. The first converts, mostly hippies from the flower power generation, took to it with fervour adopting the robes of swamis, chanting the Sanskrit Maha Mantra and giving their lives to the worship of Krishna as Divine Lord. The popular musical Hair contained references to the Hare Krishnas as did several songs by the Beatles particularly "My Sweet Lord" with the Hare Krishna mantra in the background. George Harrison remained a follower until his death and in 1973 donated the beautiful Tudor property, Bhaktivedanta Farm in the UK to Iskon. Reflecting his Hindu spiritual background Bhaktivedanta Swami Prabhupada describes us all as eternal sparks of the divine imprisoned by karma in the cycle of samsara. Without salvation through Krishna there is no hope of release from samsara so nothing is as important as seeking union with Krishna. Iskon's followers were expected to surrender their capacity for critical thinking and anyone who questioned was to be avoided as a threat to divine consciousness. Krishna consciousness and chanting absorbed every aspect of life to the exclusion of everything and everyone else, hence parents were willing to abandon their young children to the Iskon system. Brabhupada's books are an odd mix of inspiring and ominous, the seeds of what is to come being detectable in them.

As a spiritual tradition from outside the West Iskon was described by leaders of Christian churches as a cult: ironic given that the early Christian church was also regarded as a dangerous and subversive cult and persecuted as such. Perhaps the adage that the distinction between a terrorist and a freedom fighter is a matter of perception is applicable here too? If one person's cult is another person's true spiritual light how and on what basis can one be told from the other? Perhaps all religions possess some cult like aspects, particularly at the time of their founding by charismatic spiritual leaders be that Jesus, Buddha, Baihullulah or Mohammad, and India continues to produce charismatic religious leaders like The Mother, Sai Baba, Guru Majaraj ji or Sadhguru, attracting both loyal followers and passionate critics. Provision of service and food to the poor and vulnerable is a commendable facet of the Hare Krishnas but there is another much darker side and it has been dogged by scandals involving institutional sexual abuse, blatant sexism, misogyny and racism, taking children from their parents and destroying many lives. Now passing through the American courts are survivor's accounts of rape, abuse, hunger, being forced to attend gurukulus (religious schools) in India away from their families. This sorry tale has much in common with the sexual abuse scandals emerging in Christian churches, Catholic and Protestant, and seems to be associated with religions and large organizations of all kinds.

Iskon has grown in to a huge wealthy organization with branches, temples, farms, restaurants and devotees in every continent. Its regulatory principles of no eating of meat, fish or eggs, no intoxicants, no gambling, and no illicit sex, claim purification for its adherents to become liberated from the bonds of karma and samsara by realizing union with God as Krishna. Sex, even between a married couple, purely for pleasure is frowned on and it amazes me that teachings on sex far more restrictive than those of the Catholic Church are willingly complied with in an age where over ninety percent of internet traffic is devoted to pornography. Iskon's teachings on birth control are even more restrictive than those of the Catholic Church. The body is described as a 'trap' that prevents us from realizing we are divine sparks of God and sex and women are regarded as the gateway to imprisonment by rebirth in samsara.

I purchase **The Science of Self Realization** from the young swami as he stands on the broken pavement with the noise and chaos of Chennai swirling around him. He is fine featured young and earnest with sincere faith in Krishna, and for that he has been asked to deny himself not only meat, but alcohol, coffee, drugs and sex, to take on a life of constant worship of and service to Krishna. How is it possible to reconcile the austere puritanical teachings that Iskon puts forward as its public face with its darker underbelly? The accusations of drug peddling, sexual abuse, and even murder lying in the shadows of this organization are serious, and completely at odds with its stated aims and ideals. All religious traditions seem to have dark baggage in some form or another so my resistance to organized religion digs in a little deeper. Perhaps it is the case that all of them are inevitably infected with the flaws of human nature and betray their founding ideals? It is immensely sad that ideals of love and service from a profound spiritual Indian tradition, taken to the West with sincere intent to 'save' a misguided and godless society should by the end of the twentieth century become embroiled in the same depressing accusations that afflict so many religious organisations everywhere. The more fervent and sincere a spiritual group is the more vulnerable it seems to be to fanaticism and a blinkered certainty of its own rightness. That can lead to the well-trodden path of crusades, or inquisitions, or witch burnings, or religious wars, or suicide bombers, or separating three years old children from their parents in America and sending them to schools in India to ensure religious purity.

When a foreign spiritual tradition is planted in a totally alien culture in a rigid uncompromising fashion does that inevitably bring destruction? **The Poisonwood Bible** by Barbara Kingsolver, the daughter of American Christian missionaries in the Congo, explores in novel form the awful legacy that can unfold in situations of cultural difference, religious fervour, and missionary proselytizing, reflecting similar elements as Iskon. Rejecting religion is easy to do as these facts increasingly come to light, manifesting in all religions in some form or another. Many bringing Indian spirituality to the West such as Vivekenanda, Yoganananda, Ramakrishna, Krishnamurti and Sri Aurobindo, and the Maharishi and his Transcendental Meditation movement in the 1960's, did not trigger such catastrophic consequences. It is difficult to know what to make of this. Are organizations such as Iskon cults that lure the gullible, or is real wisdom to be found obscured by the mistakes of rotten apples in the barrel? Rotten apples appear in every religion, and every organization that involves a collection of people, is it possible to not throw the baby out with the bath water? It is not just religions of all varieties that have been exposed as cesspits of abuse but the scouts, schools, army training colleges, university residential colleges, and orphanages. Anywhere there is a collection of people with power over other people. If every group shown to be guilty of abuse were annihilated there would barely be an organization left on earth. Is it possible to reject and remove all that is dark and wrong in organizations such as religions and yet retain that which is good and valuable?

Exploring spirituality has pulled in opposite directions and India heightens that tension. On the one hand there is a profound mystery lying behind the world of form and matter. Spiritual traditions and quantum physics both point to that from opposite sides. It is in the explanation of that mystery, and the attempt to transcend death that the power of religion lies. The baggage of religion however makes it difficult to embrace any ideas closely entangled with religion including samsara and rebirth. Samsara, as a way of making sense of life, suffering and death is compelling but the religions associated with it often are not. As soon as spiritual inspiration becomes solidified in to institutional religion, power struggles, dogma, superstition, and exclusivism inevitably contaminate the spiritual inspiration. The **Science of Self Realization** deepens this quandary. It contains much that is profound but the conviction Swami Prabhupada has of his own rightness is chillingly reminiscent of zealous evangelical Christians who believe that Jesus is the only way to be 'saved' from eternal damnation or Muslim clerics declaring fatwahs on those who challenge Islam.

We continue along the broken footpaths alive with vibrant colour, smells, and life, to find ourselves at Chennai's Maneekshawar Temple its tower of brightly painted sculptures standing out above the rooflines of modern ugly concrete buildings. The lurid painted figures look kitsch and gaudy presenting strong contrast to the **Upanishads** or the **Bhagavad Gita** that make little reference to the bewildering array of deities and rituals accompanying Hinduism as a religion. Every religion contains ugly aspects of some kind and so drawing superficial conclusions based on aesthetic distaste for brightly painted statues misses the point. Many a Catholic church also displays garish plaster statues of a white skinned Jesus dripping blood, or displaying his sacred heart, or the Virgin Mary depicted with bright blue robes, a pure white skin and wearing a bright gold crown. The massive temple doors are shut, a few beggars crouching sleepily in the hot sun putting no energy in to their daily struggle to collect rupees. We decide to wait for the temple to reopen at four pm so go shopping nearby where an abundance of cheap goods, mostly from China, dominates. Beautiful brass pots like those in Nepal are nowhere to be found and plastic items are everywhere. Large pots of identical shape to the lovely large brass and earthenware vessels of previous times are caste in a hideous pink plastic and piled up between mobile phone cases and shiny vinyl handbags. The wonderful chaos of Indian streets hums with life, sari clad women stroll nonchalantly along as cars, motorbikes, and auto rickshaws dodge around them, horns a constant background cacophony. Nobody is run over and the great stream of humanity going about its daily life is a parade of colour vitality and noise. The brilliantly coloured kurtas and saris of the women are beautiful, and the women serene and lovely with long black hair plaited down their backs entwined with strings of fresh sweet smelling jasmine flowers. The women often ride on the backs of the motorbikes perched precariously sidewards in their gorgeous saris, whereas others sit primly astride motorbikes wearing kurtas and baggy pants, dignified and gracious as they make their way through the nightmare traffic.

In amongst all this seething mass of humanity a woman squats at the door of a dishevelled ATM booth with the dirty glass door hanging half off, broken concrete steps leading up from the ground and stickers for Visa and Mastercard peeling from the sign above the entrance. She is clearly blind, her sari stained and faded to a dull grey, her hands and skin lined and dirty, her white hair pulled back from a strangely beautiful face. Every few metres is another person begging. An elderly man is shuffling along on his bottom waving a small tin container, his legs shrivelled and useless. A woman standing at the entrance to a diamond store makes motion of her hands to her mouth indicating she needs money for food while plump women in brilliant saris and kurtas stream through the door to ogle the jewellery without appearing to notice her. The first impulse is to scramble for the wallet to try and give a tiny fix to this great legion of need and suffering that is so apparent everywhere. Guilt and helplessness surge with the constant reminders of samsara's uneven allocation of luck and resources, particularly when one has in one's wallet a relative great abundance. The expression 'compassion fatigue' describes well that combination of guilt, frustration and resignation in response to the endless need everywhere.

Giving money to every begging person in a place where there are so very many is not possible. Some of these beggars may well be employed by the equivalent of a beggar pimp who collects their takings and controls their begging. Children are sometimes deliberately blinded to make them more efficient at begging as may have happened to some we see whose eyes have a strange milky quality. Compassion fatigue sets in for me too and after the first guilt ridden handing over of rupees the amount and frequency I give diminishes and I'm shocked to find myself able to walk past and barely notice the lame, the sick and the needy in the passing crowd. That is troubling, the enormity of the problem breeding resignation then indifference. Turning one's back becomes a survival mechanism in a society where poverty and suffering are so obvious everywhere. Perhaps the doctrine of karma also plays its part in the easy indifference with which so many appear to regard the poverty and beggars in their midst: they are there because that is where their karma placed them. A classic example of blaming the victim and self-justification for doing nothing to help them, neatly combined. The idea of karma can and is used to justify the unjustifiable but it is not necessarily so. Karma can also invite a response of loving care, it being someone's karma to give service as part of their spiritual evolution in the form of karma yoga. As the **Bhagavad Gita** puts it: "Who burns with the bliss and suffers with the sorrow of every creature within his heart, making his own each bliss and each sorrow...He who in this oneness of love, loves me in whatever he sees, wherever that man may live, in truth this man lives in me."

The economic vulnerability of people in a society such as India where there are no pensions, no unemployment benefits and virtually no social welfare of any kind, makes me shudder and gives some explanation for the fervent petitioning of divine forces that goes on all around us. Trucks are emblazoned with "Jesus Saves" or "Praise the Lord", images of Siva, or Vishnu, or Kali, or Laxmi, or Saraswati, or any of the innumerable Hindu deities appear everywhere. Statues of Ganesha the elephant headed son of Shiva and Parvati, are in shops, dangling in cars, at street shrines, at the entrance to homes, just as they are in Nepal. His divine aid is sought to overcome obstacles and bring prosperity, a reflection of poverty and economic uncertainty driving a powerful religious cocktail of wishful thinking, hope, and faith. Many times when purchasing some item the shop owner takes the rupees and holds them briefly to his or her forehead, almost as an act of prayerful thanks, that yes there has been a sale so thank you Ganesha or Laxmi or whatever particular deity held responsible for the sale.

Most of the auto-rickshaw drivers have pictures of some deity or other pasted in their vehicle, many of them in Kerala having pictures of a blond, white skinned Jesus or Virgin Mary, stuck on the glass. White skinned angels dressed in white, with huge white wings, are also popular. Given the danger these drivers have to negotiate on a daily basis the seeking of divine protection is eminently sensible although not particularly comforting to the passengers when a large ancient bus is bearing down at great speed on the wrong side of the road as they frequently do. It is easy to become blind to the individuality of each of the countless beggars and to then walk on by on the other side of the road as the Biblical expression puts it. It is good to remember the people in Nepal and Cambodia who do not turn their backs but put their shoulder to the wheel to help in some way. David, the Welshman from Nepal and his organization mountainpeople.org, identified the need and acts directly to assist. Many of the rickshaw drivers of Kathmandu sleep in their leaky uncomfortable rickshaw completely exposed to the winter cold and wet. Most of them have insufficient clothing and no proper blankets. So David organized for hundreds of thick woollen blankets to have a head opening cut and stitched to create a makeshift poncho to be handed out with no charge to rickshaw drivers, giving them a little comfort and warmth in the night. Many of the drivers end up in Kathmandu drifting from extreme poverty and the dislocation of floods and earthquakes, to eke out an existence peddling a rickshaw until their health fails and they join the aging beggars shuffling around the Durbar squares of Patan, Kathmandu or Bhaktapur.

A friend in Kuala Lumpur, a twenty five year old Syrian refugee, has started no less than eleven charities working to assist his people driven from their homeland by the turbulent forces of war, power, and international politics. He looks exhausted. When asked why he does what he does he replied that after witnessing the carnage from the bombing of his village he has no choice: he either starts the charities or becomes a terrorist. What he is doing makes sense in a world where so much else doesn't. We met many similarly saintly people in Cambodia, determined to do their bit to alleviate the endless suffering around them. The world is full of quiet saints and Bodhisattvas alongside the worst that the world and human nature present.

Mother Theresa of Calcutta, an Albanian Catholic nun, began the Sisters of Charity who run orphanages, schools and hospices where dying people can find refuge. Indian nuns from her order are to be found the world over including wealthy countries like Australia, and in Los Angeles they staffed care homes for HIV infected children. It is shocking to read the accusations currently engulfing the order that Mother Theresa's organization sold babies, many of them not orphans but children adrift on a sea of tremendous poverty breaking apart their families, religion once again being associated with the best and the worst that human nature has to offer. The dark traits of humanity such as racism, sexism, and abuse of power, seem endemic to organized belief whether it is religion or a revolutionary cause such as the Khmer Rouge. It is easy to understand why religion is rejected by so many because it is so stained by its past and why many opt for no spiritual life because they are not willing to swallow its dogmas and baggage or the abuses associated with its institutions or its leaders.

We return to Maneekshawar Temple remove our shoes, pass by the beggars squatting outside and enter the throng streaming through its gates.

Immediately we are approached by 'guides' who speak little English, foreigners being perceived as attractive rupee earning opportunities. Inside the gaudily coloured gapauram tower the temple is impressive with a huge stone paved courtyard surrounded by colonnaded halls. At the centre are large shrines with people queuing to enter, their faces reflecting intense fervour as they line up to present flowers and offerings to stone idols that are presumably forms of Shiva. Milk is running from a stone channel spouting from a wall and worshippers are cupping it in their hands and anointing it over their heads. It will have been produced by the temple cows we noticed earlier and poured over the Shiva linghams inside the temple as an act of worship. It is believed the energy of the deity manifests in the idol or lingham and the worshipper can directly participate in the presence of the deity. As non-Hindus we are not permitted inside the dark candlelit innermost sanctum where priests in dhotis are distributing marks of ash on the foreheads of worshippers as strange hypnotic music with a powerful beat deepens the mysterious atmosphere. It reminds me strongly of the mood of Dakshinkali in Nepal and a deep connection with forces I have no understanding or experience of. I am simultaneously grateful that I am not expected to surrender to whatever is going on in the temple and regretful at having no access to it. Bede Griffiths described Hindu worship as coming from the unconscious and what was happening here at Maneekshawar Temple appears to present a primal experience and personal encounter with whatever spiritual forces the worshippers are seeking.

The self-appointed guides give up on us as customers but other people come to our side and draw lines on our foreheads with a white coloured powder, placing dots of red powder between our eyebrows as the centre for Ajna chakra. They are kind and obviously welcoming of us in a sacred space that is deeply meaningful to them. One very fat man sits in a corner with his back to the wall examining his cell phone between taking intermittent selfies of himself while others patiently queue to enter the inner shrines for darshan or worship. Darshan is a Sanskrit word related to sight, vision or appearance. In the Hindu tradition it refers to the beholding of a holy person, sacred object, natural phenomenon, or deity including an idol, image, or imagined form. Darshan, or "sight of God," implies an interaction and exchange of energy between the sacred object, deity or spiritual person and the viewer. Although it requires only the process of seeing darshan is a powerful expression of worship and spiritual experience. It can occur in a temple or shrine, in the home, in visualization, or in the presence of a guru, and people will travel long distances for it. Paramahansa Yogananda describes in **Autobiography Of A Yogi** how streams of people would seek darshan offered by his guru Sri Yukteswar. In an inner shrine one of the temple priests has a cell phone in one hand as he holds a tray with lighted candles in another, his large belly flopping over his cotton lunghi and the sacred thread worn by Brahmins as 'twice born' is strung over his shoulder. The juxtaposition of cell phones with ancient traditions and rituals is common, sometimes strangely surreal and often occurring in surprising contexts.

Our auto-rickshaw driver waiting outside the temple understands better than we do ourselves what we are searching for and delivers us to the gateway of the Ramakrishna Math. He explains he has driven people from all over the world and this is a place he takes them all. The sign at the entrance proclaims "All are welcome, irrespective of race, caste, nationality or religion". This is the best of India: tolerant, inclusive, dedicated to spirituality for the benefit of all humanity, embracing all humanity and to be shared with all humanity. Ramakrishna was born in 1836 in a pious Bengali family and from an early age displayed a deep interest in religion, in particular Kali. He was initiated in to vamachara practices of Tantra but warned his followers not to involve themselves with those. He had many mystical experiences and for brief periods embraced Islam and Christianity. His primary teaching was that all living beings are the embodiment of the divine and that there are many paths to God. His mystical experiences of oneness with the source of all being became more common later in his life, Max Muller describing Ramakrishna's account of those: "It has been revealed to me that there exists an Ocean of Consciousness without limit. From It come all things of the relative plane, and in It they merge again. These waves arising from the Great Ocean merge again in the Great Ocean. I have clearly perceived all these things."[149] His foremost disciple was Swami Vivekenanda who later took Indian spirituality to the West and contributed both to a revival of Hinduism and the development of Indian nationalism. It is in large part due to Swami Vivekenanda that Indian spirituality and practices of yoga and meditation gained entry in to Western countries.

We remove our shoes and climb the steps of the impressive building to find ourselves in a large empty hall with people quietly kneeling and praying at small side chapels dedicated to Ramakrishna and his famous disciple Swami Vivekenanda. It is not a temple and there is nothing garish or noisy about this place but rather an atmosphere of simplicity and calm sincere faith. Two school girls enter and approach a glassed niche where they kneel kiss their fingers then touch the frame of the glass in front of the statue of Ramakrishna's wife, Sarada Devi. She was one of his strongest followers and after his death contributed greatly to the preservation and dissemination of his teachings. The girls plaited black hair and hot pink ribbon bows are a bright touch of colour in this beautiful place. When searching for the toilets we stumble across an enormous and extraordinary library where anyone can read for no charge or borrow books for a tiny annual membership fee. The library is a revelation. Along the perimeter walls are shelves with large signs proclaiming Buddhism, Christianity, Islam, Judaism, Zoroastrianism, Sikhism, every section filled with an extensive collection of sacred texts. Many of the volumes are worn and ancient but all are given their place of great respect in this astounding library. There are sections for psychology, sociology, ethics, philosophy and complete collections of the works of Carl Jung and Sigmund Freud are lined up near to those of Karl Marx and Max Weber. There are books on yoga and Hindu philosophy, Tantra and Vedanta, many in English as well as Tamil, Telugu, Sanskrit and Hindi. There is a whole room of scholarly books in French, German, Spanish, Italian and Dutch. This is a place where learning of all kinds is treasured and made available for all those who seek it. I am overwhelmed with respect for this face of India that takes so seriously spirituality and knowledge.

At large tables in the centre of the room are men, and they are all men, studiously absorbed in their book of choice, many of them taking notes with rapt concentration. There are elegantly dressed men in Western style clothes seated by men in dhotis or kurtas. At one table a man in robes who might be a sadhu of some kind with ash lines drawn on his head showing him to be a follower of Shiva, is poring over a large and ancient tome with spectacles perched on his nose. The spectacles have sticky tape neatly wound around the side to hold them together. There is not a single cell phone to be seen anywhere although no doubt they are tucked in lots of pockets. There is one aged computer at the checkout desk but apart from this the whole room and its contents is like entering a time warp of dignified and earnest scholarship from an age before computers and cell phones took over our lives. Around the central desks are shelves of journals and magazines that are up to the minute in their content ranging from **New Scientist, Psychology Today** to the **Journal of Comparative Religion**. This place is remarkable and inspiring and a joy to have accidentally found in the middle of the chaos of Chennai. This is the India that can and does give to the world with great generosity a treasure house of knowledge and wisdom.

Leaving the Ramakrishna Math is to be jolted back in to dirt, noise and traffic, the gritty realities of India. I have brought with me an old Iphone to try to get an Indian sim card to make inexpensive calls. We spot an Indiatel shop incongruously perched next to a teashop, street vendors, a sleeping cow with calf, several dogs scratching at the weeping itchy sores, and a buffalo cart, as we attempt to make the purchase. No one speaks good English but it becomes clear that this is going to be an under the counter deal at which India is expert. We are sent out the door to a man sitting on a motorbike who fishes out of his pocket a pile of sim cards. Three hundred rupees and the deal is done. The kind auto-rickshaw driver steps in and gives his name and address for registering the sim card. It is popped in to the phone with a flourish, everybody laughing and happy and the endless rules and regulations of India are deftly overcome as they are everywhere often in ingenious ways. And the phone works and becomes useful. It is an experience so unlike well ordered Australia where such a transaction organized by an official cell phone outlet is unthinkable but in India just about anything can be organized for a price. The genuine smiles of all the parties to this dodgy arrangement are heart warming and that good humour and kindness are a constant presence as we trail around southern India.

After a brief detour to the ancient rock cut temples of Manilapurum our next destination is Pondicherry south of Chennai. This was the old French colonial administrative centre before Pondicherry came under the control of the British, the French administrator, Joseph Dupleix being sent home in disgrace in 1754. White Town in Pondicherry is a surprising relic of history where French is still spoken, where the street names are French and the police wear gendarme style uniforms with neat red caps. The architecture is beautiful, with gracious villas and buildings many of them with shuttered windows and pretty balconies. Our hotel is a small but charming converted French villa exquisitely but simply decorated with antique Indian furniture and a garden courtyard behind the high brick wall from the street. Purple bouganvillea festoons the walls and fragrant jasmine winds its tender tendrils up the veranda posts. It is a little cooler in the veranda's shade and large fans suspended from its ceiling beat a slow rhythm in the languid late afternoon heat. The owners and manager are French and the clientele mostly French too. The streets have lovely street lamps in what appear to be old gaslights and the overall effect is charming if not particularly Indian. The footpaths are mostly broken or dug up but the policy of restricting cars has meant walking along the streets is pleasant and relatively safe. This part of Pondicherry is an escape from the relentless dirt, noise and chaos of so much of India but it doesn't take much of a walk to find ourselves straight back there as soon as leaving the old French quarter, the latter's quiet tree lined streets and elegant mansions feeling like a different country. We stumble across a Siva Temple just a block from the Sri Aurobindo ashram and are immediately returned to the vibrant world of Hinduism with its brightly painted deities. I'm getting used to the garish statues and trying hard to look past the surface to the deeper spiritual realities they represent but think it will be impossible to ever like them. There is the usual mysterious air of deep piety going on inside the temple as worshippers line up to receive darshan and the sacred ash on their foreheads. Outside an elephant with the name of Laxmi hung around her neck is blessing worshippers at the entrance. What sort of life do these temple elephants have? Are they well treated out of public view? One wonders how they have been trained to stand outside a temple all day pretending to be a deity dispensing blessings.

Pondicherry is where Sri Aurobindo retreated when escaping from arrest by the British for his anti-colonial activities in an earlier part of his life. The story of Sri Aurobindo is a fascinating one that reflects the wider story of India itself. He was born Aurobindo Ghose in 1872 to a prosperous Bengali family who believed in the superiority of European ideas and life. He was sent to school in England and knew almost nothing of India or Indian spirituality and spoke primarily English with a little childhood Hindi for family servants. Upon return to India he became active in anti-British rule campaigns until profound spiritual experiences changed his direction and focus. Sri Aurobindo perceived all life as yoga and his system of Integral Yoga was to awaken spiritual development in every area of life. His teaching on rebirth is that its purpose is the unfolding of consciousness to evolve towards ever expanding awareness of oneness with the divine source that is pure consciousness. So the aim is not so much escape from samsara as a cycle of futile suffering in which we are trapped, but regarding samsara as an opportunity for the experiences and learning that will lead the evolving consciousness ever closer to God.

Sri Aurobindo's following comments about Hinduism embracing a vast range of religious expressions, from worship of millions of deities represented by idols to the purest abstracted monotheism, is helpful in understanding what goes on in Hindu temples and the images statues and idols that appear everywhere: "The Hindu believes that to whatever form he brings his devotion, the love of God is bound to assume and vivify it, and we cannot say that the belief is irrational. For if there is a Consciousness in the universe and transcending it which answers to the yearning of all these creatures and perhaps Itself yearns towards them with the love of the Father, the Mother, the Friend, the Lover, and a love surpassing all these, then it is idle to suppose that It would assume or create for its own pleasure and glory the forms of the universe, but would disdain as an offence to Its dignity or purity those which the love of the worshipper offers to It and which after all Itself has formed in his heart or his imagination. To these mental forms mental worship may be offered, and this is the higher way; or we may give the material foundation, the pratistha, of a statue or pictured image to form a physical nodus for a physical act of worship. In the formless also we worship God, in His qualities, in His Love, Power, Bliss, Wisdom, in the great cosmic Principles by which He manifests Himself to the eye of knowledge. We worship Him as the Impersonality manifested in these things or the Personality containing them....But it seems to us that God scorns nothing, that the Soul of all things may take as much delight in the prayer of a little child or the offering of a flower or a leaf before a pictured image as in the philosopher's leap from the summit of thought into the indefinable and unknowable and that he does best who can rise and widen into the shoreless realisation and yet keep the heart of the little child and the capacity of the seer of forms."[150]

Sri Aurobindo's story is also that of French woman Mirra Alfassa, spiritual thinker, teacher, occultist and collaborator with him in his formulation of Integral Yoga. He regarded her as of equal spiritual stature and called her "The Mother". The Sri Aurobindo ashram founded by her is close to the hotel and visiting is a wonderful experience. This is where the remarkable relationship between The Mother and Sri Aurobindo developed over thirty-six years after their first meeting in 1914. Mirra Alfassa wrote that on first seeing Aurobindo she recognized him from visions she had ten years earlier and she knew that her destiny was to be with him. "As soon as I saw Sri Aurobindo I recognized in him the well-known being whom I used to call Krishna... And this is enough to explain why I am fully convinced that my place and my work are near him, in India."[151] She goes on: "I came here..... I had an appointment for the afternoon. He was living in the house that's now part of the second dormitory, the old Guest House. I climbed up the stairway and he was standing there, waiting for me at the top of the stairs....EXACTLY my vision! Dressed the same way, in the same position, in profile, his head held high. He turned his head towards me...and I saw in his eyes that it was He. The two things clicked (gesture of instantaneous shock), the inner experience immediately became one with the outer experience and there was fusion - the decisive shock."[152]

To accept that is to accept the existence of spiritual forces outside of material reality and time, a conclusion that requires a colossal shift for me and I'm not sure what to make of it. After Sri Aurobindo's death in 1950 The Mother took over control of the publication and promotion of both his writings and her own. She had many significant visitors and friendships including Indira Ghandi, Alexandra David-Neel, artists, writers and thinkers and her impact has been enormous. In 1968 she established Auroville, a city to be created of no nationality, religion, or politics, dedicated to a human future without divisions of creed or culture. It is still there and we intend to visit. It is typical of India to allow and nurture a place such as Auroville dedicated to all humanity. Sri Aurobindo was one of India's great spiritual thinkers and visiting the ashram and Auroville is part of why we are here.

During the trip to Auroville excitement builds, it has been a long held dream to visit this place that offers such a profound vision for humanity's future, the Mother having written her founding charter for Auroville as follows:

1. Auroville belongs to nobody in particular. Auroville belongs to humanity as a whole. But to live in Auroville, one must be the willing servitor of the Divine Consciousness.

2, Auroville will be the place of an unending education, of constant progress, and a youth that never ages.

3. Auroville wants to be the bridge between the past and the future. Taking advantage of all discoveries from within and out, Auroville will boldly spring towards future realizations.

4. Auroville will be a site of material and spiritual researches for a living embodiment of an actual Human Unity.

It was originally planned for a population of fifty thousand but as of 2018 still only has around three thousand full time residents. The spiritual centre of Auroville is an enormous ball shaped building, the Matramandir, surrounded by lawns. Inside is apparently a beautiful clear, pure, sunlit space to "contemplate consciousness." I say apparently as the ordinary tourist is not permitted access to the interior unless prior arrangements have been made. Visitors get no closer than a viewing area several hundred metres away after a long hot walk. We have lunch at a small restaurant that interestingly will only accept cash in a community where money is supposed to be a thing of the past. I remember my son's remarks about his stay in Auroville that most of the hard work is undertaken by Indians but much of the credit for the vision and achievements of Auroville is claimed by Europeans, a sort of mirror of old colonial structures of power and privilege.

Auroville represents one of the last surviving relics of an idealistic age when the utopian dreams of the 1960's were believed to be realizable. The 1960's was the era of Woodstock, "The Times They Are A Changing", hippiedom, the counterculture, rejecting the 'establishment', flower power, sexual liberation, anti-war rallies, beads, caftans, experimentation with psychedelic drugs, tuning in and dropping out and Che Guevara posters featuring on University students' walls. It all seems hopelessly idealistic and naïve from the perspective of the early twenty-first century and disappointment creeps in that this place I have long admired and dreamed of visiting is something of an anti-climax. Given the short time of our visit it is unfair to come to conclusions about Auroville but it is not the unalloyed success it aims to be and my response is in part disappointment. Crime, violence, even murder have taken place in its sprawling territory and accusations of lack of transparency of financial arrangements dog it. Who exactly runs and controls Auroville is not entirely clear and decision making structures are clouded with controversy. The lack of access to the Matramandir is understandable given the large groups of tourists but nonetheless it feels spiritually remote rather than accessible and the exterior of the building is hideous: a futuristic, shiny, gold coloured, golf ball like structure erupting from a swathe of green lawns.

Perhaps my mixed reactions to Auroville mirror fading commitment to progressive social and political change. Are we all so preoccupied with mobile phones and social media that involvement in bigger causes has become fragmented and harder to sustain? Has our vision become simultaneously smaller around immediate friends and loved ones, and global as we surf the internet and consult the oracle, Google, for what we want to know? Has that made a coherent vision of a better future impossible in this postmodern age where all the old narratives of belief have evaporated along with the twentieth century? It would be wonderful to believe that the vision of Auroville offers hope for a new and better future for humanity but we don't see much that convinces that is happening. The twenty first century is one of doubt in the perfectibility of human society, and loss of vision that a world without racism, war, sexism, or social inequality as aspired to by the 1960's generation of idealistic young people who founded Auroville, can be achieved. Perhaps teaching dystopian fiction has annihilated my belief that utopias are even remotely possible. Maybe I'm just very hot and tired, covered in red dust from Auroville's roads and ready to escape back to the pretty hotel and its little pool in the shady streets of Pondicherry, a very un-Indian part of India. The name of the district of our hotel brings a shudder: White Town. Under French and English rule that is exactly what it once was, an enclave of white colonial dominance.

We are reluctant to leave Pondicherry but it is time to move on. Purchasing train tickets online is promoted by Indian Rail as the easy way to bypass the chaos and queues typical of Indian ticket counters. It proves so far from being easy as to be impossible despite consulting Google for help and checking blogs. The blogs are filled with angry and frustrated gripes from people having similar issues so clearly Indian bureaucratic nightmares will prevail. We pass through metal detector machines at the station entry that frequently beep but no one takes the slightest notice and a guard with a gun does not even turn around. Standing in a long hot queue to purchase tickets we are hoping for an air-conditioned carriage with allocated sleeping berths for the night train, but given there are so many ticket classes with confusing titles we are not overly confident. Many people kindly offer us directions to the correct platform and a stooped aging porter whisks away the largest suitcase without our request, but it is nonetheless a blessing as the heat and humidity are overpowering and sweat soaks our clothes. We watch as two very dark skinned women crouch on the train tracks with a bucket scrubbing excrement from the rails in the searing heat. They are Dalits from the untouchable caste, given, as they have been from time immemorial, the worst most demeaning tasks and they are shunned by caste Hindus. It is a shocking reminder of the power caste still has to dictate life opportunities, or for untouchables lack of life opportunities. Eventually an aging decrepit "express" train limps in to the station and we fruitlessly search for our carriage until another kind local points us in the right direction. We settle down on our little bunks with neatly folded worn sheets, a thin ancient blanket and a carriage full of gravely courteous other passengers as we head in to the night.

The early hours of the morning we are jolted in to action to get off the train, we have arrived in Madurai south India. The auto-rickshaw taking us to the hotel lurches through unlit side streets and small lanes, around cows sleeping quietly amidst a sea of plastic rubbish. Apparently street cows in India often die terrible slow deaths from the many kilos of plastic bags stuck in their guts from browsing for food. The usual skinny dogs are curled up against walls, along with huddled shapes of people draped in meagre coverings sleeping quietly before the dawn of a new day breaking soon. It is reminiscent of Kathmandu but at least the climate here will not bring achingly cold winter nights to people without warm clothing as it does there. Madurai days are hot, oppressively hot, but the nights are pleasantly warm and the air full of that peculiarly Indian tropical smell of drains, rotten food, accumulated garbage, the scent of cooking spices and jasmine flowers wafting their perfume. It is strangely intoxicating. And the people we see would almost all accept as reality, without question, that they are bound to continue incarnating on the wheel of samsara in whatever circumstances their karma has determined for them, which might be sleeping on a pavement in a back street of Madurai. Is that how people endure so apparently graciously the inequalities so obvious in this country? Does belief in karma and samsara automatically lead to a fatalistic indifference to and acceptance of social inequality and suffering? Or could belief in karma drive a greater commitment to alleviate suffering and bring about a better world? Or could it do both but it is a choice which of those paths is taken?

The next morning we explore Madurai, a centre of Tamil culture and home of the massive Minakshi Sundareshvara temple covering over fourteen acres. It was built in successive layers from the 7th to the 18th centuries, being looted and partially destroyed by Muslim conquerors in the fourteenth century and extensively rebuilt and extended in the 17th and 18th centuries. It is vast and to a non-Hindu incomprehensible. It is dedicated to Shiva, known as Sundareshvara or 'handsome God' and Parvarti his wife known as Minakshi or 'fish eyed Goddess'. Every evening an image of Sundareshvara is taken in the Palliarai Puja to the Minakshi shrine so the God can be with his wife. This is one of the most important temples in India and upwards of twenty thousand people stream through every day. It is early evening close to the time of the Palliarai Puja and the queue to enter the temple is long as it slowly progresses through the massive entrance gates or gaupurams, located at the cardinal points and covered in brightly painted stucco deities. As non-Hindus we can only enter through the eastern gate. The largest gaupurum is the size of a fifteen-story building and resembles a gaudily decorated temple. Inside is a maze of colonnaded stone halls with incredible carved pillars and shrines. It is dimly lit and a strange atmosphere of religious fervour interspersed with wandering sellers of snacks, souvenirs and guidebooks permeates this ancient building. The smell of incense and innumerable candles wafts through the still darkness as we watch a family with a young baby ardently worshipping in one shrine. Priests are performing rituals in side shrines and we wish that someone could explain to us what is happening. Unfortunately the two most sacred parts of the inner temples are once again closed to us as non-Hindus. Apparently the Shiva shrine contains an enormous and ancient Shiva lingham that we cannot view.

Suddenly there is great commotion in the outside walled courtyard area and a bejewelled caparisoned elephant surrounded by a large crowd passes by, several sadhu like figures carrying enormous flaming tridents symbolic of Shiva in the lead. Loud devotional music blares from speakers around the walls and much shouting accompanies the elephant's procession around the outside of the inner shrines separated from the street by huge perimeter temple walls. The temple elephant will have spent the day greeting worshippers and accepting small offerings. The image of Sundareshvara is contained in a silver cabinet carried behind a tall thin man dressed in jeans. He blows an enormous conch shell as they enter the temple and make their way to the shrine of Minakshi lit by towers of sputtering candles held by temple priests. The whole scene is compelling, confusing, alive with the spiritual longings and ardour of the worshippers, a display of religion utterly unlike anything in the West with its well ordered and restrained church services. Perhaps the candles, incense and bells still occasionally to be found in the Catholic mass, or Orthodox churches, are the closest parallels in Christianity. The whole question of the role of ritual arises. Do humans need ritual as a way of making concrete the abstract spiritual forces in the background of all religion? Is ritual both a conduit for superstition and a necessary dimension of spirituality and can one exist without the other?

It is a struggle to reconcile formless attributeless Brahman, the Lord of Love of the **Upanishads**, with the very literal Gods and Goddesses that appear to be the centre of worship. The **Upanishads** warn that rituals are "poor rafts to cross the sea of samsara" and describe God, Brahman, as ineffable, indescribable, without form, invisible, the sacred source of all that is: matter, consciousness, energy and time. It is a complex reality of Hinduism that it recognizes one God behind all manifestations of form simultaneous with accepting infinite manifestations of God expressed as deities who are associated with particular aspects of God: for example Saraswati is goddess of learning and Ganesha is overcome of obstacles. Something powerful and mysterious is going on here in the temple but it seems a long way from the spirituality of the **Upanishads** the **Bhagavad Gita** or ascetic holy men meditating alone in their Himalayan caves in an ecstasy of satchitananda, or truth, consciousness, bliss. The teachings of Ramakrishna, Krishnamurti, Yogananda, Vivekenanda and Sri Aurobindo, claiming the universality of God beyond all religions, are hard to reconcile with the signs forbidding us as non-Hindus to enter the most sacred spaces in the temple, something we found to be frequently the case in India. We enter the long stone colonnaded hall of the Pudumandapa group of businesses recently reopened after a devastating fire, its corridors lined with tailors, shops and the bustle of commercial life. On a side wall is an enormous black Kali idol, a string of skulls around her neck, her eyes bulging bloodshot and hideous, her tongue stuck out of her mouth. She is repellent and unnerving, and yet the goddess to whom Krishnamurti and his disciple Vivekananda addressed their worship. Once again it is bewildering what meaning can be drawn from Kali and the technicolour deities covering temples. It is a paradox of India that it possesses the most profound and intense spirituality jumbled up with cultural practices of religion that obscure as well as reveal that spirituality: it is simultaneously deeply attractive and strongly repellent to someone like me looking in as an outsider.

The next day is spent shopping buying beautiful silk shawls in brilliant jewel colours. We meet one business owner who lives with her four children above her small business, working ten hour days, seven days a week, to support and educate them. She is an inspiration. She has an enormous shining brass statue of Nandi the bull and mount of Shiva and a small shrine in her shop. After we have paid her she make some kind of gesture of thanks towards the shrine that the gods or goddesses have granted her a sale and money to support her family. Is that blind faith in an illusion or is there a "divinity that shapes our ends" and guides our lives as we live out the karma that according to Hinduism brings us back again and again in to samsara?

We take a wild and terrifying bicycle rickshaw ride across the city to The Ghandi Memorial Museum at one point crossing a multi-lane busy road then heading up it in the wrong direction. How the aged rickshaw driver had survived so long is a complete mystery given his total indifference to traffic rules. The museum is a sobering experience. My father's brother was an employee of the British Empire in India. He loved India, spoke fluent Urdu and Hindi and no doubt believed he was shouldering what Kipling referred to as the 'white man's burden,' a perception possessed by the British that they were bringing order and the wonders of European civilization to the darker peoples of the world. In the name of that racist belief in their own superiority they took over India, played princely leaders against each other and gained control of India's massive resources, supplying the mills of England during the industrial revolution with cotton and diamonds, rubies, pearls and emeralds for the British crown jewels. Opium grown in India was traded across the Empire and rammed down the throats of the Chinese whom the British defeated in the nineteenth century Opium Wars and demanded Hong Kong as reparation for daring to fight to restrict the British right to trade.

The ideology of colonialism pasted a thick obscuring veil over what was really going on: a grab for the resources of India to expand the power and wealth of the British Empire with Queen Victoria as Empress of India. My father was an administrator in the British system of control of Malaya where rubber and tin supplied the Empire, and my great grandparents had rubber plantations employing Chinese and Indian rubber tappers as cheap labour, so it feels uncomfortably close to home reading the accounts of British exploitation and dominance of India. There are no other people of European background in the museum full of Indian families learning of their own history under British rule. Large photographs of the Amritsar massacre by British troops in April 1919 are displayed, along with others showing Ghandi leading satyigraha, or 'passive resistance' protests against British rule. It is ironic that Sri Aurobindo was sent as a young boy to school in Britain because his family regarded all things British as superior to all things Indian. He grew up speaking only English with almost complete ignorance of Indian culture and spirituality and yet went on to become expert in Sanskrit and one of India's foremost spiritual thinkers leaving a great legacy for all of humanity.

We leave the Ghandi museum to depart Madurai for Kerala so once more we dive in to the gargantuan chaos of the Indian train system that employs over a million people. India's extensive rail network is cited as one of the positive legacies of British colonial rule, an ironic claim having just visited a museum exposing the abuses of British colonialism. An aged train chugs in to the station and we have lucky window seats. The windows have a peculiar structure of double sheets of yellowing glass between which mice are scurrying, going about their mousy business unconcerned by the people in the seats next to them protected by a thick pane of glass from human interference. Tea wallahs and snack sellers wander up and down the aisles between the seats pouring steaming hot sweet chai from enormous teapots. People smile and nod as we rattle through the Indian countryside. Occasionally we are stationary beside other waiting trains and can see through barred windows without glass in to crowded third class carriages with hard wooden benches for seats and most of the passengers seated on the floor. It is a reminder to hold in check our judgements about the state of our aging carriage blessed by seats and glass even if the seats are worn and torn and the windows are mouse travel routes to wherever they live in the walls of the train.

The lush green of Kerala passes by, coconut palms and paddy fields tropical and fertile, children playing happily outside their homes. Kerala is one of the most prosperous Indian states and governed by a Naxalite communist government. Education levels of girls and health care services are better here than most of the rest of India. We finally arrive in Trivandrum dragging our suitcases down the iron stairs of the station. On each step are written exhortations in English such as "hygiene is health," "eliminate disease wash your hands," and "do not spit" almost covered by the grime of dirt spit and plastic litter. The drive to the hotel is marked by the prevalence of posters promoting Naxalite communism, and an abundance of Christian churches. Many are Catholic but there are also churches belonging to the Thomasite Christians, supposedly originating with the activities of the apostle St Thomas who travelled to India in the first century CE. It is a wonderful aspect of India that it frequently accommodates with tolerance and inclusiveness so many varieties of belief, although that may well change and religious divisions again dominate like they have during earlier periods of India's history. For many Hindus Jesus is another divine example of God's intervention in the world and for others an incarnation of Vishnu akin to Krishna.

Our hotel is on a beautiful Kerala backwater looking straight out over a wildly beautiful beach to the Indian Ocean. Sadly the beach is slashed by long deep rifts of plastic garbage in some places a metre deep, washed in on the wild surf and piled along the shoreline. It is a heartbreaking sight. We saw the same in Cambodia when catching a ferry from Sihanoukville to offshore islands with some stretches of coast barely visible beneath accumulated plastic waste. In popular tourist areas of Thailand and Bali the beaches are cleaned to present a pristine and utterly false image, but you don't have to look far to find the truth that the coast of Asia is drowning in plastic washed up by the sea or flowing down rivers with few resources to fund cleaning it up and little organized garbage disposal. A visit to Mykonos many years earlier in winter had revealed similar pollution on Mediterranean beaches, only fully cleaned for the tourist summer season to present the illusion of a Greek island holiday paradise.

We are in Trivandrum for two reasons. The first is to visit the Padmanabhaswamy Temple, the other is to travel to the Sivananda Ashram near the Neyyer Dam inland from Trivandrum. Both represent differing facets of India's spirituality. The Padmanabhaswamy Temple, dedicated to Vishnu, is an exceptionally extraordinary place in a country full of the extraordinary, possessing everything that sets the spirituality of India apart from the dry culture of the West. It involves a way of looking at the world that takes for granted secret powers and hidden forces, just like in Nepal and Bali. It has mystery, intrigue, superstition, incredible legends, trillion dollar treasures, deadly cobras, strange secrets, hidden vaults of indescribable riches, curses, mantras, mystical powers, royal rivalries, brutal conflict, and saintly gurus littered through its chequered past going back in to the beginnings of an ancient history. It is a place worthy of the adventures of Indiana Jones if there ever was one. The temple is referred to in records going back to 500 BCE as 'The Golden Temple" and is mentioned in the ancient texts the Puranas and the Mahabharata. Extensive building work has been added over the centuries including the enormous gaupuram in the 16th century. The temple's main idol is Vishnu as Padmanabha asleep on the hooded serpent Ananta.

The trustees of the temple are the royal family of Travancore but in 2011 the Supreme Court of India ordered six secret vaults under the temple opened. A staggering twenty-two billion dollars worth of treasure, gold, coins, and jewels, was discovered, including eighteen foot long diamond necklaces, solid gold thrones and a huge solid gold Vishnu idol. If that were not enough there is at least one as yet unopened chamber with an enormous steel door covered with sculpted cobras that no-one has dared to open. The legend goes that if the doors are forced open disaster will befall India and perhaps the whole world. The doors are reputed to only be able to be opened by highly secret sacred mantras known only to very high sadhus, of which there are none alive today. It is speculated that the hidden chamber contains untold riches that could bring the total treasure to over a trillion dollars. Rumours abound of past attempts to open various vaults and discovering them infested with cobras. As yet that door to vault B remains unopened as arguments rage as to the correct course of action.

We stand at the entrance astounded at the tales that surround this place sitting at the end of a small obscure street in south India. Many machine gun bearing guards pace up and down and security is massive. Sadly once again we cannot enter the innermost sanctum reserved for Hindus only. It seems the famous tolerance of Hinduism only extends so far and access to God, and the manifestations of God represented by the Hindu deities in the sacred part of the mandir, are forbidden to non-Hindus. It is disappointing to discover that Hinduism exhibits the same desire to hold its understanding of God exclusively to those on the inside in the same way as the Semitic religions of Judaism, Christianity and Islam have been particularly prone to do.

Apart from its unique extraordinary wealth the Padmanabhaswamy Temple raises the same old dilemmas associated with religion and or spirituality, or the insights from substances such as ayahuasca or LSD. That is acceptance that supernatural forces and powers are real and the material world is only one dimension of a much more complex reality. Every religion categorizes those forces and powers differently, holds to different sacred texts, sacred figures, stories and legends, and sets out contrasting paths to manage them. Once entering that rabbit hole it leads to an endless maze of possibilities through which navigation often involves choosing between adopting one exclusive path of belief and thereby rejecting all the others, or having no path at all. That is an impossible choice as Rita Valencia points out: "Are we to accept that these are holy visions of a world inhabited by invisible ones of manifold names, shared by men and women who have pioneered the way into these realms and handed down genuine–albeit extraordinary—accounts of their experiences? Or are we to go the ultimate distance and ourselves apply for residence in these realms?"[153] A recent comment by Deepak Chopra is helpful to remember: "Christ-consciousness, God-consciousness, Krishna-consciousness, Buddha-consciousness...it's all the same thing. Rather than 'Love thy neighbour,' this consciousness says, 'You and I are the same beings." In Hindu terms we are all part of the Self or Brahman manifesting in samsara as the individual self.

"Like oil in sesame seeds, like butter
In cream, like water in springs, like fire
In firesticks, so dwells The Lord of Love,
The Self, in the very depths of consciousness.
Realize him through truth and meditation.
The Self is hidden in the hearts of all,
As butter lies hidden in cream.
The Lord of Love, supreme reality,
Who is the goal of all knowledge."
Shvetashvatara Upanishad

Walking back to the street corner is to re-enter the scruffy chaos of a busy road with the usual garbage, cows, dogs, beggars, a solitary sadhu, honking traffic, loud Indian music blaring from somewhere, a passing crowded stream of humanity and the vibrant world of samsara as it manifests in India. Our final destination is the Sivananda Ashram in the lushly forested Sahyadri Hills behind Trivandrum, beside the tranquil waters of the Neyyer Dam. The auto-rickshaw ride there is a mistake, aging trucks and buses hurtling past and certain death from a collision missed by millimetres. My eyes close in pure terror on many occasions, not at all comforted by the cardboard picture of a Hindu holy man swinging from above the windscreen. The same image of the same man is to be seen in many places in south India, in taxis, rickshaws, buses, propped up on shelves in shops and restaurants, and on roadside posters. He has the most penetrating gaze and an air of great sweetness. It turns out he is Ramana Maharshi, a great south Indian saint and his story typifies the respect for the inner life and spirituality so typical of India. He was born as Ventkataraman in to an orthodox Brahmin family near Madurai in 1879, and after many mystical experiences even involving loss of consciousness he came to know God through personal knowledge. He attended the Minakshi temple in Madurai daily, and then at the age of 20 he ran away to become a sannyasin. At Tiruvannamalai, in Tamil Nadu he lived for the first period in the temple of Arunachaleswara in states of deep samadhi, despite being bitten by rats and eating almost nothing. He would have starved but for the intervention of Seshradri Swamigal a local saint. In 1899 he moved to the mountain of Arunachala sacred to Shiva and lived in various caves, including the Virupaksha cave for seventeen years.

He attracted many visitors and followers, becoming known a Ramana Maharshi from 1907. He gave much of his spiritual teaching by saying nothing, and people described extraordinary experiences and insights from being in his presence and receiving darshan. The method of self-enquiry, 'who am I?' was his main teaching at the ashram that he eventually founded near Arunachala around his mother's tomb. He described an earlier near death mystical experience as "....a force or current, a centre of energy playing on the body, continuing regardless of the rigidity or activity of the body, though in connection with it. It was that current, force or centre that constituted my Self....I had no idea at that time of the identity of that current with the personal God....I was only feeling that everything was done by the current and not by me...This current or avesam, now felt as it was my Self, not a superimposition...that Avesam continues right up to now." He was said to be extremely modest and self effacing, resisting all attempts to deify him to the point of running away from his own ashram on a number of occasions to find silence and solitude.

A number of Westerners became followers and some such as Paul Brunton in **Conscious Immortality: Conversations With Sri Ramana Maharshi** and **A Search in Secret India**, and David Godman in **Sri Ramana Maharshi**, took his teachings to the wider world. His insights in to reincarnation and samsara are interesting. Reincarnation in samsara presumes the reality of space, separate identity and time, and Ramana Maharshi viewed reincarnation as a tool of understanding only for those who cannot grasp that separateness, space and time are illusions. There is no birth and death, no self and other, everything is the Self, or Brahman, as pure consciousness beyond time and form. It is so typical of India that the life of the spirit is accorded such deep respect and devotion, Ramana Maharshi being one of countless spiritual teachers that India has produced over millennia. It really is an extraordinary country.

The Sivananda Ashram is, as promised, a place of refuge and yearning for a pure spirituality that transcends religion and national identity. There are people there from all over the world, of all ethnicities, genders, creeds, ages, and backgrounds, following the path of yoga with earnest simplicity. Sivananda Saraswati was born in 1887 in Tamil Nadu and served as a doctor in British Malaya up until 1923. He returned to Rishikesh, in northern India to continue his spiritual search under his guru Vishwananda Saraswati who initiated him in to sannyasa. He continued to use his medical skills and founded dispensaries and clinics for the poor and sick, as well as taking intense spiritual pilgrimages including visiting Ramana Maharshi's ashram and Sri Aurobindo in Pondicherry. In 1936 he founded the Divine Life Society that is now a worldwide organization. One of his disciples was Swami Satyananda Saraswati, who founded the Satyananda yoga tradition that has teachers, ashrams and yoga centres across the globe. Even my small city in Australia has Satyananda yoga trained teachers who have done much to spread the philosophy and practice of yoga to every continent on earth. India's remarkable spirituality, including yoga, has become a global export available to all humanity thanks to those such as Swamis Sivananda and Satyananda. Many Western versions of yoga have lost their deep connections with Indian spirituality, and are practiced more as stretching exercises, but the Sivananda and Satyananda traditions have maintained a strong emphasis on meditation and Indian spiritual knowledge.

A rather curt Westerner waves us away from the ashram's main meditation hall where a large group of mostly Western yoga students are engaged in hatha yoga positions. We wander around the ashram for hours. In the reception area is a beautiful painting depicting a circle embracing a Christian cross, a Star of David, the crescent moon of Islam, a Tibetan Buddhist wheel of life image and the sacred Sanskrit letter Om representing the primal vibration of the universe. Around the circle is a ring of pure white doves. It is a wonderful image of tolerance and respect for all religions as containing some element of divine truth, focussing on what religions and people have in common rather than on what divides them. I pick up a pamphlet from the office and am surprised to notice that women are requested to not attend temple or puja when menstruating. My heart sinks, because here it is again: deep suspicion of women as impure and spiritually unclean when their body is simply doing what womens' bodies do.

This anxiety about menstruation crosses religions and cultures and is at the root of the Nepalese custom of chaupadi, the forbidding of menstruating women to enter temples in Bali, or Shinto shrines in Japan, or not participate in communion in some Christian Orthodox churches, or be forbidden to circumnavigate the Kaaba in Islam, and endless other proscriptions and restrictions surrounding women as described in **The Dangerous Sex** and **Purity and Danger**. This discrimination against menstruating women is a product of cultural anxieties, prejudices, discriminations and taboos typical of the baggage of religion. I'm deeply disappointed to see it still in place in a place as enlightened as the Sivanananda Ashram. Interestingly in the ashrams founded by his disciple Swami Satyananda no obvious restrictions are placed on menstruating women engaging in spiritual activities. A battle has been raging at the Sabarimala Temple in Kerala where not just menstruating women but all women of childbearing age have been forbidden since ancient times. Two women who defied this ruling in 2018 in pursuit of women's rights were threatened with violence and have been in hiding ever since to escape retribution. The shadow side of religion is powerful and Sri Aurobindo was right to thank atheism and science for helping purify religion purify of some of its worst aspects.

Our time in India is now done and the long trek home begins. It has been an amazing trip in to an incredibly rich and varied culture full of contradictions and contrasting threads of intense darks and lights. The most remarkable aspect of India is its willingness to follow and honour the inner journey, and a relentless pursuit of spiritual search. Indian spirituality and philosophy has made the exploration of consciousness a central concern for thousands of years and its focus is on inner realms of awareness as a reflection of the universal source of consciousness, Brahman or the Self, rather than on consciousness as a product of the brain as it is in the West. The world, and modern science, would do well to listen to the knowledge and insights that India has to offer.

It is in India that the path of the sadhu, sannyasin, ascetic, or renunciate, who explore the frontiers of consciousness and take the steep climb towards spiritual realms, is seen as the highest of achievements and the final goal of life. In India, a holy man or woman living and meditating alone in a cave absorbed for long periods in samadhi, inspires love and respect, whereas in Australia they might find themselves coming to the attention of well meaning social workers or placed in a psychiatric hospital. A naked ash smeared dreadlocked sadhu without fixed address wandering the streets of Sydney, or Melbourne, or New York, or London, perhaps puffing on a clay pipe of hashish, would be quickly arrested, but in India they are revered as spiritual seekers whose austerities bring blessings and protection to the world. Sahdus number around four million and bear testament to India's preoccupation with the spiritual path. Inevitably there are frauds and charlatans, a few are thieves or criminals, and some do not live up to the high spiritual or moral claims they espouse, but for the most part they represent a tradition of genuine spiritual quest. Throughout India, be it in ashrams, villages, cities, or remote caves in the Himalayas, people have dedicated their lives to exploring consciousness and utilizing spiritual technologies such as meditation and yoga. What they have learned has been expressed through the lives and teachings of those such as Ramakrishna, Paramahansa Yoganananda, Krishnamurti, Vivekananda, Sri Aurobindo, and Ramana Maharshi, who are just a few of the innumerable teachers and seekers that India has produced. Most of the world's accumulated knowledge in relation to yoga, meditation, rebirth, samsara and consciousness, have their source in India and it has been the cradle of Hinduism, Buddhism, Jainism and Sikhism. Humanity owes India a debt of gratitude for its spiritual achievements. Whether India will continue to play that role in the twenty first century and beyond as forces of social change, economic development, modernization, secularization, and global technological culture unfold is unknowable, but its spiritual legacy will endure for all time. It is a great privilege to have spent time there.

"Rituals are unsafe rafts for crossing
The sea of samsara of birth and death.
Doomed to shipwreck are those who try to cross
The sea of samsara on these poor rafts."
The Mundaka Upanishad

CHAPTER TEN

JOURNEYS AND DESTINATIONS

It has been a long and winding journey, through many kilometres of geographical and spiritual space. So how has that journey ended? In many ways it feels like it has just begun, that the destination is the journey itself that perhaps never finishes. TS Eliot's poem "Little Gidding," from Four Quartets, puts it well:

"We shall not cease from exploration
And the end of all our exploring
Will be to arrive where we started
And know the place for the first time."

Words from the Christian Bible also come to mind "we but glimpse through a glass darkly" and from St Augustine of Hippo that "our hearts are restless until they rest in thee." Are we all participants in a stupendous mystery, travelling through many, many, lifetimes and vast eons of time around the wheel of samsara towards a fuller awareness of that mystery and our place in it? Are time, space and matter the illusory props of maya as we take what the religions of India claim is the endless journey across the "sea of samsara" being born, dying, and reborn over and over again? The **Shvetashvatara Upanishad** expresses the purpose of our incarnations in the world of matter and form to be nothing less than the realization of our oneness with God:

"The world is the wheel of God, turning round

And round with all living creatures upon its rim
The world is the river of God
Flowing from him and flowing back to him.
On this ever-revolving wheel of being
The individual self goes round and round
Through life after life, believing itself
To be a separate creature, until
It sees its identity with the Lord of Love."

Are the polarities of life and death, light and dark, consciousness and form, good and evil, choice and destiny, joy and suffering, creation and destruction, all manifestations of the Self and ultimately all necessary to the unfolding of the cosmic story spun by the Lord of Love? Creation cannot exist without destruction, death cannot exist without life, perhaps growth cannot happen without suffering, good has no meaning without evil, light no meaning without dark, and as the Buddhist Heart Sutra puts it "emptiness is form, form is emptiness."[154] These dualities are symbolized by the Nataraja Shiva, who dances creation and destruction through time on the demon of ignorance in the circle of flame that is samsara.

Mystical experiences of unity with divine reality transcend all arguments about dogma, ritual and belief, or claims to exclusive ownership of truth. At the core of the illusion of separateness are we all one, Tat Tvam Asi, "thou art that" as Vedanta expresses it? Unique fragments of an indivisible whole where consciousness, space, matter, energy and time are knitted together in an awe-inspiring creation emerging from the mind of God. Through that creation does God, as the play of consciousness, become ever more self-aware by the observation of itself expressed in infinite transient forms, each of us being one tiny drop in the ocean of being? Is the purpose of the universe to evolve in consciousness through both physical and spiritual evolution? Those insights are the gift at the centre of spiritual insights having their source in India, but perhaps, as mysticism suggests they are also present at the very deepest core of spirituality in all its forms.

In an interview given not long before he died in 1993, Benedictine Catholic monk Bede Griffiths explains that a recent stroke had shut down his left brain, rational, linear thinking mind and that he had come to a completely new realization of God beyond any specific system of religion and beyond masculine conceptions of God such as "God the Father" of Christianity. He describes his experience of God as being without form or gender but if anything closer to the eternal feminine. He urges "Above all we have to go beyond words and images and concepts. No imaginative vision or conceptual framework is adequate to the great reality."[155] He opens the palm of his hand to the camera and points to his five fingers, describing each as representing one of the world's great religions: Judaism, Hinduism, Islam, Christianity and Buddhism. Separate, distinct from each other, a gulf between them. Then he traces the finger of his other hand down each of those fingers to the centre of his palm where at the deepest point of each individual separate finger, they all merge, one not being distinguishable from the others. It is there, he says, that the mystery of God is to be found, beyond the doctrines, rules, rituals, cultural forms, beliefs and differences that divide religions from each other.

Abdu'l-Baha of the Bahai faith points to the same insight: "....it is incumbent upon all mankind to investigate truth. If such investigation be made, all should agree and be united, for truth or reality is not multiple; it is not divisible. The different religions have one truth underlying them; therefore, their reality is one."[156] When Krishnamurti rejected the role of "world teacher" envisaged for him by Theosophy he explained: "I maintain that truth is a pathless land, and you cannot approach it by any path whatsoever, by any religion, by any sect. That is my point of view, and I adhere to that absolutely and unconditionally. Truth, being limitless, unconditioned, unapproachable by any path whatsoever, cannot be organized; nor should any organization be formed to lead or coerce people along a particular path. ..... I am concerning myself with only one essential thing: to set man free."[157]

Consciousness altering substances are powerful tools: although non-addictive, they are not frivolous entertainment and present potential danger if misused as do alcohol and fast cars. With that proviso they could contribute much to humanity's understanding of reality, consciousness and what lies beyond normal waking experience. Psychedelics are much feared: they render the rules and dogmas of society and religion irrelevant and make transcendent dimensions accessible whatever someone's religion or lack of it. Mysticism has also been feared for similar reasons: it involves only the conscious experience of an individual requiring no priests, no rules, no dogmas, no beliefs and no religion. Both psychedelics and mysticism offer freedom of access to experiences without social or religious mediation and control and both offer insights in to spiritual realms and consciousness.

Scientific discoveries of the observer effect, that the consciousness of the observer plays a role in the manifestation of waves of energy into particles of matter, and the mystery of quantum entanglement and non-locality, have opened doors in to spiritual territory, even if that is something science remains mostly uncomfortable with. Those discoveries relate to the insight of Vedanta Hinduism that the seer and the seen are expressions of the same consciousness, Brahman or the Self, and that energy, matter and consciousness are ultimately one: in the language of Sanksrit Tat Tvam Asi. Organisations such as the Institute For Noetic Sciences founded by astronaut Edgar Mitchell after his mystical experience, represent a serious attempt to integrate scientific method with the study of consciousness and its spiritual meaning.

Experiments in parapsychology give support to those ideas by offering evidence for such phenomena as telepathy, psycho-kinesis, pre-cognition, PSI and clairvoyance. Carl Jung's concepts of synchronicity and the collective unconscious, and Rupert Sheldrake's[158] theory of morphic fields, also recognize the primacy and unity of consciousness. All this makes it ever more vital for humans to regard our planet and each other as part of one reality of consciousness entwined in a cosmic dance together through time. If it can be demonstrated that consciousness exists independent of the brain then that will be a watershed of change in understanding of every aspect of reality the universe, life, death and ourselves. Rebirth and samsara might then become not just spiritual ideas but scientifically verifiable as possible and understanding of those could develop far beyond the religious contexts that currently inform and describe them. Perhaps science is becoming ready to embrace a different paradigm from that described in the first stanza of Sri Aurobindo's poem where he laments the extent science and its exploration of the 'how,' has hitherto ignored spirituality that explores the 'why':

"Our science is an abstract cold and brief

That cuts in formulas the living whole.
It has a brain and head but not a soul:"[159]

Sri Aurobindo claims in **The Life Divine** that science now finds itself poised on the edge of a new wave of insights and will have no choice but to address the questions of what lies behind and beyond the realm of matter, moving from an emphasis on technical mastery of the world to exploring its most mysterious secrets such as consciousness. Science's "....very soul is the search for Knowledge, it will be unable to cry a halt; as it reaches the barriers of sense-knowledge and of the reasoning from sense-knowledge, its very rush will carry it beyond and the rapidity and sureness with which it has embraced the visible universe is only an earnest of the energy and success which we may hope see repeated in the conquest of what lies beyond...," [160] If Sri Aurobindo is right we live on the threshold of great changes where the dogmas of religion become irrelevant in the light of truth, knowledge and science, and we cannot even begin to imagine where that might lead. Perhaps the future will bring not a choice between science and spirituality but harmonious mutual understanding and respect as the "two wings of knowledge" whereby humans could discover they are "not isolated beings living our desperate lives on a lonely planet in an indifferent universe"[161]but part of something far grander and more hopeful.

Every country we visited offered a different window through which to view both the possibilities and limitations of spirituality and the diversity of samsara, and there is much gratitude for all they have revealed. The barriers between the numinous, and the rigid materiality so dominant in the West are much thinner in Nepal, Bali and India, allowing a sense of mystery and unseen transcendent dimensions to become tangible. Cambodia graphically exposes shocking truths about human nature, history and the suffering that manifests in samsara, which can never be forgotten. It also revealed modest, selfless people practicing Bodhicitta as quiet saints amidst evils such as poverty, corruption, injustice and child exploitation, doing their best to overcome those.

The religions of all the countries we visited, Buddhism and Hinduism, both perceive rebirth and samsara as a cycle of suffering and misery with escape being the primary objective. Their view of samsara is as a treadmill of births, growing up, adult lives, aging, sickness and death, repeated over and over again ad infinitum, with lots of suffering and loss thrown in along the way. What then is the point of existence? The same old, same old: birth, death, rebirth, forever and ever. From that perspective life seems terrifyingly futile: no wonder getting off the merry-go-round of samsara to enter the bliss of moksha or nirvana is their central priority. In that aspect Hinduism and Buddhism are pessimistic, life being something to be escaped by ending rebirth. However rebirth and samsara are not monolithic concepts and multiple interpretations are possible. The work of Sri Aurobindo takes a much more positive perspective viewing life as a gift to experience a journey of discovery of the soul's infinite potential as a spark of the divine mystery moving towards realization of itself. From that perspective the ideas of samsara and rebirth could have much value and offer hope in relation to existence as being the 'schoolroom of the soul' with each life and its experiences being the lessons we learn from. As concepts rebirth, karma and samsara are deeply entangled with traditional religion, but if those layers could be peeled away and their innermost essence revealed, then they have the potential to enrich human understanding of the experiences of our individual lives and deaths, independent from any particular religion.

Whatever the limitations of religious formulations of samsara and rebirth an eternal destiny of eternal heaven or hell based on only one life that might be only a few years long, makes no sense. Condemning a small baby to eternal hell because it is unbaptized as became the case in the early Christian Church with its doctrine of 'Original Sin,' is incomprehensible.[162] One Buddhist friend remarked how easy it would be to attain the Christian heaven, or Islamic paradise, after only one life compared to being forced in to endless crossings of the "sea of samsara" until the shore of enlightenment is finally reached after many, many lifetimes, a great deal of suffering and many, many deaths. According to both Hinduism and Buddhism there is no choice about this, we are driven in to rebirth in samsara whether we want it or not and there is no escape until enlightenment is realized. Bodhisattvas do make an active choice to re-enter samsara to help all sentient beings, and can choose the circumstances of their rebirth but for everyone else karma dictates the process and circumstances of our next birth. According to samsara we are all on an arduous path to enlightenment where we must resolve the karmic consequences of our own actions through unimaginably long time. There is no easy quick route to an eternal heaven based on just one life, or one moment, such as accepting Jesus as saviour, confessing our sins to a priest, dying in a state of grace, or submitting to Allah. According to the concept of samsara there is also no eternal, damned for all time hell of the kind formulated by Christianity. The repeated travelling around the wheel of samsara may bring stints in some kind of hell or heaven but none of them are permanent. Opportunities for spiritual evolution towards enlightenment are always available even if it may take untold millennia to reach that via an extremely long varied and difficult journey. In terms of hell the concept of samsara is more forgiving and hopeful than eternal damnation meted out by Christianity after death to unbaptized babies, unbelievers, unrepentant serious sinners or heretics.

If time, space and matter are all ultimately illusory manifestations of consciousness, as mystics claim and modern physics contemplates as possible, Ramana Maharshi is right: belief in reincarnation as a linear sequence of lives through time is based on ignorance. However given that our lives are lived in time and our brains think in the context of time perhaps we can only understand rebirth in terms of a chronological sequence of lives. According to the Hindu perspective it takes the atman over two million lives to reach the level of a human incarnation as it progresses from expression in single celled life forms. Perhaps that is why we enter each new incarnation without any memory of the endless chain of previous lives? To be aware of those and the vastness of time through which we have travelled would be so overwhelming as to render living the life we are living now impossible. We must therefore have the memory slate wiped clean between each life, described by Plato in **The Republic** as drinking of the waters of forgetfulness from the river of Lethe prior to being reborn in a new body.

Accounts deriving from past life regressions, such as Joel Whitton's **Life Between Life: Scientific Explorations In To The Void Separating One Incarnation From The Next**, describe how during the bardo period between lives the next life assignment is planned. The circumstances of the new life are chosen to offer maximum opportunity for the resolution of karma and undergo necessary sometimes painful and difficult lessons of the soul so as to progress towards greater love and wisdom. This is described as taking place in a context not of judgement, condemnation, punishment or reward, but rather to develop compassion for self and all other fellow travellers around the wheel of samsara. Hinduism and Buddhism decree that only the enlightened are able to remember their previous lives but the practice of past life hypnotic regressions undertaken by people such as psychiatrist Dr Brian Weiss,[163] appears to give ordinary people some limited degree of access to their incarnational history. The experiences of Weiss's clients confirm that karma and rebirth are real but independent from the cultural accretions that surround them in religions. Interestingly, in accounts of near death experiences cultural context often plays a part in how they are interpreted but the experiences themselves transcend particular religious creeds in the same way as mystical experiences do.

Voltaire exclaims that the "Doctrine of reincarnation is neither absurd nor useless. It is not more surprising to be born twice than once." George Harrison of the Beatles believed "life on Earth is but a fleeting illusion edged between lives past and future beyond physical mortal reality" and "You go on being reincarnated until you reach the actual Truth. Heaven and Hell are just a state of mind. We are all here to become Christ-like. The actual world is an illusion....The living thing that goes on, always has been, always will be. I am not really George, but I happen to be in this body."[164] Leo Tolstoy expresses a similar idea: "As we live through thousands of dreams in our present life, so is our present life only one of many thousands of such lives which we enter from the other more real life... and then return after death. Our life is but one of the dreams of that more real life, and so it is endlessly, until the very last one, the very real life of God." Is it in the experiences of mystics, saints and seers across cultures and religions where a path might be revealed to spirituality free from dogma and creed? Does, as Aldous Huxley claims in **The Perennial Philosophy**, "One Reality, all-comprehensive, contains within itself all realities"? Is it the same underlying reality that all mystical experiences point to beyond words and form? Religion is mostly about cultural constructs but for mystics, they know, or claim to know, through direct personal experience. Rudolf Steiner asserts awareness of that is the next step in human evolution: "Just as an age was once ready to receive the Copernican theory of the universe, so is our own age ready for the ideas of reincarnation and karma to be brought into the general consciousness of humanity."[165]

So where has all this taken me personally? The grief and pain around losing Rob and the awful way his death came to him, remain. Suffering is a mystery that everyone experiences but it is impossible to make sense of what often appears random, unjust, meaningless and cruel, as it was for Rob and countless others. That Rob was fated to suffer his illness because it was written in to the very fabric of the genetic code dealt to him at conception seems particularly cruel and arbitrary. He had a fifty fifty chance of acquiring the genetic glitch causing the illness and the roll of the genetic dice went against him in what appears an utterly random and meaningless twist of bad luck. As the character Dolly Pickles comments in Tim Winton's Australian novel **Cloudstreet** "Lady Luck" is often "a rotten slut." Where Rob is now I cannot know, but I hope he is finding his way on his continuing journey across "the sea samsara" with much love accompanying him.

In terms of spiritual traditions the ideas of Advaita Vedanta stand out along with Sri Aurobindo's teachings of evolutionary rebirth and Integral Yoga. Sri Aurobindo's understanding of life and samsara is not as imprisonment on a hamster wheel of endless suffering from which we aim to escape as fast as we can, but the opportunity for evolution of the soul towards union with the source of consciousness. Evolutionary rebirth offers hope and turns rebirth and samsara in to positive instruments for development. Viewed through that lens they possess profound purpose and meaning for learning and growing towards increased consciousness and compassion to finally realize the soul's "identity with the Lord of Love" as described by the **Shvetashvatara Upanishad**. Instead of a passive fatalistic resignation to the cycle of samsara as a meaningless trap of illusion, suffering and the dictates of karma, life becomes a positive opportunity to realize a great purpose and generate active involvement in the world. That could be big step on the long journey Homo sapiens sapiens has travelled from monkeys to wherever the future might take us. The work of Teilhard de Chardin brings together the evolution of intelligence, consciousness and physical form with the unfolding of spiritual evolution towards the Omega Point of inevitable mergence with God as divine consciousness. It echoes many of Sri Aurobindo's ideas but without reference to rebirth which has been a heresy in the Christian church since the Council of Constantinople in 533 AD. In recent times Barbara Marx Hubbard has written extensively about conscious evolution for humanity and created the organization Foundation For Conscious Evolution to help awaken the scientific, spiritual and social advancement of humanity, drawing on the work of Sri Aurobindo and Teilhard de Chardin. It is remarkable that people as opposite in their thinking as Noah Yuval Harari, Ray Kurzweil and Teilhard de Chardin all view a post-human evolution for humanity in which technology is integral. Hope for the future of humanity will come from many sources and hopefully spirituality can help to play a positive part in that hope. Even Ray Kurzweil, who aims for immortality by embracing a trans or post human future with hybridization between human biology and technology, recognizes the "ultimate spiritual value is consciousness."[166]

There will be no signing up for membership of any religion: they are all riddled with prejudices, superstitions, dogmas, myths, rituals and beliefs that have their roots in history and culture as much as spiritual inspiration. As the **Mundaka Upanishad** warns "Doomed to shipwreck are those who try to cross the sea of samsara on these poor rafts." It will be instead be a matter of staying in the same place but with a different way of understanding, "to arrive where we started, and know the place for the first time." And the journey will continue, as it does for everyone, as the soul seeks a divine mystery beyond words and formulas of religion. In practical terms Milarepa's observation that "Life is short, and the time of death is uncertain; so apply yourself to meditation…," is good advice I intend to follow. An inner shift has flowed from these travels, creating a deep certainty that there is much, much, more to the universe and life than appears at the obvious material level. What that means and how far that goes is like opening Pandora's box to see what is inside. It would perhaps be best to leave that closed not wanting to enter a can of worms where supernatural forces and spirits require acknowledgement. I am no longer certain those do not exist but am unwilling, or am perhaps too cowardly, to directly explore them. I remain agnostic, just, but am leaning over the side of the fence to where the mystery of the universe has meaning and purpose and our place in it is part of something far, far bigger, of which our individual consciousness is an intrinsic part:

"Like oil in sesame seeds, like butter
In cream, like water in springs, like fire
In firesticks, so dwells the Lord of Love,
The Self, in the very depths of consciousness."
Shvetashvatara Upanishad

The concepts of rebirth and samsara, although entwined with religious accretions that are best let go, I can accept, or almost accept, as expressing truths at their essential core. But as soon as those truths are put in to words they begin to evaporate and dogmas, divisions, and differences slip in, so perhaps it is best to not arrive at fixed conclusions. Sri Aurobindo expressed that well: "A certain kind of Agnosticism is the final truth of all knowledge. For when we come to the end of whatever path, the universe appears as only a symbol or an appearance of an unknowable Reality...The more That becomes real to us, the more it is seen to be always beyond defining thought and formulating expression."[167]

For the most part spirituality has been imprisoned in various forms of religion, but if the religious baggage and dogmas that divide religions and people from each other could be put aside it might be possible to access the one spiritual mystery lying deep at their centre in a spirit of tolerance and knowledge, for the benefit of all sentient beings. Bede Griffiths describes this unity lying at the heart of all religion: "There is one absolute, eternal, infinite, unchanging Being, which is the unique source of all existence, of all knowledge and of all life: which is above all things and in all things and for which all things exist. This absolute Being may be conceived in different terms, but in one form or other it is the basis of all religion, not only in India but in China and throughout the East. This is what we have called the spiritual foundation of mankind and the ground of all religion."[168] Beneath the great diversity of religious beliefs and behaviour flow universal currents and if those could be identified they could hopefully carry humans forward in to a new era of unity and discovery in partnership with unfolding discoveries of science. The **Shiva Mahinma Stotram** describes that underlying unity: "As the different streams having their sources in different places all mingle their water in the sea, so, O Lord, the different paths which men take, through different tendencies, various though they appear, crooked or straight, all lead to Thee!" and "Whosoever comes to Me, through whatsoever form, I reach him; all men are struggling through paths that in the end lead to Me."

The emphasis of religion is unfortunately often towards judgement and control. The ultimate reality of a vast universe and the source of consciousness, space, time, matter, energy and life, is unlikely to be bothered by whether or not an intelligent hominid ape drinks alcohol, or abstains from pork, or beef, or shellfish, whether females cover their hair, men marry men, or Buddhists marry Jews, or someone goes to church on Sunday or Saturday or not at all. Those are the obsessions of the created rather than the creator and although those rules are often attributed to God they are more likely to be human and cultural constructs expressed through religion than of concern to the source of the universe.

Is spirituality without religion possible or is spirituality even desirable? Would ritual have any role in spirituality of the future? It might be necessary for humans to have some kind of religious structure and elements of ritual although unfortunately those usually become ends in themselves. Perhaps idols and symbols might also be needed to make present and accessible unseen spiritual realities in which case the baggage of religion might inevitably be waiting at the door. The undertow of superstition and supernatural forces lurking in the background of all religions is powerful and problematic ready to draw us back in to a "demon haunted world" and that is not what we need in the twenty-first century. The ancient impulse to project human tendencies on to gods may prove so strong as to be irresistible so humans will continue to create deities in their own image rather than search for truth. As the old saying goes if there were not a God then humans would invent one. Given the human tendency to construct dogmas and doctrines, and believe others' ideas wrong and their own right, then maybe dogmas and divisions are inescapable because they are easy to create and hard to let go and then it is only a short step to conflict and religious persecution. It might be that spirituality without religion is not even possible and naïve to hope otherwise. All these issues and obstacles do not mean we need to live in a world completely barren of any spirituality but that we need to be mindful of the pitfalls and issues that dog religion and impact on spirituality's content and practice.

That is where science could be helpful by revealing knowledge independent of religion, be it the discoveries of quantum physics, or researching mind-altering substances or mystical states, or investigating biophotons or parapsychological phenomenon. Religion in its current conflicting and culture specific forms is not equipped to address global issues that embrace the whole of our species, but spirituality that transcends religious divisions and embraces science could be of vital help and significance. Abdu'l-Baha, son of Baha'u'llah stated the Fourth Principle of the Bahai faith at the Paris Talks in 1912 as being "The Acceptance Of The Relation Between Religion and Science." It reads: "Put all your beliefs into harmony with science; there can be no opposition, for truth is one. When religion, shorn of its superstitions, traditions, and unintelligent dogmas, shows its conformity with science, then will there be a great unifying, cleansing force in the world which will sweep before it all wars, disagreements, discords and struggles—and then will mankind be united in the power of the Love of God."[169]Every belief system and religion has its shadow side and Homo sapiens sapiens has an endless capacity to create fictions and believe them, so maintaining hefty doses of scepticism is also a crucial value to maintain. These are all a few of many questions and issues for the future to resolve.

In **21 Lessons for the 21st Century** Yuval Noah Harari asserts that Homo sapiens sapiens, as a clever hominid species, will inevitably move in to a post human future where it will design itself and its future through technology. How humans manage technology and artificial intelligence that will far exceed the intelligence of its human inventors, will shape humanity's future and present enormous challenges that have only just begun in the twenty first century. Already no human can beat AI in many fields from chess to processing tax returns. For humanity to navigate its way through the unprecedented changes that are coming, understanding what we are, what if anything our lives mean, and what guiding ideas could sustain us in the next steps of our species' evolution, are of central importance. Humans are as puzzled by and afraid of death as they have always been, and now seek to prevent that by aiming for an immortality created by technology, but that is a project with unknowable outcomes that might instead create new forms of suffering and provide no clues whether life has any purpose or meaning, or what we humans are. Those are spiritual not technological questions.

Something technology can hopefully never replicate or replace is consciousness so exploring what consciousness is and whether it can exist independent of the brain is hugely important. Humanity needs to know if our identity, our emotions and our choices, are nothing but complex algorithms of brain chemistry or if there is much more to us than that. Is the brain the source of consciousness or is it rather a receiver and interpreter of consciousness but not its creator? Exploration of outer space continues but humans still know very little about the inner space of consciousness. We all have it but we have almost no idea what it is, or how matter produces it, or how our subjective experiences of beauty, love, grief, sight, taste, smell, wonder at a stunning sunset, or hope for a better world, come in to being. As Christof Koch puts it in **Scientific American**[170] consciousness is "...the central puzzle of our existence: how a three-pound organ with the consistency of tofu exudes the feeling of life." The nature of consciousness is the key: we cannot hope to truly understand what constitutes 'reality' without understanding the nature of the consciousness with which we perceive 'reality' and that understanding will determine if any validity is to be found in the concepts of samsara and rebirth. We could, at the very least, keep open minds to the possibilities of samsara and rebirth as consciousness is explored, although maybe consciousness is something so mysterious that it might never be fully understood, or not any time soon. In the mean time we paradoxically continue to chase the tail of consciousness using our minds that are expressions of consciousness to do so, unable as yet to catch it. It is essential however that we try because it is the key to who and what we are and to the true nature of reality. In the words of Ray Kurzweil, futurist, inventor and proponent of a transhumanist non-biological vision of humanity's future and a technology based immortality: "I do believe in miracles" and "the fact that consciousness came into being is a deeply mysterious spiritual kind of revelation."[171]

The mystery of consciousness and its "hard problem"[172] are not resolvable within existing paradigms of either science or religion: each in isolation in their current forms are inadequate keys to open those locks so hopefully they will overcome their mutual suspicions to work together to discover answers. Terence McKenna in **Brotherhood Of The Screaming Abyss** observes as follows: "What science has not yet done, and may never be able to do, is to span the gap between what science has revealed about the physiochemical foundations of consciousness and our subjective experiences of truth, beauty, dreams, memories, love and emotions. Building that bridge is to my mind the great challenge of the twenty-first century. I have little doubt that science will play a critical role in unravelling these mysteries, if they are to be unravelled at all. "[173] Albert Einstein would have agreed stating in 1930 "the cosmic religious feeling is the strongest and noblest motive for scientific research."[174] Western approaches to consciousness are strongly focussed on a material perspective and the brain whereas Indian spirituality views consciousness from the perspective of inner states of awareness and as the primary nature of universe. Brahman represents pure consciousness as described by the **Shvetashvatara Upanishad**:

"Know him to be the supreme magician
Who has brought all the world out of himself.
He is the Lord who casts the net of birth
And death and withdraws it again
The supreme Self who governs the forces of life.
From him the cosmos comes....He is the
Lord of Love who reigns over all life.
He is pure consciousness, omnipresent,
Omnipotent, omniscient, creator
Of time....
He is the maker of the universe,
Self-existent, omniscient, destroyer
Of death, the source and inmost Self of all,
Ruler of the cycle of birth and death."

If the differences between the views of science and spirituality could be transcended so as spirituality, mystics, meditators, scientists and those who use psychedelic substances, could unite in an open-minded quest for knowledge, then maybe humans could venture across the last and greatest frontier to discover what we are. If we do not know what we are, then there is no chance of determining what we will become. As Swami Vivekenanda wrote: "We know as yet but little of man, consequently but little of the universe. When we know more of man, we shall probably know more of the universe."[175] In an increasingly complex world of runaway change where technology will outsmart us at every step, understanding consciousness is critical. If it can be shown that consciousness survives death and exists independently of the brain, then the realm of spirituality is opened and ideas such as rebirth and samsara become worth considering. As Carl Jung observed humans "cannot stand a meaningless life" and awareness of rebirth and samsara could give the journey of our lives profound meaning as being expressions of the source of consciousness learning through repeated incarnations of the atman to know itself. Consciousness, as a unity of which we are all a part, is expressed in the "oceanic experiences" of oneness described by mystics as well as users of psychedelics. In the words of thirteenth century Persian poet and mystic Rumi "You are not a drop in the ocean. You are the entire ocean in a drop."

If light, in the form of biophotons, is revealed to play a role in consciousness that points to the ancient understanding of the world's religions that light and spiritual realities are one, whether they are named God, Brahman, Allah or the clear pure light of Buddhism. The **Bible's** book of Genesis 1:3 states "God said, let there be light: and there was light" and the 35th verse of the 24th Surah of the **Quran** states "Allah is the light of the heavens and the earth." At the heart of the **Brihadaranyaka Upanishad** is the prayer:

"Lead me from the unreal to the Real.
Lead me from darkness to light.
Lead me from death to immortality."

The eighth century **Tibetan Book of The Dead** from the Tibetan Buddhist tradition, puts it thus:
"Thine own consciousness,
shining, void and inseparable
from the Great Body of Radiance,
hath no birth, nor death,
and is the Immutable Light"

As expressions of the Self everything is one: Tat Tvam Asi. Perhaps with that awareness humans could become capable of loving each other as all the world's major religions ask us to do, and loving our beautiful, fragile planet. That is where humans could perhaps find the greatest happiness and the best that spirituality can give. All of the world's major religions are united in placing love at their core. Christianity states God is love, Hinduism refers to union with the Lord of Love, Buddhism holds the development of karuna or compassionate love as a central focus, and most of the chapters of the Islamic **Quran** begin 'In the name of Allah, the Compassionate, the Merciful." At the heart of the Jewish **Torah**, Leviticus 19:18, is the instruction to "love your neighbour as yourself." The practice of love has been sadly lacking throughout the sorry history of religious division and conflict, but nonetheless it is there, a yearning for love and union with a spiritual dimension that gives purpose and meaning and opens us to love lying at the heart of creation. In the words of Krishna to Arjuna in the **Bhagavad Gita** "Only by love can men see me, know me, and come unto me."

ABOUT THE AUTHOR

Rebecca Harrison lives in Tasmania, Australia. Apart from a few years teaching in the department of Politics at the University of Tasmania she has been a teacher of students in their final years of school. A lifelong interest in the spiritual traditions of Asia developed during her undergraduate studies of Indian religion and accompanies her passion for travel.

REFERENCES

CHAPTER ONE

[1] Michael Pollan **How to Change Your Mind: The New Science of Psychedelics,** Penguin Books, 2019

[2] Milarepa quoted in WY Evans-Wentz **Tibet's Great Yogi: Milarepa,** Oxford University Press, 1951

CHAPTER TWO

[3] Ramana Maharshi **The Teachings of Sri Ramana Maharshi** Edited by David Godman, 1989

[4] Sri Aurobindo **Rebirth and Karma,** Lotus Press USA 1990, first published 1939

[5] Carl Jung **Memories, Dreams, Reflections,** Prologue, Fontana Press, 1995

[6] **The Bhagavad Gita,** Chapter 2 verse 22

[7] Bede Griffiths **Essential Writings**

[8] Abdu'l-Baha **The Promulgation of Universal Peace,** page 394

[9] Sri Aurobindo **The Life Divine,** Lotus Press 1990, first published 1939, page 14

[10] Malcolm Jeeves and Warren Brown **Neuroscience Psychology and Religion,** Templeton Press, 2009

[11] "The countries where apostasy is punished by death" Posted Sunday 7 May 2017 13: by Louis Doré news, **Indy100.com**

[12] Karl Marx **The Communist Manifesto,** first published 1848

[13] Karl Marx, part one of **Critique Of The Gotha Program,** 187

[14] Charles Darwin **Origin of Species,** 1859

[15] Prem Rawat talk in Barcelona

[16] Plato **The Republic**

[17] Matt Haigh **Notes On A Nervous Planet** Canongate Books, 2019

[18] Carl Sagan, **Pale Blue Dot,** speech, 1990

[19] Malcolm Jeeves and Warren Brown **Neuroscience, Psychology and Religion,** Preface

[20] Alan Watts **The Book on the Taboo Against Knowing Who You Are**, Random House, 1999, first published 1966

[21] William Shakespeare **Hamlet**

[22] Ernest Becker **The Denial of Death,** 1973

[23] Matt Haigh **Notes On A Nervous Planet** Canongate Books, 2019

[24] Karen Armstrong **Buddha** Penguin Biographies, 2004, Introduction, xxv

CHAPTER THREE

[25] Ray Kurzeil outlining his personal beliefs in a **YouTube** Q&A session August 2016, "Do You Believe in God?"

[26] Frederic Lenz **www.ramaquotes.com/satori**

[27] "Samadhi in space." An interview with Apollo 14 Astronaut Edgar Mitchell, by Sarah E. Truman, **Ascent Magazine,** 2007

[28] Interview with Edgar Mitchell by Sarah Truman in **Ascent Magazine**, 2007

[29] "Astronauts report an "overview effect" from the awe of space travel—and you can replicate it here on Earth" By Olivia Goldhill, September 6, 2015 on the website **Quartz.com**

[30] Paramahansa Yogananda **Autobiography Of A Yogi,** Random House, 1996, page 166. First published 1950 by The Self Realization Fellowship.

[31] Peter Matthiessen **The Snow Leopard,** Harvill Press, 1989, page 105

[32] Lao Tzu **Tao Te Ching**

[33] Therese of Avila **The Way Of Perfection,** quoted in Cuthbert Butler's **Western Mysticism,** Harper Torch Books, 1966

[34] Therese of Avila quoted in Peers, E. Allison. **Studies Of The Spanish Mystics**, London, 1927

[35] Joseph Campbell **Myths to Live By**, Viking, 1972

[36] William Blake "**The Marriage of Heaven and Hell**" 1797

[37] Deepak Chopra interview **ForaTV,** You Tube, October 30th, 2009

[38] Dennis McKenna **Brotherhood Of The Screaming Abyss,** North Star Press 2012, page 438

[39] Dr Rick Strassman in Robert Forte (ed) **Entheogens and Future of Religion,** 1997, Page 157

[40] Baha' Ulah **Paris Talks** 1912

[41] Sri Aurobindo **The Life Divine,** The Lotus Press, 1990, first published 1939, page 16

[42] Carl Sagan **Cosmos** Ballantine Press, 2013

[43] Bernard Haisch **The God Theory** Red Wheeler, 2009

[44] "Life and mind in the universe" by George Wald published: 12/15 March 1984, **Quantum Chemistry**

[45] Sri Aurobindo **The Life Divine,** Lotus Press 1990, first published 1939

[46] Peter Matthiessen **The Snow Leopard,** Harvill Press, 1989

[47] A Hindu Sanskrit term meaning the basis or essence of all material things in the universe.

[48] Swami Vivekananda **Raja Yoga**

[49] Nikola Tesla **Man's Greatest Achievement,** 1907

[50] Karl Tate in "How Quantum Entanglement Works" April 2013 at **www.livescience.com**

[51] June 8, 2009 "Quantum Mysticism: Gone but Not Forgotten" By Lisa Zyga, **Phys.org**

[52] Max Planck **The Observer,** London, January 25, 1931

[53] Albert Einstein **The World as I See It**, Philosophical Library, New York, 1949, pp. 24 - 28

[54] University of Glasgow 13 July 2019, "Scientists unveil the first-ever image of quantum entanglement". **Phys.org.**

[55] Per Snaprud "The Consciousness Wager" **New Scientist** July 2018

[56] Michael Pollan **How to Change Your Mind: The New Science of Psychedelics,** Penguin Books 2019

[57] The 'hard problem of consciousness' a term coined by David Chalmers.

[58] Kristof Koch published with the title "What Is Consciousness? "**Scientific American**, pages 60-64, June 2018

[59] "Biophoton Communication: Can Cells Talk Using Light? **MIT Technology Review**, May 22, 2012

[60] Paramahansa Yogananda, **Autobiography of a Yogi** Self Realization Fellowship, 2004, Page 166

[61] Sri Aurobindo **The Life Divine,** Lotus Press 1990, first published 1939, page 22

[62] Lama Anarika Govinda **The Way of The White Cloud,** Rider Press, 1984

[63] Peter Matthiessen **The Snow Leopard,** Harvill, 1989

[64] Tulku Urgen Rinpoche **Tricycle.org** "A Mind Like a Clear Pool: Realizing happiness through training the mind" By Sogyal Rinpoche, Fall, 2002

[65] John Wheeler, **Cosmic Search,** Volume 1, number 4

[66] Sri Aurobindo **The Life Divine** The Lotus Press, 1990, first published 1939, page 5

[67] Sri Aurobindo **The Life Divine,** The Lotus Press, 1990, first published 1939, page 22

[68] **Shvetashvatara Upanishad**

[69] A central idea of the **Chandogya Upanishad**

[70] **Brihadaranyaka Upanishad**

[71] Paramahansa Yogananda **Autobiography Of A Yogi** Self Realization Fellowship, 2004

[72] Das Wesen der Materie [The Nature of Matter], speech at Florence, Italy (1944) (from **Archiv zur Geschichte der Max-Planck-Gesellschaft**, Abt. Va, Rep. 11 Planck, Nr. 1797)

[73] Peter Matthiessen **The Snow Leopard,** Harvill, 1989

[74] Paramahansa Yogananda, **Autobiography of a Yogi** Self Realization Fellowship, 2004

[75] Matthew Talbot **The Holographic Universe,** Harper Perennial, 2011

[76] JBS Haldane **Possible Worlds,** first published 1927

[77] The choices presented by Morpheus to Neo in the movie **The Matrix**

[78] Andrew Stein "Can Machines Feel?" **Maths Horizons,** 2012

[79] "A human head transplant would be reckless and ghastly. It's time to talk about it." By Paul Root Wolpe **Vox.com** Updated Jun 12, 2018

[80] **https://www.sciencealert.com/scientists-build-an-artificial-neuron-that-fully-mimics-a-human-brain-cell**

[81] Ray Kurzweil **The Singularity Is Near**, 2005

[82] Benny Shanon **Antipodes of The Mind – Charting The Phenomenology of The Ayahuasca Experience,** 2002

[83] Wofgang Pauli **Atom And Archetype,** Taylor and Francis, 2001

CHAPTER FOUR

[84] Sir John Woodroffe translation of the **Mahanirvana Tantra** first published 1913, published by NuVision Publications, 2007, pages 21-22.

[85] **Cambridge Declaration on Consciousness**

[86] David Kinsley **The Sword And The Flute: Kali And Krsna, Dark Visions Of The Terrible And The Sublime in Hindu Mythology**, University of California Press, 2000

[87] David Kinsley **The Sword And The Flute: Kali And Krsna, Dark Visions Of The Terrible And The Sublime in Hindu Mythology**, University of California Press 2000, page 158

[88] Hermann Hesse **Siddhartha,** Simon and Schuster, 2008

[89] "Cula-Malunkyovada Sutta: The Shorter Instructions to Malunkya (MN 63)" **Access to Insight**, Retrieved April 7, 201

[90] Ringu Tulku **The Ringu Tulku Archive**

[91] David Nichtern **Waking From The Daydream**, Wisdom Publications, 2016
71Isabella Tree "Radical Tantra" **The Economist,** November/December 2015

[93] Lama Anagarika Govinda **The Way of The White Cloud** Rider Press, 1984

[94] Isabella Tree in "Radical Tantra" **The Economist,** November/December 2015

[95] Isabella Tree "Radical Tantra" **The Economist,** November/December 2015

[96] Dr. Nida Chenagtsang, "Sexuality in the Tibetan Buddhist Tradition" in an interview with Lyudmila Klasanova, **Buddhistdoor Global,** 2018-06-20

[97] Robert Beer **The Encyclopedia of Tibetan Symbols and Motifs,** Serindia publications.

[98] Isabella Tree "Radical Tantra" **The Economist,** November/December 2015

[99] Bede Griffiths, **A Human Search: Bede Griffiths Reflects on His Life: An Oral History** a documentary by John Swindells 1993

[100] **https://www.bbc.co.uk/religion/religions/buddhism/beliefs/karma.shtml,** 2017

[101] Quoted by Peter Graff in, "Faiths Ask of Quake; 'Why Did You Do This God?'", **Reuters News,** 2004, December 30th

[102] Arnaud de Borchgrave, "Allah off the Richter scale," **The Washington Times,** 2005 January 2009

[103] Julian of Eclanum quoted in **Born Bad: Original Sin And The Making of The Western World** by James Boyce, Schwartz Publishing 2014, page 18

[104] David Kinsley **The Sword And The Flute: Kali And Krsna, Dark Visions Of The Terrible And The Sublime in Hindu Mythology** University of California Press, 2000

[105] Sri Aurobindo, **The Life Divine,** The Lotus Press 1990, first published 1939 page 36

CHAPTER FIVE

[108] Isabella Tree "Radical Tantra" in **The Economist,** November/December 2015

[109] **www dimmid.org** "The Relevance of Bede Griffith's Vision For Today" Dr Anandam Lourdu, January – June 2014

[110] His Holiness the Dalai Lama,

[111] ABC Radio National, "All in The Mind" program, Sunday 9 November 2003, Natasha Mitchell reading from Benny Shanon's **Antipodes of The Mind – Charting The Phenomenology of The Ayahuasca Experience,** 2002

[112] "Letting Daylight into Magic: The life and times of Dorje Shugden," Stephen Batchelor **Tricycle** Spring1998

[113] Brendan O'Neill editor of **spiked-online.com,** July 28, 2010 at **www.reason.com**

[114] Lama Anagarika Govinda **The Way Of The White Cloud,** Overlook Press, 2005, (originally published 1966) page 276

[115] Karl Marx **A Contribution to the Critique of Hegel's Philosophy of Right Introduction** Written: December 1843-January 1844; First published: in **Deutsch Französische Jahrbücher,** 7 & 10 February 1844 in Paris

[116] **Gita: The Science of Living** by Jayantilal S Jariwalla

[117] Bede Griffiths **Bede Griffiths Essential Writings,** 2004

CHAPTER SIX

[118] William Shakespeare **Macbeth**

[119] Douglas Stewart "The Goldfish Pond"

[120] Ruth Tucker in **Jerusalem to Irian Jaya: Biographical History of Christian Missions,** Zondervan, 2004

[121] ABC news report, Hobart, Tasmania, April 2017

[122] Lauren Davis, 2014 interview **"This is the most disturbing animal behavior David Attenborough has seen"** at https://io9.gizmodo.com/this-is-the-most-disturbing-animal-behavior-david-atten-1498010055

[123] **https://kashgar.com.au/blogs/gods-goddesses/kali-a-most-misunderstood-goddess**

[124] Reported 14/07/2015 "Witchcraft in Nepal" in **AsiaNews** by Christopher Sharma

[125] Dan Mc Dougall from Khurja India, in **The Guardian Online,** 5th March 2006

[126] Lama Anagarika Govinda **Way of The White Cloud,** 1984, page 276

[127] Gordon Jensen and Luh Ketut Suryani **Trance and Possession in Bali,** 1993

[128] Sri Aurobindo **The Life Divine,** The Lotus Press, 1990, first published 1939, page 36

[129] Carl Sagan **The Demon-Haunted World: Science As The Candle in The Dark** Brilliance Corporation, 2017

CHAPTER SEVEN

[130] **Bali Now** magazine: "Understanding Reincarnation, The Balinese Way" by Jean Couteau, December 1st, 2014

[131] Carl Jung **Memories, Dreams, Reflections,** page 19

[132] Mary Douglas **Purity and Danger: An Analysis of Concepts of Pollution and Taboo,** 1966.

[133] HR Hays **The Dangerous Sex,** 1964

[134] Deborah Cassel's article in **The Australian** "Caged People: the tragedy of Bali's mentally ill" February 13, 2015.

[135] Fred B. Eiseman **Bali: Sekala And Niskala** Tuttle Publishing 1990

[136] Wikipedia

[137] **Hinduism Today** April /May/ June 2012, by Rajiv Malik

CHAPTER EIGHT

[138] Joseph Conrad **The Heart of Darkness**, first published 1902

[139] Thomas Hobbes **Leviathan,** first published 1651

[140] Lauren Davis, 2014 interview "This is the most disturbing animal behavior David Attenborough has seen" **at https://io9.gizmodo.com/this-is-the-most-disturbing-animal-behavior-david-atten-1498010055**

[141] CP Snow "The Two Cultures and the Scientific Revolution", delivered May 7 1959, in Cambridge at that year's **Rede Lecture.**

[142] Milgram described his research in 1963 in the **Journal of Abnormal and Social Psychology** and later in detail in his , **Obedience to Authority: An Experimental View,**. 1974.

[143] **Tricycle** magazine, from "The Enemy Within" **by** The Dalai Lama, summer 2002

[144] Alan Watts **The Book on the Taboo Against Knowing Who You Are,**1966

CHAPTER NINE

[145] In August 1929 Krishnamurti dissolved the 'Order Of The Star' of the Theosophical Society in a speech with those words in the Netherlands.

[146] Swami Vivekananda **Complete Works**, Volume V, Fifth Edition, page 77

[147] Carl Jackson quoting Vivekananda in **The Founders, Vedanta for the West: The Ramakrishna Movement in The United States** Indiana University Press, 1994

[148] Sri Aurobindo **The Life Divine,** The Lotus Press, 1990, first published 1939, page 11

[149] Müller, Max (1898). "Râmakrishna's Life" **Râmakrishna his Life and Sayings,** pp. 56–57

[150] Sri Aurobindo, **CWSA,** Vol. 01, p. 572-74

[151] The Mother, **CWM,** volume X111, pages 38-39

[152] The Mother, 20/12/1961 **The Mother's Agenda,** volume 2

[153] "A Leap of Faith" August 16, 2009, by Rita Valencia **www.TimesQuotidian.com**

CHAPTER TEN

[154] **The Heart Sutra**

[155] Bede Griffiths. **Bede Griffiths: Essential Writings** 2004

[156] Abdu'l-Baha, **The Promulgation of Universal Peace,** 1912, pages 105-106

[157] Wikepedia, **Krishnamurti**

[158] Rupert Sheldrake **Dogs That Know When Their Owners Are Coming Home,** Penguin Random House, 2011

[159] **Les poèmes de Sri Aurobindo** (bilingual edition) also in **More poems** – 76 and **Collected Poems** – 168 all published by Sri Aurobindo Ashram, Pondicherry, diffusion by SABDA

[160] Sri Aurobindo **The Life Divine,** The Lotus Press, 1990, first published 1939, page 16

[161] Lynne McTaggart **The Field: The Quest For The Secret Force Of The Universe,** page 226

[162] James Boyce **Born Bad: Original Sin And The Making Of The Western World,** Schwartz Publishing, 2014

[163] Brian Weiss **Many Lives, Many Masters** Simon and Schuster, 1988

[164] **Hari Quotes**, compiled by Aya & Lee, George Harrison

[165] **5 lectures, Berlin and Stuttgart, January-March 1912 (CW 135)**

[166] Ray Kurzeil outlining his personal beliefs in a **YouTube** Q&A session August 2016, "Do You Believe in God?"

[167] Sri Aurobindo **The Life Divine,** The Lotus Press, 1990, first published 1939, page 14

[168] Bede Griffiths, "Christian Ashram" in **Essays towards a Hindu-Christian Dialogue** (London: Darton, Longman and Todd, 1966), p79

[169] Abdu'l-Bahá **Paris Talks,** 1912, London: Bahá'í Distribution Service (published 1995)

[170] Kristof Koch, "What Is Consciousness? "**Scientific American,** pages 60-64, June 2018

[171] Ray Kurzweil in a **YouTube** Q&A session responding to the question "Do You Believe in God?" August 2016

[172] David Chalmers **Facing Up To The Problem of Consciousness,** 1995

[173] Dennis McKenna **Brotherhood Of The Screaming Abyss,** North Star Press, 2012, page 283

[174] Albert Einstein **The World as I See It,** Philosophical Library, New York, 1949, pp. 24 - 28

[175] Swami Vivekenanda quoted in **Understanding Consciousness: Recent Advances,** published by Ramakrishna Mission Institute of Culture, Kolkata 2009, page 103. Published proceedings of the fourth biennial International Seminar on Consciousness held in Kolkata India in 2008. It gathered together mystics, philosophers, scientists and physicists from around the world.

Printed in Great Britain
by Amazon